CASS LIBRARY OF INDUSTRIAL CLASSICS
No. 20

THE COTTON TRADE
OF
GREAT BRITAIN

CASS LIBRARY OF INDUSTRIAL CLASSICS

No. 12. W. Cooke Taylor
Notes of a Tour in the Manufacturing Districts of Lancashire (1842).
With a new introduction by W. H. Chaloner.
Third Edition

No. 13. Sir George Head
A Home Tour through the Manufacturing Districts in the summer of 1835 (1836).
With a new introduction by W. H. Chaloner.
Second Edition

No. 14. James Bischoff
A Comprehensive History of the Woollen and Worsted Manufactures (1842).
New Impression   Two Volumes

No. 15. John Holland
The History and Description of Fossil Fuel, The Collieries, and Coal Trade of Great Britain (1835).
New Impression

No. 16. Richard Guest
A Compendious History of the Cotton Manufacture (1823).
New Impression   4to

No. 17. G. I. H. Lloyd
The Cutlery Trades. An historical essay in the economics of small-scale production (1913).
New Impression

No. 18. Archibald Prentice
History of the Anti-Corn-Law League (1853).
With a new introduction by W. H. Chaloner.
Second Edition   Two volumes

No. 19. J. C. Kohl
England and Wales (1844).
New Impression

THE COTTON TRADE

OF

GREAT BRITAIN

Its Rise, Progress, and Present Extent

JAMES A. MANN

FRANK CASS & CO. LTD.
1968

Published by
FRANK CASS AND COMPANY LIMITED
67 Great Russell Street, London WC1

First edition   1860
New impression   1968

SBN 7146 1405 X

Printed in Great Britain by
Thomas Nelson (Printers) Ltd., London and Edinburgh

THE COTTON TRADE OF GREAT BRITAIN:

ITS

RISE, PROGRESS, & PRESENT EXTENT,

BASED UPON THE MOST CAREFULLY DIGESTED STATISTICS,

FURNISHED BY THE SEVERAL GOVERNMENT DEPARTMENTS,

AND MOST EMINENT COMMERCIAL FIRMS.

BY JAMES A. MANN, F.S.S., M.R.A.S.

ETC. ETC.

DEDICATED BY PERMISSION
TO THE PRESIDENT, VICE-PRESIDENT, AND COUNCIL OF THE COTTON SUPPLY ASSOCIATION, MANCHESTER.

LONDON: SIMPKIN, MARSHALL & Co.; MANCHESTER; JOSEPH THOMSON & SON.

1860.

TO THE

PRESIDENT, VICE-PRESIDENT AND COUNCIL

OF THE

COTTON SUPPLY ASSOCIATION,

MANCHESTER.

GENTLEMEN,

It is with a feeling of considerable diffidence that I dedicate to you these pages, from a consciousness that your intimate knowledge of the subject will render their deficiences at once apparent.

As a tribute to the important interest you represent, I offer this Dedication, the acceptance of which on your part, from your individual eminence in the commerce of our country, and the national purpose for which you are associated, cannot but be both a pleasure and an honor to

Yours very faithfully,

JAMES A. MANN.

KENSINGTON,
MARCH, 1860.

PREFACE

The importance of correct statistical information to the Merchant, to enable him to purchase the raw material and sell his manufactures in the best market—to the Political Economist, to enable him to grasp the intricacies of the trade with which he intends to deal, or to the Historian who would trace its phases and features—is everywhere admitted; and whether we would study the history of the trade in cotton or any other article, we must learn it as anatomy is learnt; in short, we must first study thoroughly the bones if we would successfully trace the intricate ramifications of nerves and arteries. The object in view in the compilation of this work is to furnish the Merchant, Political Economist, or Historian, with the statistics bearing on the cotton trade of Great Britain, in as concise yet comprehensive a form as the data at our command will permit.

The statistical tables which form the basis of the work may be fully relied on; they have been carefully collated from official or the most reliable sources; the object has been throughout to obtain all the available statistics of weight and value, to the exclusion of undefined denominations of measure, such as bales, and except in those cases where "the trade" have become used to their employment they are excluded.

Although some of the tables are not strictly of the trade of Great Britain, they will be found in all cases to have a bearing on the question of the demand and supply of that trade.

The letter-press is divided into three books or chapters, which may be thus defined:—

Book No. 1. Traces the ancient history of the cotton manufacture—its introduction and progress in India, China, Africa, America, and Europe—its tardy development in Great Britain—the mechanical inventions of Wyatt, Paul, Kay, Hargreaves, Arkwright, Crompton, and Watt; their causes and effects—and the progress of the trade to the close of the eighteenth century.

BOOK No. 2. Treats of the progress of economy in the manufacture, with a review of the actual effects thereby produced on the trade—glances at the present expense or cost of the several departments of manufacture as compared with that under the old and rude systems—traces the features of the trade in its progress during this century—and the effect it has produced on places and people—and exhibits a picture of its present extent and greatness.

BOOK No. 3. Is devoted almost exclusively to the question of supply of the raw material, giving a review of the more prominent facts in regard to supply from the United States, East Indies, Brazil, Africa, West Indies, and other parts—with a few closing remarks on the extent of the home and export trade of Great Britain.

In the department referring to the supply of cotton from India in Book No. 3., are included certain remarks relating more particularly to the cotton manufacture of that empire; as exerting a great influence upon the future demand for British manufactures, they are not thought irrelevent or unworthy of a place in these pages; the whole of that department formed the subject of a paper read before the Royal Asiatic Society on the 21st January in this year, and is therefore better given in its entirety.

The Map of India, fronting page 64, will exhibit particularly the means of transit enjoyed by the several districts of India, while the accompanying table (to which the numbers on the map refer) will show the area and population. It is hoped that together these will assist to a view of the advantages of India, as yet to be developed, while they evidence the progress making in internal communications to meet the transit difficulties, which have hitherto been considered the greatest obstacles to the development of the export trade in cotton in India.

The Diagram fronting the work will show the relation of the four great elements of supply, demand, stocks, and prices, over a space of thirty-four years; the figures employed in its compilation will be found in Tables No. 29 and 36; and it is to be hoped, if it serves no other purpose, that it will indicate to the Cotton Broker, Merchant, or Manufacturer, the insecurity of allowing so great a declension in the stocks of the raw material as that now existing.

It is right to state that it was the original intention of the author merely to have compiled the statistical tables illustrative of the trade; but that, at the request of several friends, he was induced to edit a few remarks to lead the mind of the reader in their perusal, and to publish them in the form they now assume. As such, then, these pages are presented in their crude state. The author is cognizant he has much indulgence to crave for their incomplete and desultory character, put together without sufficient regard to order; but if he has committed any errors in the use of his figures, it is by inadvertance and not intention or want of care.

The author takes this opportunity of expressing the great obligation he is under to those gentlemen who have so liberally accorded him their time and assistance (with whom must be shared any credit which may be due for the completeness of the statistical tables). His special thanks are, however, due to A. W. Fonblanque, Esq., of the Board of Trade; C. C. Prinsep, Esq., of the Statistical Department of the India House; Dr. J. Forbes Watson, Reporter on the Products of India at the India House; J. A. Messenger, Esq., Inspector General of Imports and Exports; A. C. Fraser, Esq., Custom House; J. Carpenter, Esq.; H. B. Joyner, Esq.; Thomas Bazley, Esq., M.P. for Manchester; Henry Ashworth, Esq., of Bolton, Lancashire; Messrs. Stolterfoht, Sons and Co., Liverpool; Richard Burn, Esq., Manchester; Messrs. George Holt and Co., Liverpool; Charles Speakman, Esq., Manchester; G. R. Haywood, Esq., of the Cotton Supply Association; J. C. Ollerenshaw, Esq., Manchester; Messrs. Niell Brothers and Co., of New York; Messrs. Platt Brothers and Co., Oldham; James Landon, Esq., of Broach (East Indies), and London; Alexander C. Brice, Esq., of Bombay, Cochin, and London; Messrs. Thomas Houldsworth and Co., Manchester; and Messrs. Du Fay and Co. Manchester; while, at the same time, he has not failed to avail himself of the valuable information afforded by such works as are extant upon the subject, and many periodical price currents published by merchants and others.

INDEX TO STATISTICAL TABLES.

TABLE No. 1. — Shows the quantity of Raw Cotton Annually Imported, Exported, and Taken for Consumption in the United Kingdom; with the Rate of Duty and Revenue collected therefrom, from 1781 to 1859.

TABLE No. 2. — Shows the Annual Average Prices of Wheat; "United States Uplands," "Brazil and Pernambuco," and "East India Surat" Cotton; and of No. 100's, and No. 40's Best Seconds' Mule, and No. 30's Water Twist or Cotton Yarn, from 1782 to 1859

TABLE No. 3. — Shows the Official and Declared Real Value of Cotton Goods and Yarns Exported from the United Kingdom, from 1785 to 1859.

TABLE No. 4. — Shows the quantity of Raw Cotton Exported Annually from the United States of America; the Average Price per lb.; and the Total Value in American and Sterling Money, from 1791 to 1858.

TABLE No. 5. — Shows the quantity of Raw Cotton Exported from the Port of Calcutta, and its destination, from 1795 to 1834.

TABLE No. 6. — Shows the quantity of Raw Cotton Exported from the Roadstead of Madras, and its destination, from 1824 to 1834.

TABLE No. 7. — Shows the quantity of Raw Cotton Exported from the British East Indies (distinguishing the three Presidencies, Bengal, Madras, and Bombay,); and its destination, from 1834 to 1858.

TABLE No. 8. — Furnishes a Resume of the Principal Features of the entire British Cotton Trade; and particularly illustrates the Value of the Home and Export Trade, from 1834 to 1858.

TABLE No. 9. — Shows the Declared Real Value of Textile and other Articles (distinguishing Cotton, Wool, Silk, and Linen Manufactures,) Exported from the United Kingdom, from 1820 to 1859.

TABLE No. 10. — Shows the Prices of Beef and Mutton at St. Thomas's Hospital, from 1688 to 1860.

TABLE No. 11. — Shows the Amount and Annual Cost of the National Debt, from 1691 to 1859.

TABLE No. 12. — Shows the quantity of Raw Cotton Imported into the United Kingdom from each of the producing countries, from 1815 to 1859.

INDEX TO STATISTICAL TABLES.

TABLE No. 13. — The Crops of Raw Cotton in each of the United States (Cotton Growing States), from 1824 to 1859.

TABLE No. 14. — Shows the Annual Average Weight of Bales of Cotton Imported into the United Kingdom, from 1816 to 1859.

TABLE No. 15. — Shows the distribution of the Crops of the United States, from 1826 to 1859.

TABLE No. 16. — Shows the number of Bales of Cotton Imported into the Port of Liverpool, from 1785 to 1859.

TABLE No. 17. — Shows the quantity of Raw Cotton Imported into the United Kingdom, from India, from 1783 to 1859.

TABLE No. 18. — Shows the quantity and value of Cotton Manufactures Exported from the United Kingdom to India; and the quantity of Raw Cotton and Cotton Manufactures Exported from India, from 1840 to 1858.

TABLE No. 19. — Shows the Imports from, and Exports to India, from 1827 to 1858.

TABLE No. 20. — Shows the Imports from, and Exports to China and Hong Kong, from 1827 to 1858.

TABLE No. 21. — Shows the quantity of Raw Cotton Imported from each of the British Possessions, from 1831 to 1858.

TABLE No. 22. — Shows the quantity and destination of Raw Cotton Re-exported from the United Kingdom, from 1827 to 1858.

TABLE No. 23. — Shows the quantity (in detail) of British Cotton Manufactures Exported from the United Kingdom, from 1820 to 1852.

TABLE No. 24. — Shows the quantity and value (in detail) of British Cotton Manufactures Exported from the United Kingdom, from 1853 to 1858.

TABLE No. 25. — Shows the Declared Real Value of British Cotton Manufactures Exported from the United Kingdom to each country, from 1820 to 1858.

TABLE No. 26. — Shows the quantity of Cotton, Wool, Silk, Flax, and Hemp Imported into the United Kingdom, from 1820 to 1859.

TABLE No. 27. — Shows the quantity of Cotton (in bales) Imported into the United Kingdom, from each source, from 1801 to 1859.

TABLE No. 28. — Shows the Supply of, and Demand for Cotton (in bales) in Europe and America, from 1827 to 1859.

TABLE No. 29. — Shows the Monthly Average Price of Fair Uplands (American) Bowed Cotton in the Liverpool Market, from 1826 to 1859.

TABLE No. 30. — Shows the quantity or value of Foreign Cotton Manufactures Imported, Exported, and Consumed in the United Kingdom; with the Amount of Revenue collected thereon, from 1831 to 1858.

TABLE No. 31. — Shows the Value of Raw Cotton Exported from each of the Presidencies of Bengal, Madras, and Bombay, from 1834 to 1858.

INDEX TO STATISTICAL TABLES. vii

TABLE No. 32, — Shows the Official and Declared Real Value of Imports into, and Exports from the United Kingdom; distinguishing Raw Cotton Imported, and British Manufactured Cottons Exported, from 1801 to 1859.

TABLE No. 33. — Shows the quantity of Raw Cotton Exported from the Port of Alexandria (Egypt), and its destination, from 1855 to 1859.

TABLE No. 34. — Shows the quantity of Raw Cotton Exported from the British East Indies, and its destination, from 1850 to 1858.

TABLE No. 35. — Shows the quantity of Raw Cotton Exported from the United States of America, and its Destination, from 1851 to 1858.

TABLE No. 36. — Appendix to Diagram. — Shows the figures employed in the compilation of the Diagram; showing the quantity of Raw Cotton Imported, Exported, and taken for Consumption, with the quantity held in stock, in the United Kingdom, from 1825 to 1859.

NOTE.—The OFFICIAL VALUES given in the Tables are calculated at a fixed price settled by the Government so early as the close of the seventeenth century, when prices were very different to those of the present day; these prices are so perfectly anamolous as to render the Official Values of worth only as a criterion by which to judge of the progress of quantities. In the case of Imports, until the year 1854, there was no other calculation or return of values made by the Government.

The DECLARED REAL VALUE applies only to Exports of British Produce or Manufactures from the United Kingdom, and is the actual value returned by the exporting merchant.

The COMPUTED REAL VALUE applies only to Foreign Produce Imported into, and Re-exported from the United Kingdom since 1854, when the system was first instituted; it is the value calculated at the average price fixed annually by the Customs' authorities.

ERRATA.

Page 2. line 11, for " was spun from it," read " was spun for it."

Page 25, bottom line, for " Donelli," read " Bonelli."

Page 50, Table at the head of page, the total for 1840 should be 54,447, in place of 45,447.

Page 81, line 3, for " Table No. 20," read " Table No. 21."

Page 88, line 5, for " 21," read " 22."

Page 90, line 8, for " No. 22 and 23," read " Nos. 23 and 24."

Page 90, line 2 from the bottom, for " 20," read " 25."

THE COTTON TRADE

OF GREAT BRITAIN.

BOOK 1.

In the most uncivilized states of mankind the process of manufacturing vegetable as well as animal substances for use must early have attracted the attention of the people. Even in the most barbarous times the requirements of life in such a state would lead to the employment of substances combining flexibility and strength, for which nothing better could be obtained than the skins of animals and vegetable fibres. In the earlier period of the world skins would probably form the clothing of man, but still for many purposes they would be unsuited; and the very intertwining of strips of hide for the manufacture of a rope would suggest the great utility of any fibrous matter, particularly flax and other such self-evidently useful substances. To the inhabitants of the temperate and tropical zones, too, the great weight and toughness of skins would make patent the advantage of any material which could be made of the necessary strength, and at the same time light and flexible. Our mother, Eve, employed the leaves of a neighbouring fig tree to hide her shame; and, with this exception, we know nothing of the mode adopted to dress the person, whether for comfort or vanity, until about 1715 years before our era, at which period the linen manufacture in Egypt, according to the Bible, had reached considerable perfection. But before the manufacture of linen was established in Egypt, the cotton manufacture was no doubt extant in India. In one of the hymns of the Rigveda, said to have been written fifteen centuries before our era, reference is made to *cotton in the loom* in India, so that at this early date some considerable proficiency had there been attained in the manufacture of textile fabrics.

India is, according to our knowledge, the accredited birth-place of the cotton manufacture, and it seems probable that the process of spinning and weaving was carried on at the earliest date of which we have any record, in much the same manner as it is there in the present day. The strictly conservative character of the Asiatic, the profusion of labour in the present mode of manufacture, the primitive form of implements, and the carelessness of the cultivation, all tend to this view. Whether the quality of the native cotton has improved or deteriorated is a matter of doubt; but this is certain, in former times large irrigation works existed there, and equally so that the poorer cultivator, by a combination of circumstances, is in the present day considerably imposed upon by his superior, either in power or pecuniary advantage.

Considering the disadvantages of their primitive mode of manufacture, it is somewhat a matter of admiration that the natives of India should have arrived at such proficiency in the delicacy of the fabrics manufactured by them. Muslins (so called from *Mosul* in Mesopotamia), were among the earliest articles of foreign trade in the East; those manufactured by the natives, particularly at Dacca, are still unequalled in fineness by either our hand or machine wove fabrics. Tavernier said "they are so fine that you can scarcely feel them in your hand;" and some of the finer muslins have been woven from thread of such extraordinary delicacy that a single pound of cotton was spun from it into a length of two hundred and fifty miles.* Though the manner in which this wonderful delicacy of texture was wrought is very surprising, it is not astonishing that the natives of India should have excelled in the manufacture. In such a climate the delicacy and fineness of the garment must necessarily have been of first consideration, and when we regard how greedily fabrics eminently combining these qualities must have been sought after by the wealthy and licentious nobles of India—not fallen India of modern times, but the India of poetry and romance, of splendour and glory!—every stimulus to excellence in this direction must have been afforded by their luxurious mode of living and their vanity. Utility and economy were to be the characteristics of the energetic and thrifty European, but to the Asiatic no expenditure of labour or material was too great which could add in the slightest to their wishes in this respect.

The earlier condition of India and its cotton manufacture are fields for speculation. To attempt any conclusive argument on the subject would be mere empiricism; but the opinion may be ventured, that at the climax of the former greatness of India, the population would not have been less than that of the present day, or, indeed, it may for some time past have even diminished, and our knowledge of their social, moral, and religious institutions support this view. During the period in which those circumstances existed which wrought its downfall, the people of India, as a whole, must undoubtedly have been considerably impoverished, and this would not only tend to check an increase of population, but also to diminish the demand for cotton manufactures. The long period for which the manufacture has existed there to our knowledge should, under a prosperous condition, have given rise to a greater consumption; and perhaps the fact that the plant is now found throughout all India is as conclusive testimony as any we have of the antiquity of the trade and its extent. In these surmises is not of course embraced the period in which India has been under the civilizing auspices of the British Government—the progress which civilization has made in that period has doubtless raised the energies of the people and caused an increase in the consumption of cotton goods.

Of the origin or extent of the earlier export trade of India, and afterwards of China, little more is known. We have reason to believe that five centuries before our era cotton was exported from India; for in the reign of Amasis, 569-525 years B.C., cotton was known in Egypt, where it is not probable any then was grown. Herodotus writing, 445 B.C., speaking of the usages of the Indi, says (lib. iii, cap. 106) "the wild trees bear fleeces for their fruit surpassing those of the sheep in beauty and

---

* To prevent misconception, it may be remarked here that Messrs. Houldsworth, of Manchester, have *spun* yarn in length nearly equal to 400 miles to the pound.

excellence, and the natives clothe themselves in cloths made therefrom," and (lib. iii, cap. 47) calls it *tree wool* (εἴριον ἀπό ξύλου). From India the manufacture seems to have reached Persia, where, according to Strabo (lib. xv), who died A.D. 25, it grew in Susiana, a province of Persia, at the head of the Persian Gulf, and was manufactured into cloth. At the Christian era the growth and manufacture were carried on in Egypt; and Pliny (His. Nat., lib. xix, cap 1) mentions, A.D. 70, that the cotton plant was grown in Upper Egypt towards Arabia. Arrian, who wrote in the second century (Arrian Indi, c. 16, p. 582), stated that cotton cloths were among the articles received from India by the Romans of his time, though at this date the importations must have been of a desultory character, as no mention is made of the different kinds by any writers of the period, or in the Roman law *de Publicanis et vectigalibus*, which detailed all the different kinds of merchandize then imported; indeed until *Justinian's Digest of the Laws*, in which, in a list of goods then imported, is enumerated (A.D. 552) Indian cotton goods, we do not find notice taken of them by any writer, though other goods are repeatedly mentioned, and the reason seems to have been, that while these goods could not compete with silks as articles of luxury, they did not, being comparatively dearer, displace woollen and flax manufactures, particularly as these latter must from long employment have been adapted to the tastes and wishes of the people.

In the *Circumnavigation of the Erythæan Sea* by Arrian, written in the second century, cotton goods are first distinctly mentioned as an article of trade, and particular mention is made of the imports and exports of several Indian towns in their trade with the Arab Greeks. The Arab traders brought Indian cotton to Aduli, a port on the Red Sea—the ports beyond the Red Sea had an established trade with Patali (on the Indus), Ariakè and Barygaza (the modern Baroche on the Nerbudda), and received from them, among other things, cotton goods. Barygaza is said to have exported largely the calicoes, muslins, and other goods, both plain and figured with flowers, made in the provinces of which it was the port, and in the interior of the more remote provinces of India. The muslins of Bengal were then, as in the present day, superior to all others, and received from the Greeks the name of *Gangitiki*, from being made on the borders of the Ganges. Surat was famous for its coloured chintzes and piece goods, but the Baroche muslins were inferior to those of Bengal and Madras, as were the printed chintzes of Guzerat to those of the Coromandel coast.

While India thus carried on not only an internal manufacture but an export trade, China appears to have cultivated the cotton plant in entire ignorance of its use, though silk was not only spun and woven but also exported to the Roman empire, from the people of which considerable sums were received in return; and it is supposed that the cotton fibre was not turned to any account there till the sixth century of the Christian era, and not even until the eleventh century was the manufacture of any extent. Its introduction met with strong opposition from the spinners of wool and silk, an opposition which was not overcome, it is supposed, until 1368; since which, however, it seems to have steadily progressed, and now the immense population of that empire, where formerly, and even to the ninth century, none but silk garments were known, are principally clothed in manufactured cottons, by which, no doubt, the article silk has been considerably liberated for export to the more opulent nations of the West. A small export trade in cottons (particularly *Nankeens*, so called from the city of Nankin) likewise arose in China, but has long since begun to languish. The imports of this peculiar manufacture into the United Kingdom reached its greatest height about 1824, when 1,010,494 pieces were imported. Since that date our Imports have become gradually smaller, and at present the trade is almost annihilated.

Though India is the accredited birth-place of the cotton manufacture, the inhabitants of Western and Southern Africa, it is extremely probable, carried on the manufacture before any foreign goods could have found their way into the country. America also had her cotton manufactures at an early period, for the European conquerers, when they first invaded Mexico, found the people using cotton manufactures, mixed and unmixed with fine hair. They were well acquainted with the art of dyeing, for some of these manufactures which were sent as a present to the Emperor Charles V. created great curiosity from figures of animals and other devices being dyed upon them; they also used cotton in the manufacture of a species of paper, and one of their kinds of money consisted of a peculiar cotton fabric manufactured for the purpose. When Christopher Columbus landed, 12th October, 1492, at Guania, one of the Lucaye Islands, the first land he saw after crossing the Atlantic, his vessels were surrounded by canoes filled with natives bringing cotton in skeins to exchange. It was singular that these yellow men, of a race till then unknown to the old world, should possess ideas of commerce truly innate; nevertheless their advance, which was equalled throughout most of the West India Islands, is not so marvellous when we consider that according to our preconceived ideas of the peopling of the world the inhabitants in the remotest corners of the globe must all have migrated thither, and that to have passed the boundless oceans they must have either enjoyed considerable enlightenment or a marvellous instinct. It is stated that five days after Columbus landed at Cuba, the island he at first thought the mainland, he saw there cloths made of cotton of which the native women wore dresses, and a sort of network, in the language of the country called "Hamacas" which they stretched between two poles, and in which they slept at night. They had also there, so great a quantity of spun cotton distributed in spindles, that that of a single house was estimated at 12,000 lbs. weight. Oviedo states the same of Haïti—and at the discovery of Gaudaloupe in the same year, cotton thread in skeins was found everywhere, and utensils with which to weave it; and here, as at Haïti and Cuba, the idols were of cotton. The cultivation of the plant in Central and South America is evidently of great antiquity; and if we recognize the race of Zoltyns, people who ought to be placed first in the annals of the New world, if it is true, as they deduce it from the Aztec *hieroglyphics*, that it belonged (in the year 544 of our era) to another nation situate to the north, and who came after a migration of 104 years to settle in the Valley of Anahuac, the famous town of Mexico, we learn that the use of cotton among these people was as common and almost as diversified as it is now among the nations of Europe—they made of it clothing of every sort, hangings, defensive arms and innumerable other things, and a tribute paid by the provinces to the Emperor was in a quantity of cotton; indeed it appears the cultivation was restricted only by the limits imposed by nature in the climate. Peru had, according to all accounts, also acquired the art of manufacture at a very early date, and we must unquestionably recognise in Peru and Mexico the two empires of the earlier American civilization. It is recorded that in the former place the dress of the Inca or sovereign, from the formation of the empire at an unknown date, had been made of cotton, and of many colours, by virgins consecrated to the worship of the sun.

To return to the European trade, it seems almost inexplicable that while silk and other goods from India and China regularly found their way to Rome, the manufacture of cotton fabrics must, to our knowledge, have lingered thirteen hundred years on the shores of the Mediterranean before it crossed over to Greece or Italy, and more so when we see that in the former place not only had cotton goods been for centuries imported, but as early as the close of the eighth century the raw material was imported and used in the manufacture of paper. The date of the introduction of the cotton manufacture into Europe is veiled in obscurity, but it is generally assigned to the period of the conquest of Spain by the Moors in the eighth century. In the reign of Abderahman the Great, about the year 950, the cotton plant is said to have been naturalized in Spain, and the manafacture was carried on at Seville, Cordova, and Granada, where it continued to flourish for several centuries. Barcelona was famous in particular for her manufacture of sail cloth. The term *fustaneros* (from which the word *fustian* is taken) was given in Spain to the weavers of cotton goods of a stout make, or as the Spanish word signifies *substantial*. The mutual hatred which existed at the period between the Moors and Christians prevented its extension into other parts of Europe, for when, in the latter end of the fifteenth century, the Saracens were expelled from Spain, the manufacture of that country became extinct with them. The trade, however, carried on with the African coast doubtless helped to propagate the manufacture in that country, though, as before remarked, there is every reason to believe it had previously existed there.

The manufacture did not appear in Italy until the fourteenth century, when the fustians and dimities of Venice and Milan were much esteemed, and among the most valuable articles exported to Northern Europe; and at this period the manufacture of yarn is said to have been begun in Turkey. The progress in Europe, which, up to this time, was very circumscribed, now became more rapid, for half a century later it had crossed the Alps and was established in Saxony and Suabia, whence it was carried into the Netherlands. At Bruges and Ghent a large trade arose. In 1430 we have mention of fustians being manufactured and imported into Flanders from Prussia and Germany, and thence exported to Spain. Antwerp, which in 1560 carried on a large trade, imported considerable quanties of fustians from Germany, which, with cotton wool obtained from Portugal, it exported to England. Thus, in the sixteenth century, the European trade was extending rapidly, but we must remember that its production was still confined almost entirely to fustians, which were heavy and clumsy cloths, half cotton and half flax, while the finer cloths or muslins were yet obtained from India.

In 1253 linen was first manufactured in England by Flemish weavers, and though we have account of raw cotton imported as early as 1298 it probably found its way from Portugal, and was wholly employed in the manufacture of candlewicks. At the beginning of the fourteenth century nearly the whole of the cotton, woollen, and linen fabrics consumed in England were manufactured on the continent, and a great quantity of British wool was exported to Flanders and Holland. Edward the Third, however, took measures to invite foreign skill to the country, and the result was the immigration of some Flemings in 1328, who, settling in Manchester, laid the basis of the British woollen manufacture in the manufacture of what were called *Manchester cottons*,—the pioneer of the great cotton era,—and we may believe, that the impetus thus given to the trade in woollen fabrics, aided and paved the way for the great mechanical improvements, which gave to the British textile manufacture the start of all other nations. In 1560 cotton was imported into England from the Levant, and at the period some anxiety was evinced to compete in the manufacture with other countries, though yet principally in woollen fabrics, for in 1582 a commercial treaty was entered into with Turkey, a Levant company established, and a commission of enquiry sent to Constantinople and other parts of Turkey, to learn any secrets in the art of manufacturing, dyeing, &c. No material benefit resulted to the country from these measures, and the slight impetus given to the trade about the period is owing rather to the number of Flemings who were driven to the country in 1585. In 1641 the cotton imported came almost exclusively from the Levant, a large proportion probably from Cyprus and Smyrna; and it was then that the cotton-woollens, fustians, dimities, and other articles were exported to the continent.

Though it was in 1530 that the spinning wheel was invented by Jurgen, up to the beginning of the seventeenth century the distaff and spindle continued to be used as in the earlier times; the weaving was by the old loom, the same as that introduced by the Flemings three hundred years before. While the woollen and linen manufactures progressed more rapidly, the manufacture of cotton remained almost stationary; indeed, looking to the statistics left to us, the quantity of the raw material imported even diminished, thus:—

	Cotton wool imported. lbs.	Manufactured goods imported. £.	
1697	1,976,359	5,915	official value.
1701	1,985,868	23,253	"
1710	715,008	5,698	"
1720	1,972,805	16,200	"
1730	1,545,472	13,524	"

We have not, however, the statistics of the quantity of cotton yarn imported, so that we cannot determine the point; and, indeed, from a newspaper of 1739, in which the progress of the manufacture of the antecedent twenty years is looked upon as immense, we might infer that the import of yarn was considerable, and that a large quantity of linen yarn was mixed with all descriptions of cotton goods.

In 1738 commences the history of those wonderful inventions which, giving the power of almost unlimited production to our people, have revolutionized the manufacturing world. Though the distaff had been laid aside for the spinning wheel, the process of spinning by the latter means was so slow, that a person could spin only a single thread; and when we say that a man employed eight hours a day could only spin three quarters of a pound of yarn of a low count or quality, and that therefore to spin the nine hundred million pounds, or that at present consumed in Great Britain, would alone require the constant application of four million persons. We shall be able to recognize the extreme rudeness of the then mode of manufacture and its productions at the period, being then little in advance of that existing in the most ancient times of which we have record. The cost of spinning counts from 10 to 60, at the period of which we are speaking, ranged from 1s. to 13s. per pound, or say, as the counts were very low, the moderate average of 3s., which would make that item alone in our manufacture now amount to the enormous sum of £135,000,000, or double the total value of the whole of the present multifarious, beautifully fine, and costly productions therefrom; and then only admit of paying the spinner at the rate of 2s. per diem, while we have it on record that in 1760 they earned really only 2s. to 3s. per week—weavers and dyers of course much higher—but on an average (as estimated by Mr. Baines) about 5s. per week, than which they now receive not only much higher but more advantageous wages. We will endeavour to trace the several improvements which have assisted to produce the present state of seeming perfection, and in following them we shall be able to appreciate the immense advantage wrought by such apparently insignificant means. In this year a patent was taken out by one Lewis Paul, a foreigner, for a machine for *spinning by rollers*, invented by a John Wyatt, of Birmingham, and it forms the basis of all the spinning machinery in our present stupendous factories. The great advantage of the instrument, however, was not apparent at the time, nor does it appear that beyond the principle was it complete, for it seems to have failed to bring in any profit to the parties concerned, though a spinning engine with rollers was constructed in 1741, by Wyatt, at the Upper Priory, Birmingham, and turned by cattle ; in 1743, up to which date India yarns had been wholly employed in the manufacture of all the finer qualities of goods, another of a like construction was erected at Northampton, for a Mr. Edward Cave, the projector and proprietor of the Gentleman's Magazine, and contained 250 spindles, turned by water : and this in like manner appears to have been barren of results. It is probable that without a corresponding increase in the power of weaving, over which perhaps even the laborious process of spinning had the advantage, the demand would not exist for the increased production, for the manner in which the shuttle was then thrown was very tedious and attended with great labour, and so rude were the whole appliances, that the weaving of a width exceeding 36 inches, required two hands in the operation at the loom. In the same year, however, commenced the era of improvement in this branch of the manufacture. Mr. John Kay, of Bury, invented the *fly shuttle* and *picking peg*, which enabled one man, unaided, to weave double the quantity he had theretofore done. In lieu of throwing the shuttle by hand, which required the constant stretching of the arms to the sides of the warp, the lathe (in which the shuttle runs) was extended a foot on either side, and by means of two strings attached to the opposite ends of the lathe, and both held by a peg in the weavers hand, he was able with a slight and sudden pull to give the proper impulse to the shuttle. Next followed Mr. Lawrence Earnshaw in 1753, who, it is said, invented a *spinning machine and cotton reel*, which he destroyed, on the plea that it would be the ruin of the working class. In 1758 a second patent was taken out by Lewis Paul, for an improvement in the *carding* process, and the arrangement of the rollers. This patent, which, like the previous one, expired without any benefit to the inventor, contained many admirable points, especially in the mode of carding by rollers, which formed the basis of a great improvement made and patented afterwards by Arkwright, by which the carding or roving was made continuous, and the operation performed principally by the machine. In 1759 Mr. Robert Kay (son of the inventor of the fly shuttle and picking peg) invented the drop box, which enabled the weaver to use at ease one of three shuttles, and thereby produce a fabric of three colours with nearly the same expedition as he could weave a common calico.

The period thus embraced from 1738 to 1760, though strictly after the era in our cotton trade, may be perhaps more truthfully considered the transition state. These inventions of Wyatt, Paul, Earnshaw, and the Kays formed the principles the benefits of which others were to reap by improving upon them. The erection of machinery to employ profitably the magnificent ideas embodied in them, required considerable capital, which was not forthcoming, and consequently their advantages remained undemonstrated. But though so fruitless to the inventors, and at the time apparently so barren of effect upon the trade, the period and the circumstances were not lost upon the country; the minds of the people were prepared for the reception of the improvements which were to work out the practicability of in a great measure superseding hand labour, and employing in its stead the combination of inert matter devised to assist man, and the prejudices against which could not be overcome but by time. The practicability of an extension of production, and of demand, as well as the question of supply of the raw material, were all being arranged; and in proof of the interest then attaching to the subject, it may be stated that in 1760 the Royal Society of Arts offered a premium for the first invention of a machine for spinning six threads of wool, cotton, flax, or silk, at one time, and that would require one person only to work and attend it. The manufacture too was being as it were centralized. About 1741, Manchester merchants began to give out warps and raw cotton to the weavers, receiving them back in cloth, and paying for carding, roving, spinning, and weaving. The weaving of a piece containing twelve pounds of 1s. 6d. weft occupied a weaver's family about fourteen days, and he received for the weaving 18s., spinning the weft at 9d. per lb., picking, carding, and roving, 8s. Manchester did not, however, rise into celebrity for its cotton manufactures until about 1759.

In 1741 the imports of raw cotton wool into the United Kingdom was only 1,645,031 lbs., and the official value of goods exported £20,709, while for the seven years following 1743 the movements were as follows:—

	Imported. lbs.	Exported. lbs.	Consumed. lbs.
1743	1,132,288	40,870	1,091,418
1744	1,882,873	182,765	1,700,108
1745	1,469,523	73,172	1,369,351
1746	2,264,808	73,279	2,191,529
1747	2,224,869	29,438	2,195,431
1748	4,852,966	291,717	4,561,249
1749	1,658,365	330,998	1,327,367

The improvement apparent up to 1748 was not fully maintained, for in 1751 the import was only 2,976,610 lbs., and the official value of cotton goods exported £45,986. The progress, doubtless, of the manufacture of many of our continental neighbours, up to this period, must have quite equalled, if not exceeded that of our own. Taking France as a case in point, in 1688 the import of raw cotton from the Levant into that country was 450,000 lbs., and of cotton yarn 1,450,000 lbs.; while in 1750 the imports were of raw cotton 3,831,620 lbs., and cotton yarn 3,381,625 lbs.

Legislative enactments, which had hitherto indiscriminately imposed restrictions, now endeavoured to foster and encourage the home trade, and in 1757 a duty of 4d. per lb. was imposed on cotton yarn imported from India, the duties and prohibitions on certain other goods still remaining unaltered; but with this, the total value of the cotton manufactures of the country was only about £200,000. In 1762 the secret of dyeing *Turkey red* was introduced by Mr. John Wilson, of Ainsworth, and in the year following bleaching came generally into use. British muslins were also first manufactured by Mr. Shaw, of Anderton, near Chorley, though with small success from the limited supply of yarn suited to the purpose. The art of printing calicoes, which had been introduced since 1675, was in 1764 for the first time practised in Lancashire.

The grand idea conceived by Wyatt had now slumbered a quarter of a century, for although it had, as we have before observed, been employed in two particular instances, and doubtless at frequent times in a smaller way, there existed a want, without which it could not be profitably employed—it was that of an inventive genius to perfect the detail, to which Wyatt appeared unequal—when, in 1763, one Thomas Highs, a reed maker of Leigh, is said to have invented the spinning jenny, so called after his daughter Jane. Great uncertainty, however, prevails on the point, but whether such were the case or not, it does not appear that he thoroughly understood its merits, or even turned it to other account than as a mere curiosity. Mr. Baines surmised, and with reason, that it is probable Highs was aware of Wyatt's design, and as he appears to have abandoned his craft for that of a mechanician, was employed in endeavours to improve upon it; but though his success was small, he seems to have originated ideas, which thereafter, through a combination of circumstances came into the hands of the genius Arkwright. In the following year, James Hargreaves, a poor weaver of Blackburn, is supposed to have conceived the original idea of the *spinning jenny*, patented by him in 1770, but which he had at a much earlier date put into practice, in 1767, at which time he and his family spun the weft for their own use, though he endeavoured to retain the secret, its practicability was so well understood, that he became the subject of persecution, and was attacked by a mob of the working people, who broke into his house and destroyed the jenny, and ultimately forced him in 1768 to flee with his family from his native place to Nottingham, as the inventor of the fly shuttle had done before him. In the same year, however, he entered into partnership with a joiner, Mr. Thomas James, who raised sufficient money for them to erect a small mill, which, fitted with the machine, enabled them to give the twist necessary to reduce the roving or slubbin, into the form of yarn, and admitted of a number of spindles being worked by one hand; at first the number of spindles was eight, at the time of the patent (1770), they had been increased to sixteen, then twenty, and thirty, and continued to increase till its supercession by the present form of machine.

Hargreaves, scarcely second to Arkwright in the matter of genius, was not possessed of the knowledge the latter enjoyed of the mode of working his invention to his own benefit, for it appears that he made several machines for other parties previous to having patented his invention; and as may be imagined, in such a time when the opinion, not alone of the working people, but the general public, was averse to the adoption of machine power, which they ignorantly imagined would cause the starvation and ruin of the humbler classes, it gave a key by which the jealousy of the other manufacturers could set at nought Hargreaves' patent right. Having failed in an offer made by a delegate in their behalf, they continued their aggressions on his patent, and permitted an action commenced by Hargreaves to proceed, which he was forced to abandon on that ground alone. Thus was poor Hargreaves like others, by the gross selfishness of his opponents, ousted from the benefits that in fairness accrued to him; and though he does not seem to have died in the straitened circumstances which have been stated, he yet enjoyed but small fruit from his labours in the interest of his country.

We now reach the crisis when not one alone, but several, are engaged on the improvement of the process of manufacturing cotton. Up to this date a large number of minor inventions for spinning wheels and appliances many of great merit, had been brought to light, principally by the encouragement of the Royal Society of Arts, which had offered several premiums and prizes for the attainment of improvements in the spinning of textiles ; and though we have recorded Hargreaves as the inventor of the spinning jenny, it must be remembered that this machine, though very ingenious, was but a modification of the spinning wheel, and applicable only to the spinning of cotton for the weft, being unable to give to the yarn the necessary degree of firmness and hardness to fit it for employment as the longitudinal thread or warp in the manufacture of cloth. In 1769, Mr., afterwards Sir Richard Arkwright, patented the *spinning* or *water frame*, which, while drawing out the carding or roving, gave to it the twist and pressure necessary to produce the hardness and firmness which fitted it so admirably to the purposes of the warp; it was at the same time also capable of producing in equally vast quantities yarns of finer quality. This invention, while embodying the principles of Wyatt and Paul's, then extinct patents, was so totally different in detail, and so relatively superior to that to which Highs laid claim, as not in any way to detract from the undoubtedly superior genius of Arkwright. It consisted of two pairs of rollers, turned by means of machinery, the lower one of each pair being furrowed or fluted longitudinally, the upper ones covered with leather, and pressing upon the lower, enabled them to take hold of the carding or roving of cotton, which as soon as it had begun to pass through was received by the second rollers, which revolved with (as the case may be) three, four, or five times the velocity of the first pair. By this admirable and simple contrivance the roving was drawn out into yarn of the necessary degree of tenuity, a twist being given to it by an adaptation of the spindle and fly of the common flax wheel; thus requiring only that a person should feed it with rovings, and join any threads which might happen to break during the process. While struck with the simplicity of the contrivance, it is difficult to say which to admire and praise most,—the profound and fortunate sagacity which led to so great a discovery, or the consummate skill and master mind by which it was so speedily perfected and reduced to practice.

The effect of these two most important and valuable inventions was in time to cause a total revulsion in the character of the operations of the spinners. Spinning had previously been carried on almost entirely as a domestic manufacture; but now the manufacturers who had adopted the practice generally of giving out the warp and cotton for the spinning of the weft, with which the weaver manufactured the required cloth, discovered that a yarn of better quality, made by machine, could be had at a cheaper rate, the warp being supplied from the spinning frame, and the weft from the jenny. And were it not that the sordid jealousy and the insatiable cupidity of the old manufacturers succeeded in wresting from the originators the well-deserved fruits of their labours, we should regard with unmixed pleasure a period so rife of intellectual conquest and wonderful effect.

With the precedents in the case of Kay and Hargreaves before his eyes, Arkwright deemed it expedient to remove to Nottingham, where Hargreaves had now found security, which he did along with Kay, the clockmaker, in 1768. Nottingham thus became the cradle of the three greatest inventions in the art of spinning and weaving cotton. Having arrived there, he was fortunate enough to meet with some men of capital; resulting in a partnership with Messrs. Need and Strutt (the latter the improver and patentee of the stocking frame), and in the following year, the machine was perfected and the patent taken out.

We have thus seen the process of reducing the roving of cotton by attenuation and twisting into the form of yarn; but the processes of first *carding* and afterwards *roving* the cotton were still very imperfect and required much hand labour, and thereby assisted in preventing that extension of the trade to be looked for as a result of such wonderful improvements. Although there is proof that Paul patented in 1748 the identical process of carding by cylinders, the invention had been allowed to fall into obscurity; but now that other branches had progressed sufficiently to attract attention to the subject, and to prove the necessity for a revision of the manufacture, the long forgotten idea of Paul's was reclaimed, and brought forth for improvement and active employment. The machines erected by Paul at Northampton had passed into other hands, and it is remarkable that the carding cylinders had been purchased by a hat manufacturer of Leominster, and employed by him in the carding of wool in his business; and that its re-application to the cotton manufacture in Lancashire did not occur till 1760. Mr. Peel, the grandfather of the late Sir Robert Peel, is said to have been among the foremost to adopt it, and, with the assistance of Hargreaves, to have erected a mill with cylinders at Blackburn; but from the labour required to feed it and strip the fleece off the cards, which operations had to be performed by hand, it was soon abandoned, and only came into general use after further improvements had been perfected, and about the same time that spinning machines were generally adopted. The operation of *feeding* was improved by Mr. John Lees, a quaker, of Manchester, who invented a contrivance by which a given weight of wool being spread upon an endless cloth, wound upon two rollers, was by it conveyed to the carding cylinders. In 1773, it has been said, James Hargreaves invented the *crank and comb*, which facilitated the taking off of the cotton in a continuous roving from the cylinders by machinery. It consisted of a plate of metal finely toothed at the edge, which, being worked by a crank in a perpendicular direction, with slight but frequent strokes on the teeth of the card, stripped off the cotton in a continuous filmy fleece, which, as it came off, was contracted and drawn into and through a funnel at a little distance in front of the cylinder, and thereby reduced into a roll or *sliver*, which, passing between the rollers, was compressed into a flat riband, and fell into a deep can, where it was coiled up in continuous length until the can was filled. This beautiful contrivance was, however, embodied in Arkwright's patent taken out in December, 1775, and from some testimony, adduced by Mr. Baines, appears to have been the result of his genius. It forms the next epoch with which we have to deal. The improvement and combination of all these varied material which was effected by Arkwright, and formed the substance of his second patent of 1775, and the admirable adaptability of the embodiment and combination to the purpose, presents unmistakable proofs of Arkwright's mechanical genius. By it the raw cotton was put in an entangled and knotted mass, the fibres lying in every direction, which, being spread, was conveyed by an improved method, invented by Arkwright on Lee's form of feeder, to the carding cylinders, where they were carded, and became regularly placed as they should lie in a piece of yarn; here the crank and comb took it off in filmy continuous fleece, which was drawn through a funnel to compress it to the needful size to pass through the roller, which sent it forth in the form of ribands or cardings ready for the *drawing machine*. This important operation of drawing was undoubtedly Arkwright's original idea, and forms perhaps the most important operation in the whole manufacture. It has the two-fold object of *straightening* and *laying* the fibres at their full length, and of equalizing the thickness of the *cardings*. It is effected first by drawing out the cardings, and then doubling and redoubling the slivers or ends so as to make them of the same substance as at first; thus, while the drawing out of the fibres loosely straightens them so as to fit them for the preparation of fine thread, the drawing and doubling averages the irregularities, and renders it of an uniform and continuous thickness. The number of times that the operation of drawing and doubling may be repeated depends first on the kind of cotton used, and then on the quality of yarn required. If of long and strong staple it requires to be doubled more than if weak and short, and the harder and finer the yarn wanted the more drawing will the sliver require. The sliver is thus prepared for the *roving frame*, consisting of three pairs of rollers, which, revolving with different velocities, *stretch* it out to the required tenuity, and then allow it to fall into an upright can revolving rapidly on its axis, which, imparting to it the necessary *twist*, it is ready for winding on the bobbins.

With this admirable series of machines, manufacturers were compelled to yield to the conviction that yarns of a cheaper and better quality could be produced by machine than by hand labour, but still continued with insatiable and sordid jealousy to oppose their introduction in every way, and moreover leagued themselves together in a refusal to purchase the manufactured yarn, the result of which was that Messrs. Arkwright and Co. became encumbered with a large and valuable stock, and inconveniences and disadvantages of no small consideration followed. Whatever were the motives which induced its rejection, they were driven to attempt by their own strength and ability the manufacture into woven fabrics. Their first trial was in the manufacture of stockings, in which they succeeded, and soon established the manufacture of calicoes. But another and still more formidable obstacle arose: the orders for goods which they received were suddenly countermanded, the Officers of Excise insisting on the additional three-pence per yard, making the duty six-pence as on foreign calicoes; besides which, the calicoes when printed were prohibited, and a large and very valuable stock of calicoes necessarily accumulated. An application to the Commissioners of Excise was attended with no success; the proprietors, therefore, had no alternative but to apply to the legislature for relief, which, in 1774, after much money had been expended, and against a strong opposition of the manufacturers of Lancashire, they obtained. Such malicious, and blinded policy as that of the manufacturers in this opposition is unequalled in the annals of commerce; it forms a prototype of the period, and its successful combat serves all the more to illustrate the strength of mind possessed by Arkwright to overcome difficulties. When the decision was promulgated, the fame of Arkwright resounded through the land; capitalists flocked to him to buy his patent machines or permission to use them, and he sold to many adventurers residing in the counties of Derby, Leicester, Worcester, Nottingham, Stafford, York, Hertford, and Lancaster, many of his patent machines. Though the opposition continued to smoulder, a mighty impulse was given to the manufacture; the weavers found they could obtain an unlimited supply of yarn, and besides, use cotton in lieu of linen warps, which permitted a greater reduction in the cost than had hitherto been known. The demand for these goods consequently increased, the shuttle flew with increased energy, and the weavers earned immoderately high wages. But here it seems probable, in consequence of the increase in demand, prices of the raw material must have temporarily increased, and, while holding out an inducement for an extension of the cultivation abroad, or an increased import, must also have checked the bound of demand; for, looking at the increase in the power of production, and the consequent falling off in the demand for hand labour from a not equivalent increase of material, we should expect a total stagnation of employment among the spinners; but as the weaving and spinning had up to this date been combined very much under one roof, and the shuttle had frequently drooped for want of the yarn, the increase in the demand, small as it was, was able, in the statu quo state of the loom, to afford an equivalent extension of demand for the labour liberated under the improved process of spinning.

The great and wonderful *factory system* here takes its birth, for although there had previously existed mills for the manufacture of silk, they were isolated cases, forming no part of a system. Hitherto the manufacture required no larger apartment than that of the weaver's cottage; but the ponderous water frame and carding engine required not only more space, but a stronger building, and more power for their application than could be exerted by the human arm. The employment of these machines, too, required a greater division of labour, the material in them going through many more processes; and had its removal from house to house been necessary, a greatly-increased waste and loss of time would have been the inevitable result, so that it became obvious a great advantage was obtained in carrying on all the many operations in the same mill, —an economy of power in every department, as in all the detail, was the result. The whole formed a system in itself, dependent in a lesser degree on extraneous and fluctuating aid, superintended by the master spinner himself, who could, by his command of means, employ any improvement that might arise with more facility than could have been done under a sub-division of the processes of manufacture. Like Wyatt, Arkwright had abandoned the animal power for that of water, and the employment of the latter had become general, all the mills erected being on the falls of considerable rivers, except in a few instances where Newcomen's and Savery's engines had been employed, with ill-success from their waste of fuel and continued disorder.

Arkwright is said to have first directed his attention to the matter of spinning machinery about 1767, when, having connected himself by marriage with a family of Leigh, the native place of Highs, he appears to have met with, and employed one Kay, a clockmaker, of Warrington, who, having been engaged in the manufacture of some rollers and other pieces of mechanism for Highs, it is probable he was the source whence Arkwright received the germ of the invention he afterwards perfected and patented. In 1769, he erected his first mill at Nottingham, and in 1771 the large one at Cromford, in Derbyshire. The fairness of the means by which Arkwright reaped the mede of success, almost solely his, has always been a matter of controversy; there is much bitterness in the generality of writings upon the subject, arising, not unlikely, from the jealousy with which any successful man is ever regarded, especially where, in comparison, others have not shared in the pecuniary advantage. It does appear an act of injustice to endeavour to detract on that account from the fame which Arkwright deserves for his inventive genius and unerring skill and judgment. His memory we should cherish; a substantial benefactor to the country, his reward was none too much, that those of others were less was not his fault. The simple fact that Arkwright, when comparatively a poor man, was able to demonstrate, even theoretically, the working of the conceptions, and to obtain the assistance which others with equal advantages failed to command, is ample evidence of his perfect superior mastery of the subject. In recalling his faults, let us not forget the state of commercial morality at the time, and an old true saying " that circumstances in a great measure make the man." Apart from the question of the strict originality of the first principles of all the parts of his machine, their working out and improvement to such perfection, as to render the manufacture by machinery a source of profit, in face of the ignorant opposition of popular opinion, which no one previously had done, was the link, without which it had been, hitherto, but a component of the great design, as any one material of which the machine might be composed, would be.

Though Arkwright was rapidly acquiring a fortune, he had yet to contend for his rights; his success continued to excite the cupidity of the cotton manufacturers, particularly of Lancashire, still in league against him. From the obscure wording of his patents, and the fact of many of the principles being claimed as the invention of other parties, it was in 1781, when he lost an action instituted against a Colonel Mordaunt for an infraction of his patent rights, that his second patent was thrown open to the public. Goaded by the decision in this instance, he prepared, in 1782, a document representing his claim upon the country for consideration, intended to have been presented in the House, but confined to circulation for some unexplained reason, and never formally brought before the legislature. In the following year his partnership expired with Messrs. Need and Strutt, and in 1785 he made another attempt to establish the validity of his patent by an action for infringement in the Court of Common Pleas. A decision in his favour being given by Lord Loughborough, an application was made nominally by the crown, but actually by the associated cotton manufacturers for the issue of a writ of *scire facias*, to try the validity of the second patent, and came off in the Court of King's Bench. On the 24th June, a sentence of nullification of the patent was passed; and an application made for a new trial was refused, so that the inventions became public property, which, had the patent continued in force, would not have been the case till 1789.

In thus noticing the fruits of Arkwright's patents, we have departed somewhat from chronological order ; it is however perhaps justified by the perspicacity to which it has tended. Though the inventions of Hargreaves and Arkwright had established the spinning of cotton by machinery, they were yet unadapted to the production of the finer qualities of yarn which the manufacturers of British goods required in order to compete with the qualities imported from India; the water frame spun twist for warps, but it could not be advantageously used for the finer qualities, as yarn of greater tenuity had not strength to bear the pull of the rollers when winding itself on the bobbins, though by repeating the process of drawing and doubling, it would be possible to produce yarn of sufficient fineness. The great waste of labour and time rendered a combination of the two machines eminently desirable ; and it was in 1779, three years after Arkwright had taken out his second patent, that Samuel Crompton, of Hall-in-the-Wood, near Bolton, invented the admirable machine which, combining the essential principles of Arkwright's frame with the property of stretching possessed by the machine invented by Hargreaves, has come to be known as the *mule jenny*, and to be so universally adopted, as entirely to supersede the spinning jenny, and to be employed to a far greater extent than the water frame. By means of the mule jenny, the roving was first drawn out by the rollers as in the water frame, and then stretched and spun by spindles without bobbins after the rollers had ceased to give out the rove, thereby making the yarn finer and of a more uniform degree of tenuity; for it will be seen, when delivered by the rollers, the yarn would be thicker in some parts than in others, and these thicker parts not being so effectually twisted as the smaller parts, were consequently softer and yielded more readily to the stretching power of the mule, and by this means the twist became equalized throughout. The mule jenny was a very complex piece of machinery, and required all its parts fitted and adjusted with great nicety. At first it was constructed with only twenty spindles, but by successive improvements, has been increased to as high as 1,200; these are regularly arranged on a moveable carriage, which, when in motion, recedes from the rollers at a rate somewhat greater than that at which the reduced rovings are delivered from them, the yarn receiving its twist by the rapid revolving of the spindles; and when the rollers are made to cease giving out the rovings, the jenny still continues to recede, but with a slower motion, the spindle revolving much more rapidly than before in order to save time. The distance which the spindles recede from the rollers while both are in motion is called a *stretch*,—this is usually about fifty-four or fifty-six inches; the space through which the mule or carriage moves greater than and during the giving out of the rollers is called the *gaining of the carriage;* and the further space accomplished by the carriage after the rollers are stopped is called the *second stretch*. This having been completed, and the yarn sufficiently twisted by the rotation of the spindles, the mule disengages itself from the parts of the machine by which it has been driven, and the attendant spinner returns the carriage to the rollers again to perform its task, the yarn thus manufactured being the while wound on the spindles in a conical form, and is called a *cop*.

Crompton, whose name with Arkwright's must ever be associated with the rise of the manufacture, appears to have been the very antipodes of Arkwright in disposition. Retiring and unambitious, he did not take out a patent for his mule-jenny, which it has been asserted he invented without any previous knowledge of Arkwright's frame; he endeavoured to retain his secret in order to work himself a competency; in this, however, he did not succeed, and a grant of £5,000 formed his sole reward. The original mule, with several improvements in the detail for effecting the manufacture of still finer qualities of yarn, as well as for speeding the rate of spinning, was the same in principle as that employed in the present day. The extent, however, of its powers in the rude form was to produce counts no higher than No. 80's (or 80 hanks of 840 yards each to the pound), while 800's have since been spun by it. To illustrate the important effect the introduction, improvement, and employment of the mule jenny has exerted on the price of the manufactured article, we need only remark that Crompton, according to his own statement, received for spinning No. 40's 14s., No. 60's 25s., and No. 80's 42s. per pound, while at the present day, allowing 9d. as the cost of the material employed, the margin for the same purposes would be respectively 4d., 7½d., and 1s. per pound.

At this period (1779) we have in the riots at Blackburn evidence that the use of machine labour was beginning to produce an effect on the working classes. It was on the 9th of October that the mob arose and scoured the country for miles around, destroying all the jennies and other machines with which Hargreaves and others had supplied the weavers and spinners. Nor was it only the working people who joined in this devastating outrage; for the middle and upper classes too, ignorantly supposed that the only tendency of the power afforded by the machines was to cause a contraction of the demand for hand labour, not having yet learned that the improved and cheapened manufacture would inevitably cause a corresponding increase of demand. But among all this ignorance, we find it was even then acknowledged that some partial good was derivable from their employment; for such jennies as worked not more than twenty spindles were spared, and those which exceeded this were generally cut down to the prescribed limit or altogether destroyed. Perhaps we may attribute this to a combination against the larger manufacturers who, of course, in the economy of their system, were enabled to undersell in a measure those who employed the smaller number of spindles; and it may be recorded, as illustrating the wide-spread popularity of the rioters' cause, that the destruction of a mill belonging to Arkwright at Birkacre, near Chorley, was even permitted in the presence of a powerful body of police and military. The effect may easily be imagined; capitalists and manufacturers found their security could only be purchased by flight to a more genial neighbourhood, and many afterwards settled in Manchester. Mr. Peel, the grandfather of the late Sir Robert Peel, a skilful and enterprising spinner and calico printer, having had his machinery at Oldham thrown into the river and destroyed, retired in disgust to Burton, in Staffordshire, where he erected a cotton mill on the banks of the Trent. It was many years ere Blackburn recovered from the effects of this disturbance, which nearly extinguished the manufacture in the neighbourhood.

Notwithstanding this opposition, however, which was doubtless aggravated by the then general distress, the cotton trade of the country was now established and rapidly extending; and as a result of the facility afforded by the mule for the manufacture of the finer counts, the muslin trade in the following year began to flourish, as well as the art of bleaching and printing, which legislators endeavoured to foster and retain. In 1782 an act was passed prohibiting the exportation of engraved copperplates and blocks, or the enticing of any workmen employed in printing calicoes to go beyond the seas, under a penalty of £500 or twelve months' imprisonment. In the year following, Arkwright's machinery for spinning, with the assistance of the atmospheric engine, was first used in Manchester, and an act passed reducing the duty on foreign muslins, calicoes, and nankeen cloths imported, to 18 per cent. ad valorem, with 10 per cent. drawback on exportation, while in the same year bounties were given on the export of British printed and dyed cottons, viz.:—

Under the value of 5d. per yard before printing, ½d. per yard.
Over 5d. and under 6d. ,, ,, 1d. ,,
Over 6d. ,, 8d. ,, ,, 1½d. ,,

besides the drawback of excise duty; it was however very soon after repealed. The enactments passed by the legislature, too, about the period in the matter of the cotton manufacture, were very diffuse,—the result of Pitt's legislation. In 1784 bleachers, printers, and dyers were compelled to take out licences under an annual tax of two pounds; while a tax of one penny per pound was imposed on all bleached cottons, which was, however, repealed in the following year. If we may judge by the rapidity with which these and other enactments were rescinded, the period seems to have been fraught with absurdities; for in this year Pitt brought forward his famous "fustian tax," which caused such great consternation and commotion in Manchester and its neighbourhood, that fifteen houses, employing 38,000 persons in different branches of the cotton trade, petitioned against it—and the master dyers and bleachers announced "that they were under the sad necessity of declining their present occupation until the next session of parliament;" and, as a natural consequence, in the next year it was repealed, the event being celebrated in Manchester by a grand procession. The art of printing, which was receiving great attention at the hands of Messrs. Peel and others, was heretofore effected solely by blocks and plates; but in this year a Mr. Bell, of Glasgow, invented the machine by which printing could be effected by cylinders; it was, however, afterwards greatly improved upon by Mr. Lockett, of Manchester.

The position of the art of weaving at this period, as may readily be imagined, was far in arrear of that of spinning, for although several minor improvements had been effected, the operation still required little less labour than in the rudest states of the art. In 1784, Dr. Edmund Cartwright, of Hollander House, Kent, commenced his endeavours to perform the operation by machine; and it is worthy of remark, as illustrating the relative positions of the two operations, that in a conversation at a meeting of some Manchester gentlemen, it was argued, that as it would be impracticable to employ any mechanical agency for the purpose, when Arkwright's patent should come into operation effectually, the quantity of material spun would be so great that hands could not be found sufficient to weave it. Having contended that the same excellence would in time be arrived at in weaving as in spinning, which met decided contradiction, Dr. Cartwright resolved upon entering on the subject himself practically and unaided, and the result was the production of a very rude model of the afterwards famed *power loom*, which he himself thus graphically described in its incompleteness:—" the warp was placed perpendicularly, the reed fell with the weight of at least half-a-hundred weight, and the springs which threw the shuttle, were strong enough to have thrown a congreve rocket; in short, it required the strength of two powerful men to work the machine at a slow rate, and but for a short time." Led by this invention, he was induced to undertake the manufacturing with power looms at Doncaster, but the concern was unsuccessful, and he was at length forced to abandon it. Thus this machine, the parent of the present power loom, was originally rude in its construction, and the labour requisite, from the necessity for stopping the machine very frequently in order to dress the warp as it unrolled from the beam, rendered it even after the mechanism had been somewhat improved, as expensive to work as the ordinary hand loom; neither was it during the century permanently improved upon. It ended in the total wreck of Cartwright's fortune, which was said to have been forty thousand pounds; to mitigate which, parliament granted £10,000 as compensation for his endeavours in the interest of the country.

As evidence of the jealousy with which our manufacture was guarded at the time, the act of 1782 was in this year (1785) put in force, and a German named Baden, tried at Lancaster, and fined £500 for having visited Manchester, and seduced cotton operatives to Germany. In the following year another person was fined £200 for having had in his possession a quantity of machinery with a view to export it to Germany, and for having seduced workmen to go abroad with it. The career of one John Holken, inspector-general of cotton and woollen manufactures in France, who died in this year, affords an illustration of the inutility of such persecution, as that before cited; having effected his escape from Newgate with Captain Moss before trial, he succeeded effectually in eluding pursuit, passed over to France, and his applications for pardon proving ineffectual, he established at Rouen a cotton manufactory, by which he amassed great wealth, and gave, by his example, a considerable impetus to the manufacture of that country.

Among other drawbacks to the rapid advancement of the British cotton trade was the laborious process of *bleaching*, which occupied six to eight months; and though in 1774, this process had been shortened by one-half, yet with this improvement the great length of time requisite rendered it an effectual bar to our successful competition in the foreign markets. The art of bleaching was, doubtless, originally introduced from the east, where it had been practiced immemorially; the old process was simply by the application of sour milk, and exposure to the light. This was improved by Dr. Home, of Edinburgh, about the middle of the century, by the adaptation of water acidulated with sulphuric acid; but at that time the art was so little understood in this country, that all the linens manufactured in Scotland, were sent to Holland to be bleached, and were kept there more than half a year, undergoing in the bleach fields around Haarlem the tedious processes just described. The bleaching properties of *chlorine*, formerly termed *oxymuriatic acid*, which had been discovered by Scheele, the Swedish philosopher, in 1774, had not till 1785 been turned to account in the bleaching of cloths. In this year the celebrated French chemist Berthollet, having found that it answered the purpose, made known the great discovery, which at once diminished the time required for bleaching from months to days; and even hours. But it is to James Watt, the mechanician, that we owe its introduction into this country. Having learned the art from Berthollet in Paris, he returned to England at the close of 1786, and introduced the practice into the bleach fields of his father-in-law, Mr. M'Gregor, of Glasgow. The application of oxymuriatic acid, however, imparted a very disagreeable odour to the cloth, and it was not until several years after that Mr. Henry, of Manchester, and Mr. Tennent, of Glasgow, discovered that the addition of lime destroyed the offensive odour without injuring the bleaching qualities of the acid.

Even with the increasing demand, caused by the improvements to which we have referred, the greatly increased supply of cotton manufactures at several periods caused great uneasiness in Manchester; and in 1787 a very large import of muslins and calicoes having taken place from India, a memorial was forwarded to the Board of Trade, praying that restriction might be placed on the East India Company's sales, in reply to which it was stated that the greater part of the goods had been exported. In 1788 a feeling of depression overtook the manufacturers from the great increase of manufactures and consequent competition, which was naturally assigned as the effect of the large importation of Indian goods; and government was solicited to allow a drawback as an encouragement to the export of English products. As evidence of the rapidly increasing supply of the raw material, as compared with the demand, we may see that the price of the raw material actually declined, while the quantity consumed increased, as will be subsequently shown, fully evidencing greater eagerness or ability in the production at that time, than is generally recorded.

We must now rapidly pass over the improvements which were made to the end of the century, being more in the finish of the detail than in any new principle, sup-passing those already shown. Several improvements were made in the mule by a man named Baker, and one Hargreaves, of Toddington; and in 1790, Mr. William Kelly, of Lanark Mills, applied the agency of *water power* to the *mule*. So soon as this potent agent came to be employed, Mr. Wright, a machine maker of Manchester, invented the *double mule*; while Arkwright applied the *steam engine* to his machinery, as Mr. Drinkwater had done in the year previous. Mr. Kelly also invented in 1792 a *self-acting mule*, which dispensed with a considerable amount of hand labour in the process. It was, however, at the time abandoned; but, by these additions, it was made capable of working four hundred spindles. In 1793, Mr. Kennedy made some considerable improvements in the wheel work of the mule, which greatly accelerated the action of the machine. And we must not omit here to notice the efforts, made though unsuccessfully, to improve the power loom and lessen the expenses of its employment. In 1790, Messrs. Grimshaw, of Gorton, erected a weaving factory at Knott Mill, Manchester, under a license from Dr. Cartwright, and endeavoured to improve the power loom at great cost to themselves, in which they did not succeed, and the factory being burned down, they abandoned the undertaking. In 1794, another power loom was invented by Mr. Bell, of Glasgow, which was, however, likewise abandoned; and on the 6th of June, 1796, Mr. Robert Miller, of Glasgow, took out a patent for a machine of the same nature, which was of considerable worth, but doomed to be early superseded by other improvements.

Having then recorded the epochs in the progress of the trade, we may proceed to take a retrospective glance up to the close of the century. We have briefly noticed the origin, in as far as the materials left to us will permit, and have shown, beyond a doubt, that not only the cultivation of cotton, but that the art of manufacture has existed in Asia now more than three thousand three hundred years. We have seen that, independent of its rise and progress there, a similar development has taken place in America; we have every reason to believe that in all those portions of Africa near the sea, the cultivation had been at some early period established; and have not failed to note its languid and sickly existence in Southern Europe. There exist in these facts, to one who studies the matter, many inconsistencies, perhaps irreconcilable, and though, for all material and useful purposes, we might ignore the subject, it is one, nevertheless, worthy the researches of the student and the lover of early history, as bearing much upon the condition of the inhabitants of the world in former ages. But while we survey the rise and progress of the trade from the pinnacle of greatness to which it has arrived, we must acknowledge, apart from the suppositions to which they might lead as to the advance made by other nations in former periods, that in the progress of the world, the present intellectual supremacy of one, or the rude and base animal desires of the other, are but the result of adventitious circumstances, or if not adventitious, circumstances over which the power of man, taken individually, had no control. We shall also be ready to admit, therefore, that a combination of natural circumstances, or the product of natural causes, have alone given to the European the energy with which to attain the present high standing among the people of the world. And could we but see the past, we should probably be able to trace the duration and extent of advance of the great powers of the time in a measure to the climate in which they originated and thrived. I may be accused of departing from my subject, but I hold it necessary to form some idea hereon, vague as it must necessarily be, before we can appreciate the position or relative value of our trade, or presume to surmise the place it holds, either as to the past, or in the present condition of the world, or the prospects of its future extension in our particular instance, or in other countries.

Our own condition, at a period very recent, would but ill-compare with the then inhabitants of the New World or of India; our moral condition, with all the advantages of climate, was absolutely below the latter, and the position of the manufacturing art in America, at the date of its discovery, or in India, surpassed even that of our woollen manufacture; and to this day, with all our appliances, we cannot surpass in fineness the muslins of the East, or the solidity and elegance of the *Hamaca's*, the Brazilians and Caribbees were wont to weave. When our people were in primeval darkness, East and West were in comparative light. Little could Columbus have deciphered the book of destiny opened before him, when these Caribs, in their primitive state, offered to trade in cotton yarn; he could not have for a moment thought that the fine threads would become some years afterwards a source of riches, surpassing all those treasures the Spaniards sought to obtain from the mines of the two America's. India, too, is the source whence we received indirectly our ideas of trade; it was the manufactures of that country, as of China, that inspired the minds of our forefathers with the wish for luxuries according to the received notions of the times. The period in which the manufacture was carried on in India, formed comparatively speaking, the dawning of our day; the sun was then travelling from another and past era in the world's commerce. The Indian manufacture was the forecast of that light, which, intensifying on its road hither, gained the needful warmth to dispel the early mists of morn, and develop the embryo state; and strengthened by the energy of the European, it has given rise to a new era of commercial splendour never before witnessed.

Though the transactions of the period are now shrouded in the obscurity of the past, we yet have sufficient data left to show that from India we received a considerable portion of our cotton yarns and goods in earlier years. A table, furnished in 1836 by James Cosmo Melville, Esq., of the India House, to Dr. Ure, shows the decline in the imports of yarn from India from 1700 to 1760:—

	lbs.		lbs.		lbs.
1703	114,100	1726	54,300	1740	3,339
1704	72,938	1727	27,254	1741	20,055
1705	39,155	1728	11,424	1742	11,366
1706	48,120	1729	18,816	1743	9,904
1707	219,879	1730	32,351	1744	14,593
1713	135,546	1731	20,496	1750	14,112
1714	12,768	1732	46,405	1751	4,704
1718	37,714	1733	70,976	1752	336
1720	21,350	1734	5,924	1755	37,632
1721	50,624	1735	91,394	1756	6,061
1722	10,800	1736	40,274	1757	4,357
1723	24,025	1737	2,083	1758	12,869
1724	21,588	1738	3,024	1759	4,390
1725	5,809	1739	8,445	1760	2,814

Thus, while in 1710 the total imports of cotton wool from all parts were 715,008 lbs., the imports of yarn from India in 1707 amounted to 219,879 lbs.; and when the imports of raw cotton had increased, in 1764, to 3,870,392 lbs., the Indian yarn imported in 1760 had decreased to 2,814 lbs.; and we must not omit to recall the fact, that a large contraband trade was being prosecuted in Indian yarn at the period, the figures of which would doubtless greatly eclipse those now given.

To the Genoese is probably due the credit of having introduced the raw material into this country, and to the Flemings the requisite skill with which to employ it; but to our countrymen are reserved those flights of mechanical genius which must always be regarded as having given to us the primogenitorship in the cause of civilization.

The importance of the mechanical part of those inventions acting directly upon the manipulation of the fibre, will be fully demonstrated in their wonderful effects; but we shall also have observed of how little avail the ingenious discoveries of Arkwright, Hargreaves, and Crompton would have been had not some substitute been found for the inadequacy of the animal power. When machine labour came first to be employed, the application of atmospheric and steam engines was unprofitable from their incompleteness; but fortunately for the trade and prosperity of our people, the manner in which to apply the accumulative force of water was well known, and superseded animal power almost ere it had been employed; the mills were consequently generally built on the falls of considerable rivers, and available land in that position greatly improved in value. This power, likewise, would have proved totally inadequate to subsequent requirements, but the adaptation of Watt's engine to the turning of the various machines in the manufacture met all requirements, admitting of an almost indefinite production of power; it also allowed of the sites being chosen among the people suited to the employment, and in localities having the advantage of an abundant supply of water, coal, and iron. The introduction imparted to the trade new life and vigour; and should any one, pondering over the causes which have led to the prodigious expansion of the cotton trade, omit it from his calculation, he will have erred much in the thesis. Its inexhaustible power and uniform regularity of motion supplied the most urgent want of the time, and without which probably at this day not alone our cotton manufacture, but general commerce would have formed as insignificant an appearance as in those earlier times. We may indeed recognise its successful application towards the end of the century in the statistics of the period.

Looking at these statistics, we have seen that up to 1745 the imports of the raw material had not reached 2,000,000 lbs., and the slight increase we have shewn as having occurred thereafter up to 1748 was ascribable, we may believe, to the temporary impetus given by the inventions some years previously of Wyatt and Paul in spinning and of Kay in weaving,—more particularly that of the latter, which came universally to be adopted. In 1764 the import was 3,870,392 lbs., and the official value of British manufactured cotton goods exported £200,354; the increase, then, up to the end of the century, may be seen as follows:—

From 1771 to 1775 the average annual import of raw cotton was 4,764,589 lbs.
,, 1776 ,, 1780 ,, ,, ,, 6,766,613 ,,
,, 1781 ,, 1785 ,, ,, ,, 11,328,989 ,,
,, 1786 ,, 1790 ,, ,, ,, 25,443,270 ,,
,, 1791 ,, 1795 ,, ,, ,, 26,683,002 ,,
,, 1796 ,, 1800 ,, ,, ,, 37,350,276 ,,

and the intermediate detail given in table No. 1. serves further to illustrate the matter. While the importations of the first fifty years of the century seem only to have increased 50 per cent., in the latter half the increase was equal to 1,782 per cent, or nearly *thirty-six times* as great. We will note the great bound of demand in 1785, the year in which Arkwright's patent was thrown open.

Between 1780 and 1790, the quantity of cotton increased *five-fold*. The per cent of increase decenially from 1741 appears to have been—

1741 to 1750..81 per cent.	1771 to 1780.. 75¾ per cent.
1751 to 1760..21½ ,,	1781 to 1790..319½ ,,
1761 to 1770..25½ ,,	1791 to 1800... 67½ ,,

And this extraordinary impetus is the result, then, of those ingenious inventions which the preceding pages have attempted to depict,—a phenomenon in commerce surpassed only by the present rate of advancement of our trade.

The cotton trade, unlike most others, was no nursling of government protection. In the suddenness of the impulse with which it arose it had to contend against stubborn and erroneous popular prejudices, which were at the time decidedly opposed to the science of economical production as applied to the arts, while the recipients of bounties in other fostered trades looked with jaundiced eyes on the intruder, which threatened then to outstrip all its compeers. Legislators watched ever anxiously the wealth in prospect as affording a fair field whereon to apply the heavy hand of financial oppression, but it overthrew other established and opposing branches of trade, and absolutely forced legislators to withdraw oppressive taxes levied during the American war, and concede to it the proper mede of governmental support. The bounties, however, by which it has been assisted, have been almost *nil*, and for a long time the prohibitions were actually as much against the British manufactured goods as those of foreign manufacture; and the duties which were first imposed upon the raw material in 1798, produced so miserable a sum compared with the trade lost by its imposition as to have rendered it decidedly hurtful, not alone to the trade itself, but to the country, and perhaps to the revenue. Yet the trade has overcome all obstacles, and continued to prosper and flourish beyond all precedent, and to be the means, not only of supplying all our wants, but has raised up a prodigious demand from other countries, which gives profitable employment to the people.

The progress of this export trade may be seen from table No. 3; the following figures will, however, show the more salient points:—

In 1765 the official value of British Cotton goods exported was				£248,345
,, 1766	,,	,,	,,	220,759
,, 1780	,,	,,	,,	355,060
,, 1785	,,	,,	,,	864,710
From 1786 to 1790 the annual average was..				1,232,530
,, 1791 ,, 1795 ,, ,,				2,088,526
,, 1796 ,, 1800 ,, ,,				4,211,828

The actual economy which caused this great revulsion of trade cannot be better made evident than by the simple fact that, while about 1780, Crompton received 42s. per lb. for his No. 80's yarn (which was equal then to about 60s. for 100's, which, at that period, however, it was impossible to spin in this country), the prices received at several subsequent periods up to the close of the century, which we take from table No. 2, would appear to have been:—

1786 for those same No. 100's	.. .. ..	38s.	per lb.
1790 ,, ,,	.. .. ..	30s.	,,
1795 ,, ,,	.. .. ..	19s.	,,
1800 ,, ,,	.. .. ..	9s. 5d.	,,

in short the same article was selling in 1800 at *one-sixth* of the value in 1780, or twenty years previous. And here we may record the prices received by the East India Company for their imported yarns taken from another table furnished by J. C. Melville, Esq., to Dr. Ure, thus:—

1707..1s. 11¼d. per lb.	1743..7s. 2¼d. ,, Some
1730..2s, 4¾d. per lb.	few bales sold at 12s. 8d. per lb.
1735..3s. 0d. ,,	1745..6s. 0½d. per lb.
1737..3s. 5½d. ,, ⎧Some few⎫ 8s. 1d. per lb.	1750..3s. 5½d. ,,
1738..3s. 9¼d. ,, ⎨ bales ⎬ 8s. 8d. ,,	1755..3s. 10d. ,,
1739..5s. 5½d. ,, ⎩ sold at ⎭ 21s. 2d. ,,	1757..2s. 9¾d. ,,

illustrating either an increasing demand up to 1743, when the maximum price was reached, or a finer class of yarn having been imported; and although the fact of a rather diminished than increased rate of import, would suggest the latter as the cause, we have the best reason for believing that the figures represent an actual increase in the demand and prices. The figures at the same time further serve to show the coarse nature of the yarns spun at the time,—these Indian yarns were generally employed in the manufacture of *fine goods*, and yet, from the prices quoted, they could not have exceeded No. 16's or 20's, though some small quantity towards the later years may have been as fine as No. 50's, which sold for about 40s. per lb.

A considerable reduction took place, too, in the price of the raw material, notwithstanding the greatly increased demand. The supplies, which, up to the middle of the seventeenth century, were from the Levant and Mediterranean, more particularly from the infancy of the knowledge of navigation, were greatly increased by considerable quantities being imported from the West Indies. In 1778, the Royal Society of Arts gave a gold medal to Mr. Andrew Bennett, of Tobago, for the best specimen of West India cotton, and from this period to the end of the century (up to which date we have no statistical data to enlighten us on the quantity received from each source of supply) the West Indies were our most regular and largest suppliers. In 1780, the finest grained and cleanest cotton came from Berbice, and in the following years Brazilian cotton was first imported from Maranham in a dirty state. The rate of supply seems to have amply adjusted itself to the requirements of the trade, and this is amply borne out by the annual average prices of West India and Berbice cotton, which appear to have been as follows:—

1782..31d. per lb.	1787..31d. per lb.	1792..25d. per lb.	1797..29d. per lb.
1783..25d. ,,	1788..23d. ,,	1793..20d. ,,	1798..33d. ,,
1784..19d. ,,	1789..17d. ,,	1794..20d. ,,	1799..37d. ,,
1785..21d. ,,	1790..17d. ,,	1795..23d. ,,	1800..29d. ,,
1786..32d. ,,	1791..22d. ,,	1796..25d. ,,	

by which we perceive that, excepting a temporary increase at the time that Arkwright's patents were thrown open, the price had even declined, until the impetus given to demand by the application of steam power again caused an upward movement. Supply, indeed, was so liberal that uneasiness was felt by the traders, and it is recorded that in 1782, a panic occurred in Manchester in consequence of 7,012 bags or about 1,400,000 lbs. having been imported between December and April. America had not then commenced to supply us with cotton; indeed it is believed that up to this time it was not grown to any extent in North America.

Notwithstanding, however, the onward progress we have depicted in demand and supply, the trade was not without sudden and frequent convulsions; though the advance had been extremely rapid, the mercantile community were inclined to extremes in their proceedings, which, under such circumstances, adjusted themselves in violent re-actions. The causes were many which led to these irregularities, and perhaps not the least may have been the continual improvement springing up, rendering expensive works comparatively valueless, from the backward and clumsy principles on which they were constructed. Mr. R. Finlay stated to a committee of the House of Commons, in 1833, that he had seen many overthrows in the cotton manufacture. In 1788, he thought it would never recover; in 1793, it received another blow; and in 1799, a severe one. The revulsions he referred to, however, were the natural consequences of the conduct of the manufacturers, and perhaps inseparable from the period and a new trade. When the great discoveries became known, and the economy they produced, capitalists came to the trade with the idea of taking as much of this advantage to themselves as possible, and by all their means endeavoured to maintain such an arbitrary and artificial scale of prices, offering thereby a premium for others to follow their example; and so long as this could be maintained numbers would pour into the manufacture, until, by such corrections, the competition which their selfishness had invited was the cause of a sudden re-action and decline in prices, ending perhaps in their almost entire ruin. These fluctuations doubtless furnish the key to the sudden alterations and decline we see in prices in No. 2, especially in the years 1792 and 1798.

BOOK II.

The mechanical inventions in the eighteenth century formed so important a part of the cause of the great and unprecedented development we have described in the cotton trade, that I could not, if I would, have omitted them from my notice of its rise and progress, forming, as they do, the basis of the new era. And although the progress in the improvement of those machines has continued almost uninterruptedly in the present century, and fully cognizant of the magnitude, of the subject I feel that I could not present of it an approximation to a complete history, nor properly estimate the value of its relative effects. The impossibility of obtaining the assistance of a person practically conversant in the matter has prompted me, not without regret, to expunge the subject from my paper. It is, however, wrapped in considerable obscurity, and certainly deserving a tome.

In all the departments of spinning, weaving, dyeing, bleaching, and printing, the same development has been equally effected, though the process of weaving, which at the close of the century, formed the most difficult part of the manufacture, from the yet rude application of Dr. Cartwright's power loom, and the expense attending the frequent stoppage of the machine, for the purpose of dressing the warp, has rendered the improvement in that department comparatively of more importance. Through the ingenuity of several persons, the power loom was early perfected by a re-arrangement of the mechanism, and the process of dressing and sizing the warp, and the early difficulties surmounted, so that it came generally into use, and finally supplanted the hand machine. It is in its present form a triumph of mechanical skill, and so very compact that a large number of them may be seen at work in one room, four looms only requiring the attendance of one weaver. But these machines are only employed in the fabrication of plain goods; the more costly woven, coloured, figured, or fancy goods are manufactured almost entirely upon an improved form of the *Jacquard loom*, so called after the inventor, one Jacquard, a straw hat manufacturer of France, who fled thither under the persecution to which he was subjected in his native place on account of his invention; and although the beauty of the contrivance is almost unequalled, there is, perhaps, no department in the manufacture in the present day which presents greater scope for improvement. Indeed, I believe that, ere long, the application of electricity will greatly facilitate the process and vastly economise the cost, especially of elaborate patterns. An invention of Mr. Donelli, now in this country, certainly seems to meet the case, and it is earnestly to be hoped it may do so, for it would inevitably cause a great reduction in price, and consequent extension of demand. In spinning, the inventions of Arkwright and Crompton still form the principles of the machines employed; though the improvements which have been effected are almost numberless, and still continue to add to their usefulness. The *water frame* is for the greater part employed in the manufacture of low counts. Some of the *mule jennies* are on the *self-acting* principle, dispensing almost entirely with hand labour, except to join the broken ends; these are, however, only employed in the manufacture of coarse numbers, say up to 60's, though on a late improvement they can be used up to 80's. But, as evidencing the vast improvement in the mechanical parts of the mule, qualities have been spun up to 800's, or equal to 382 miles to the pound weight; this last count was spun by Messrs. Houldsworth, but only in a very small quantity, from a little very fine cotton found in a bale of Sea Island. 700's have not been exceeded as a marketable article, and this is employed only in the manufacture of very fine lace. 300's is the highest count that can be expeditiously and satisfactorily woven by machine. Some samples of fabulously fine yarn have, however, been produced by the mule. Messrs. Thomas Houldsworth & Co. exhibited some at the Exhibition of 1851, in short lengths of six or eight inches, stated to count 2150's, but admitting the correctness of the calculation by which this extraordinary delicacy of texture is asserted, which by the way would be 2,150 by 840 yards=1,806,000 yards, or 1,026 miles to the pound, it could only serve as a curiosity to show the tension of the fibre, for it could never be wound upon a spindle. It was found in this experiment that the fineness of the simple fibre of the cotton used, assuming each of them to be one and a half inches in length, averaged about No. 8,000, according to the English cotton yarn standard of 840 yards to the hank; and, consequently, that in one pound weight of such cotton there were 161,280,000 fibres, which, placed end to end, would reach 3,817 miles; or one grain in weight of which would extend 960 yards. Messrs. Mair, of Glasgow, exhibited a piece of muslin, manufactured from No. 540's yarn, which is considered the finest muslin that has ever been manufactured by machine.

Notwithstanding that I am compelled thus to dismiss the subject of the history of these magnificent ideas and improvements in the mechanism of the manufacture, which have tended not only to stimulate and enlarge that trade, but to maintain our position as the first commercial nation in the world. It is fortunate that the statistics I have been permitted to cull from various sources will abundantly illustrate the wondrous power they have exerted, and the wealth which has accrued to us therefrom. The economy they have originated has permeated the whole system of our trade; nor has it been confined to this, the contagion has spread into other countries, indeed, I may say is pervading the whole civilized world.

As instancing the relative values of the material prepared by hand in the old times, and the economy the improvements have effected, an old MS. written by Wyatt in 1743, informs us that spinners then received for spinning counts respectively about—

40's	60's	80's
6s. per lb.	13s. per lb.	20s. 6d. per lb.

While, when Crompton had completed the first rough form of his mule jenny, we find he received for spinning the same counts, 14s., 25s., 42s., and these latter prices stand as compared with those of the present day, thus—

| | 1779 |||| | 1859 ||||
Count.	Cost of spinning.	Raw material, 18 ounces.	Total market value.	Cost of spinning, spinner's profit, &c.	Raw material, 18 ounces.	Total market value.	Count.
40	14s. 0d.	3s. 3d.	20s. 9d.	0s. 6d.	0s. 7d.	1s. 1d.	40
60	25s. 0d.	3s. 3d.	34s. 0d.	0s. 8⅕d.	0s. 8d.	1s. 4½d.	60
80	42s. 0d.	3s. 3d.	54s. 3d.	0s. 11d.	0s. 10d.	1s. 9d.	80

The quality of the yarn spun by hand, however, in 1743, must have been somewhat inferior to that spun by Crompton in 1779. And we fortunate people are supplied with the latter quality, but of finer finish, at *one-twentieth* part of the price charged eighty years ago ; and, moreover, receive the article in all its ramifications of manufacture at a proportional decline.

It is less than a century since the trade in cotton was very insignificant, not alone in its own extent, but its relative proportion to the trade of the country, consuming only 2,000,000 lbs. weight of the raw material, conducted in a rough, rude manner, requiring not the assistance of those appliances, the preparation of which now gives so extensive an occupation to all other branches of trade. No necessity then existed for working mines of coal and metals, for cutting down forests to build merchant navies for carrying hither the raw material and other articles required in their preparation, nor the transit abroad of those manufactures in exchange for luxuries, which the wealth derived in their sale permits of our now taking over and above the value of the raw materals. Looking at the monstrous strides made in that trade, and the accompanying development of civilisation since its origin, one is almost led to ascribe to it this advance in civilisation ; but in doing so, we should be ascribing to it an all-powerful influence above its merits, making it the cause rather than the effect. The manufacture had been the subject of savage industry among all the semi-developed nations of antiquity, and probably existed early in the history of mankind ; yet in all that period no advance was made, so far as we can tell, in rendering it useful even to an approximate extent of that caused by the European era of economy. We should rather ascribe the discovery in our country to the advance made in civilization and science at the period, and the increasing importance of the demand for the textile fabrics, acknowledging, at the same time, the advent of our success in the start we received by those discoveries. At the period, however, the intricate rudiments of both science and the useful arts had many explorers, and almost as a thunder cloud burst with overwhelming force from the pent up elements, lighting up a path of immense and glorious splendour. Though some considerable wealth must have at the time been acquired, a large portion of the capital which was forthcoming wherewith to prosecute the channel opened up, took its origin from the increased value of almost every product of the land by the stimulus given to trade. The trade indeed arose at a most critical period in our history ; the conquests of the British had raised up the ire of the world against them ; the American colonies had just been lost to us ; the year 1773, when Arkwright and Hargreaves were maturing their grand discoveries, saw the American war just breaking out, and the whole sequel of revolutionary conquests looming thickly in the distance ; the defensive position necessary to be maintained threatened fast to bear down the energies of the people ; and, indeed it is difficult to conceive how but for the development it is justly our pride to dwell upon, the funds wherewith to meet the immense war expenditure incurred thereafter till the commencement of this century, could have been raised. And it was in this dire emergency that the British cotton trade proper took its birth; mayhap the hard school in which it was reared has added to the stability of the whole fabric, by drawing out the otherwise latent energies of the people. In its origin and progress Mr. Baynes graphically likens it to "a little rill issuing like a silver thread out of the mountain side, gathering strength as it descends, laughing, sparkling, bounding and leaping over every obstacle which opposes its progress; it increases in volume as it rushes onwards; the rill becomes a brook, the brook a rivulet, and a number of the streams united form the mighty river which, rolling majestically onwards to the great ocean, fertilizes and enriches the countries through which it flows." And truly it presents in its progress, rapid development, and present stupendous extent,—a phenomenon in commerce unequalled in the annals of the world. Conjecturing the pigmy character of the trade a century since, and then realizing the present colossal fabric, it strikes the imagination with awe; for its magnitude is unequalled, whether we consider it as the source of immense individual and national wealth, the amount of capital to which it gives employment, the large proportion it forms of our entire trade, the stimulus it has given to other departments, the millions of people directly and indirectly engaged in it, the comfort to which it has tended, the effect the intercourse necessitated by it has exerted upon civilization, or its particular effect on places and people either socially, politically, or morally. And we may glance at these separate heads as affording an idea of its actual importance.

The collection of 547,317 tons of the simple fibre cotton, at a distance of upwards of four thousand miles, and even thirteen thousand miles, the conveyance home, the redistribution of about 78,189 tons in an unmanufactured state, the conversion of the remaining 469,128 tons into yarn and woven manufactures of all kinds, and their disposal at three times the original cost of the raw material when landed on our shores, presents a field unsurpassed for the acquisition of wealth. But these duties come to be divided among as many different classes of our countrymen, striving to outdo each other as much as their foreign compeers; and this competition, though doubtless tending to an increased consumption and trade, when carried to a legitimate extent, is susceptible of being overstrained. The efficiency of the trade as a source of wealth depends upon a combination of many circumstances, the result of the discretion and foresight of those engaged in it; and we shall see perhaps from the figures in table No. 8, that these circumstances have lately assumed a form engendering a dangerous dilation of trade, and opposed to its fullest production. We will therefore, for the sake of comparison, take the aggregate of each of the five quinquennial periods, ending respectively 1838, 1843, 1848, 1853, and 1858, and we discover the margin for wages, the cost of implements, buildings, premises, dye and other drugs, interest and profit, and every expense attending the manufacture, was—

	1834-8.	1839-43.	1844-8.	1849-53.	1854-8.
	£	£	£	£	£
Value of manufactures	203,472,942	206,354,480	209,978,931	244,397,313	287,450,156
Cost of raw material actually consumed	65,059,075	60,072,831	59,325,874	83,089,646	112,180,596
Surplus for expnses &c.	138,413,867	146,281,649	150,653,057	161,307,667	175,269,560

for working up the raw material in quantity as follows :—

	1834-8.	1839-43.	1844-8.	1849-53.	1854-8.
	lbs.	lbs.	lbs.	lbs.	lbs.
	1,793,209,371	2,371,616,156	2,807,296,602	3,356,800,000	4,258,600,000

or equivalent to—

| 18·53d. | 14·80d. | 12·88d. | 11·53d. | 9·87d. |

a rate of successive decline equal to—

| .... | 20 per cent. | 13 per cent. | 10 per cent. | 14½ per cent |

We see thus, at a glance, the proportion of surplus for the cost of manufacture at these several periods, and are irresistably driven to the conclusion, that at no former period has the profits of the manufacturer been at so low an ebb as in the last period. Now there are certain causes that may mitigate this, and these are — abundant and cheap food, rendering the item of wages less ; the low price of the materials employed; or facilities of production, lessening the expenditure. In the most important item of breadstuffs, the average prices per quarter of wheat in the like periods has been—

	1834-8.	1839-43.	1844-8.	1849-53.	1854 8.
	s. d.	s. d.	s. d.	s. d.	s. d.
As per Table No. 2	50 11	61 10	55 5	43 5	63 4
Of Mutton, as per Table No. 10	3 8	3 8½	3 11½	3 7½	4 5

And it is undeniable that every necessary of life has been higher than at any of the former periods, and the rate of wages proportionately so; the same remark applies, though not with equal force, to the dyes and other articles employed. And looking at the bank rate of discount as the criterion of the value of money, we discover that, excepting the year 1847, the rate in the earlier years ranged below four per cent, and from 1849 to 1852 below three per cent, while from 1852 to the end of 1857, it steadily increased until it reached ten per cent; since which it has declined to the present low rate. The facilities of production or economy in the manufacture resolves itself now almost entirely into the *speeding* of the machinery, and has made fair progress, such as might account for the decline shewn in 1843, 1848, and 1853 ; but as in the case of spinning, this progress, as it reaches perfection, is gradually lessening—that is, as far as the mechanical part is concerned. The speeding, for instance, of spindles does not produce a proportionately increased quantity of yarn, from the more frequent occurrence of breakages and mishaps. The qualities of the manufacture, or expense of finish, has unquestionably become more lavish ; and as a whole, everything goes to prove that the manufacturers' expenses have even increased, while the margin for that purpose has palpably lessened. The only manner in which the manufacturers have gained strength to sustain the incubus, must have been in the comparatively steady employment of their machinery. But putting aside the question of increased expenditure, and adopting the rate of progressive economy indicated in the previous twenty years—as 20 per cent, 13 per cent, and 10 per cent, and allowing for the increased quantity worked up, or the more uniform and continuous employment of the mills, the rate of economy would not be more than nine per cent in the last quinquennial period ending 1858, or making the surplus that should have been reserved to cover expenses and adequate profit 10⅓d. per lb., or on 4,258,600,000 lbs.= £186,313,750 ; whereas the sum shewn as left for that purpose was only £175,269,560, or a loss of £2,208,838 per annum in the last five years. The business of manufacture may not be one in which exorbitant profit should be made, but there should be over and above providing for all contingencies, and paying a fair interest on capital, a fair margin of profit to those engaged in it. Adopting the capital of the manufacturers (*i.e.* of spinners and weavers) employed as about *sixty millions* in the last quinquennial period, the interest taken at five per cent, and profit at an equivalent sum, the amount of these two items should give *six millions per annum*; and this embraces only the departmeuts of spinning and weaving, the numberless other divisions of the manufacture can only be roughly estimated, as they are so widely diffused and so intermingled with silk, wool, and other textile trades. But supposing, for the sake of argument, that one half the amount of capital is employed in them, and that therefore the interest and profit in these branches be taken at another *three millions*, we have a total of £9,000,000, and of this, *profit* forms one half, or *four million five hundred thousand pounds per annum*. In the last period, we shall see that forty-nine per cent has been sacrificed to competition—that is, unless in the former periods which form the basis of our theory, the profits of our manufacturers were unduly large.

The capital to which the British cotton trade gives employment is prodigious; no correct data can be obtained of its extent. Mr. Ellison, in his excellent "Hand-Book of the Cotton Trade," made an estimate upon the basis of 23s. to 24s. per spindle, and £24 per loom. Upon this mode of reckoning, it will appear that for every factory hand there is equal to £90 sunk in machinery, showing the extent to which manual labour is now assisted.

2,210 mills* containing 28,010,217 spindles, costing 23s. 6d. each, would give	£33,000,000
298,847* looms at £24 per loom	7,250,000
*These are the figures returned by the Factory Inspectors in 1856; the number of both spindles and looms has, however, since wonderfully increased.	
Estimated floating capital	15,000,000
And Mr. Ellison also estimates the cash in the hands of bankers	10,000,000
Total capital embarked in the operations of spinning and weaving.	£65,250,000
Probable capital employed by manufacturers in subsequent processes of bleaching, dyeing, printing, &c.	30,000,000
Probable floating capital of importers of raw material	6,500,000
„ „ shipowners	3,000,000
Total, independent of all subsidiary trades ministering indirectly.	£104,750,000

to which may even be added £2,000,000 as the capital of the buying and exporting merchant. The miscellaneous character of all the numerous trades ministering directly and indirectly to the prosecution of this industry, renders it impossible to estimate their extent of capital. From the large stocks held by retailers in the country, the capital in that branch alone must be considerable, perhaps more than one year's consumption, or *twenty millions sterling*.

The proportion which the cotton trade forms of the entire of our national industry, it is impossible to guess at; the large proportion it bears of our entire export trade is amply evidenced in table No. 9. We find the quinquennial average of the declared real value of exported cotton manufactures, as compared with other articles, to be as follows:—

	Cotton.	Woollen, Linen, and Silk.	Total Textiles.	Exports of all kinds.
	£	£	£	£
1820-24	16,921,770	8,419,169	25,340,939	36,781,519
1825-29	16,973,897	7,377,181	24,351,078	36,048,359
1830-34	18,616,850	8,473,914	27,090,764	38,635,243
1835-39	23,210,917	10,761,762	33,972,679	49,206,309
1840-44	23,820,152	11,555,021	35,375,173	52,175,999
1845-49	24,901,744	12,390,931	37,292,675	58,637,161
1850-54	30,536,617	17,293,606	47,830,223	84,002,394
1855-59	40,659,014	21,018,620	61,677,634	116,126,064

showing the proportions to have been—

	Cotton Manufactures.	Other Textile Manufactures.	All other Articles.
1820-24	46 per cent.	23 per cent.	31 per cent.
1825-29	47 ,,	21 ,,	32 ,,
1830-34	48 ,,	22 ,,	30 ,,
1835-39	47 ,,	22 ,,	31 ,,
1840-44	46 ,,	22 ,,	32 ,,
1845-49	43 ,,	21 ,,	36 ,,
1850-54	36 ,,	21 ,,	43 ,,
1855-59	35 ,,	18 ,,	47 ,,

If we were to regard the progress and development in our general trade as the result of the discoveries and improvements in the manufacture of cotton, with which, in the earlier years above shown, it could not keep pace, the value of the progress we have already shown in that manufacture in the last eighty years, prodigious as it appears, would dwindle into comparative insignificance, not only in amount, but, latterly, in the rate of progression, for the above figures would show the rate to have been:—

	Cotton Manufactures.	Other Textile Manufactures.	All other Articles.
1825-29	3-10ths per cent.	....	....
1830-34	10 ,,	15 per cent.	7 per cent.
1835-39	25 ,,	27 ,,	27 ,,
1840-44	2 ,,	7 ,,	6 ,,
1845-49	4 ,,	7 ,,	12 ,,
1850-54	23 ,,	39 ,,	44 ,,
1855-59	33 ,,	22 ,,	38 ,,

This immense development in our general trade has been by some attributed to the impetus received from the discoveries in the cotton manufacture; with this, as before stated, I do not agree. The advance made in civilisation at the time, the knowledge of science, and of the application of the useful arts generally, caused equally the development in the cotton trade and general commerce. While we do not seek to underrate the importance of those discoveries, the trade they gave rise to, or the important effect they have exerted on the trade of the country generally, we will observe that, as a manufacture in which the main value imparted to it is in the labour expended on it, and as an easily acquired auxiliary to the comfort of the nations inhabiting the frigid and temperate zones, it presented the field, holding out the greatest indcement to the application of economy in the employment of power, and consequently that in which the greatest advantage would be gained by its application. The effect, nevertheless, has been immense on all departments of trade, the application of economical machine power has equally assisted other departments where the necessity existed, though the progress in this particular manufacture has much exceeded all others, and the wealth it has raised up has given rise to an immense demand for other luxuries.

The incalculable importance of the cotton trade in ministering to the comfort of millions of the human race is amply evidenced by the fact that its produce now forms an inseparable element in their wants. Contributing alike to the comfort of both rich and poor the cotton cloth which covers emaciation in the squalid haunts of the poor is made from the same material as the gaudy draperies which adorn the luxurious saloons of fashion, or those superbly delicate fabrics which encircle as with gossamer folds the rounded forms of beauty. But, though in the sense in which we mean it, the humbler classes are they who have received the most munificent advantage from its development; those tasteful luxuries of the more fortunate in pecuniary wealth confer a considerable boon on those to whom they are denied, in the occupation it gives to labour and skill in their manufacture. How many poor homeless creatures, prostrated by starvation, enervated by bodily disease, or the cankering sorrows of the world, would have succumbed but for the protection this simple fibre has afforded against the inclemency of our winter. How many homes glow with warmth and plenty from the product of this industry, and but for which perhaps many more sad tales of cold starvation would be surged up from those hidden haunts of sorrow in the homes of our poor.

Though the numberless and intricate ramifications into which the manufacture divides itself does not permit of our forming an idea of the number of people to whom it gives employment even in our own small islands, still the admirable census returns of Great Britain enable us to comprehend its extent in the two fundamental departments of spinning and weaving.

The information furnished to parliament at different periods furnishes considerable information on these points, and we will therefore present an analysis as far as will be interesting, and it appears as follows :—

Year.	Nnmber of factories	Number of Spindles.	Number of Looms.	Amount of Moving Power.			Number of Persons.		
				Steam.*	Water.	Total.	Male.	Female.	Total.
1835	.....	....	109,626	....	....	....	....	....	....
1839	1,819	....	....	46,827	12,977	59,804	113,815	145,570	259,385
1850	1,932	20,977,017	248,627	71,005	11,550	82,555	141,501	189,423	330,924
1856	2,210	28,010,217	298,847	88,001	9,131	97,132	157,186	222,027	379,213

* Consuming 15½ tons of coal per annum per horse power, or equal to a total of 1,359,355 tons of coal.

And we cannot but be struck by the insignificance of the number here shown as employed, when compared with the immense production to which it gives rise. But this happily forms but an atom of those receiving sustenance from its fruitful influence. It has been estimated that for each of these workers there are employed three nonworkers, not being subject to factory inspection, raising the number of those immediately employed in the manufacture to *one and a half million;* but this is still but a tithe of the immense number to which it indirectly gives employment. The population of the towns immediately concerned in one or other of the great staple manufactures, shows the relative progress to have been—

	Cotton.	Silk.	Wool.	Wool & Silk.	Flax.
1801	319,072	74,880	169,495	36,238	39,548
1811	406,982	95,367	195,515	36,478	45,146
1821	546,052	124,231	260,691	49,705	48,530
1831	743,259	161,300	350,857	60,505	67,031
1841	983,001	190,926	425,555	61,846	87,286
1851	1,220,104	227,622	507,886	68,195	102,252
Annual rate of increase in ½-century	2·719 o/o	2·249 o/o	2·219 o/o	1·273 o/o	1·918 o/o

No more weighty argument perhaps could be adduced of the beneficial effects of the cotton trade than the density of population in those districts which have come to be the centres of the manufacture. A glance at the chart which accompanies the last Census Returns, will amply show that in and around these, which we may call Liverpool, Manchester, and Glasgow, the prosperity must have exceeded that of any other department in the kingdom, if the density of the population in their vicinities may be taken as any indication.

The destinies of countries and towns, as with states and kingdoms, have always been dependent on the tracks of commerce. Cities have been made and unmade, and kingdoms elevated or depressed by simple and silent changes in the course of trade. The mighty ruins in Asiatic plains mean often nothing more than the adoption of some new route by a line of caravans, leaving a proud and stately emporium stranded and desolate; and in our Northern clime a tract of swampy and marshy land, on which no signs of trade existed, has been mainly reclaimed to agriculture and commerce, and become populous and wealthy by the diversion of that track in the one simple article—cotton. It has been the happy destiny of the port of Liverpool to be the place of ingress for almost the whole of the enormous supply of American cotton to this country; and as a consequence, the circumstance has assisted materially in the prodigious rise it has made in the last century. In 1555 the population was only 138; we may mark its progress:—

1555....	138	1777....	34,107	1831....	165,221
1693....	4,851	1790....	55,732	1841....	223,003
1730....	12,074	1801....	77,708	1851....	258,346
1760....	25,787	1811....	94,396		
1770....	35,600	1821....	118,972		

and with the adjoining townships or suburbs, exclusive of seamen, even amounts to 376,065. The rapid strides made in the trade are equally apparent from the following figures, obligingly furnished by George J. Jefferson, Esq., the Treasurer of the Mersey Dock and Harbour Board:—

	Vessels.	Tonnage.	Dock Duties.
1752	—	—	1,776
1768	1,808	—	3,566
1769	2,954	—	4,004
1800	4,746	450,060	23,380
1810	6,729	734,391	65,782
1820	7,276	805,033	94,412
1830	11,214	1,411,964	151,359
1840	15,998	2,445,708	178,196
1850	20,457	3,536,337	211,743
1859	21,214	4,451,969	366,939

Every one knows that Manchester is now the focus whence comes almost the whole of the cotton manufactures, which every where meet the eye; but few, however, unless immediately connected with the trade, can form any idea of the magnitude of the productive power constantly employed in that manufacture, and, still less, of the small number of operatives, comparatively, by which that power is wielded. There are also numerous other towns around Manchester creeping quickly into importance, and which may, ere long, in the course of development become amalgamated with the great city. Taking, however, the city of Manchester, we shall discover an immense increase in the population, all of whom, directly or indirectly, are connected with the staple manufacture.

Thus, in 1757, the population of the township was estimated as only			16,000
In 1788 it had risen to			42,821
Manchester, Salford, and the suburbs in 1801 were returned at			109,166
,,	,,	1811 ,,	132,099
,,	,,	1821 ,,	180,948
,,	,,	1831 ,,	261,584
,,	,,	1841 ,,	339,734
,,	,,	1851 ,,	439,797

and while these people, with those in the surrounding towns, by their joint exertions, assisted by all the appliances the knowledge of science can suggest, are able to spin and weave the greater portion of the entire cotton imports, they form, notwithstanding, as we have already seen, but a tithe of the number employed; but these two simple and primary processes of spinning and weaving are effected by an employment of productive power equal to that of *six million* people, if engaged in the operations of hand spinning and weaving continuously throughout the year, if unassisted by science; and yet, in the whole number of factories in which this powerful task is performed, the number of hands employed was, at the date of the last returns (1856), but 379,213. We may safely say that Manchester is the receiver and dispenser of *thirty millions sterling per annum*, an immense consumer and producer; the districts ministering to its efficacy and power, however, spread far and wide over the length and breadth of the land; and this, though the greatest is but one of the seats of the trade, for, as tastes alter and the desire for luxuries increases, other kinds of manufactures than those peculiar to Manchester come into augmented demand, so other departments adding to the beauty and value of the article are equally progressing, forming new or enlarging old ones as nebuli in the great system. The most important of these are Glasgow and Paisley, in the former a large amount of the operation of dyeing is now carried on, particularly of what is called the *Turkey red dye*, a very fine red colour in considerable demand in the Oriental markets, as well as the important task of bleaching and the manufacture of muslins and thread.

Though it is in towns that prosperity so accumulates as to attract attention, whole districts equally share in it, and Lancashire as the country in which the principal concentration of the trade has taken place by reason of its natural advantages, presents in the increase of its population the most extraordinary features of the whole country, containing 1,219,221 acres; the increase, as shown by the last census returns, appears to have been:—

1801...... 683,252	1831......1,360,946
1811...... 840,095	1841......1,698,609
1821......1,067,287	1851......2,067,301

These instances of prolific increase of population in those places where the trade has established itself, while carrying great weight with them in solving the question of the prosperity to which it has given rise, must not be considered solely the effect of that trade. It may be the first cause; yet many other circumstances, some engendered by it, but many arising from local natural advantages, have contributed to the development. But the relative value of property as compared with the present time presents equally remarkable features. Henry Ashworth, Esq., in an able paper, delivered to the Society of Arts in 1858, instanced two cases which serve prominently to illustrate the subject:—

The entire county of Lancashire was, in 1692, returned for the Land Tax at a value of £97,242

While the valuation, in 1853, for the County Rate was £6,913,073

showing an improved value of *seven thousand per cent.*

And the Hundred of Salford taken by the same valuation was, in 1692 .... £25,907

While the valuation, in 1853, for the County Rate was £3,051,347

or an increased value of *eleven thousand seven hundred per cent.*

But perhaps the most extraordinary instance of development is apparent in the Township of Chorlton-upon-Medlock,—

The return for the Land Tax of which, in 1692, was £256

While, in 1853, the valuation for the County Rate had increased to £143,151

or an increase of *fifty-five thousand seven hundred and seventy-three per cent.*

And, indeed, in every description of produce and property an equal tendency to development is presented. Taking the price per quarter of the great necessary of life, *wheat*, the annual average of decennial periods appear to have been—

	s. d.		s. d.
In 1687	24 0	Average 10 years 1790-9	55 11
Average 10 years 1730-9	28 0	,, ,, 1800-9	82 2
,, ,, 1740-9	27 5	,, ,, 1810-9	88 8
,, ,, 1750-9	31 11	,, ,, 1820-9	58 5
,, ,, 1760-9	35 8	,, ,, 1830-9	56 8
,, ,, 1770-9	45 0	,, ,, 1840-9	55 11
,, ,, 1780-9	45 9	,, ,, 1850-8	44 11

And that I may not be charged with presenting an ex-parte statement, I annex the average price of beef per stone :—

	s. d.		s. d.		s. d.
1690-9	1 11¼	1750-9	1 10½	1810-9	5 1¾
1700-9	1 8	1760-9	2 1	1820-9	3 8
1710-9	1 9½	1770-9	2 5	1830-9	3 2½
1720-9	1 9½	1780-9	2 7½	1840-9	3 3
1730-9	1 8	1790-9	3 3¾	1850-9	3 0⅝
1740-9	1 10¼	1800-9	4 10¼		

These figures speak volumes, embracing as they do the century and a half in which we have made the great advance as a commercial nation ; we cannot but be struck with the marked regularity of the rate of advance and decline. Thus, we find in the case of wheat, that from 1687 up to the close of the second French revolutionary war the price had gradually and irresistibly advanced, in which the price of meat amply sympathised. Since that period the prices have continued to decline ; but we find that it has been the greatest in the case of wheat, and discover in this the effect of commercial intercourse and free trade. The facilities opened up for the import from other countries, has prevented a continued rise, which the still increasing demand would have imposed upon us but for the enlightened administration with which we are blessed.

From the immediate connection of the causes which have promoted the development of the cotton trade and the trade of our country generally, as well as our national wealth, it becomes impossible to separate or assign the proportion of the effect on the general trade and prosperity to which the cotton trade directly or indirectly gave rise, and much more difficult is it to guess the extent to which that particular trade has contributed to produce the general wealth which we see every where around us ; but whatever proportion is ascribable to it, or its cause, we may see that the advantage accruing from the trade is immense. The economy effected in the manufacture forms as much wealth to the nation,—not wealth acquired merely by one class, but pervading the entire mass of the people,—the scope of which it is a little difficult to comprehend. The distribution of everything in the universe is consummately beautiful. Wherever, as in our case, the intelligence of a people causes an expansion of knowledge, a desire to acquire wealth, by persevering energy, and the employment of the mind and body with the luxuries it brings, there the demand for all the natural products which they work, transform and render more productive, as a consequence, increases relatively in value ; and though we have always acquired considerable wealth from our foreign trade, yet, had it all been so obtained, the extent of our true wealth or surplus of production over consumption would be that of our possession of the precious metals or other imported produce ; but this, great as it is, forms but a small part of the national wealth. By the increased productiveness and value of all property to which we have alluded, an immense wealth has taken its birth, which is, however, convertible only within the kingdom, and dependent on the continuance of that demand for its existence, and, so long as the increased value is acknowledged and obtainable, that value is the national wealth. This increased value has proportionately raised the cost of luxuries, the demand for which formed the first cause, but it has been so amply met by the economy of production as to be almost imperceptible ; indeed, the wealth it has raised up is so immense, and credit consequently so good, that though property has become enormously dear, yet that very increase in its value, and the wealth it has raised up, is such as to render it a cheap commodity. Credit being good, money, the means wherewith to obtain it, is cheap. Now, paper money supplies a large proportion of our wants; and again, much of our wealth is loaned out, and rendered productive simply upon an undertaking between the parties. This wealth then of our people, while greatly assisting in our commercial operations, is only rendered productive by a continued employment of the energies of the people to the satisfaction of legitimate passions. The increased demand for property, while increasing its value, and acting eventually on the cost of all the productions, has permitted of a greatly increased rate of consumption, and extended to the labourer his share in the sweets of the world, while the economy has permitted of his wants being cheaply and more fully supplied. The demand for luxuries, for the possessors of wealth, in the increased value of property, and its further extension by thrift, necessitates so active an employment of the whole mass of the people as to permit of the payment also of a higher rate of wages.

Certain things we see have increased in value—these are stationary or natural products,—the extent of which cannot be increased with their greater productiveness and value; others have fallen in value by the economy in the production, discovered and exercised, exceeding the increased demand. The increase in the value of the former forms a large part of our national wealth, but forming, as they do, the basis of the production of the other, were it not for the institution of credit, and the immense proportion of wealth seeking employment, that value would militate much against the cheapened production and consequent demand upon which that wealth hinges. The product of the cotton industry as the second necessary of life, and as that in which the most radical employment of the economy could be exercised, must necessarily have formed a most important part in these changes, which have raised us to the wealthy position we hold.

The national debt of the United Kingdom affords some basis on which to found speculations as to the extent of the national wealth. The table No. 11, furnishes the needful data; we see, by it, that the progress of the debt has been as follows:—

	Debt.	Interest.	ℙ cent.		Debt.	Interest.	ℙ cent
1691	£3,130,000	£232,000	7·41	1781	£189,258,681	£7,451,052	3·94
1701	12,552,486	1,219.147	9·71	1791	241,675,999	9,513,507	3·94
1711	22,398,425	2,274,377	10·15	1801	517,511.871	19,819,839	3·83
1721	54,405,108	2,855,380	5·25	1811	678,200,436	25,484,765	3·76
1731	50,738,786	2,219.986	4·38	1821	827,984.498	31,105,319	3·76
1741	48,382.439	2,099,950	4·34	1831	782,716,684	28,329,986	3·62
1751	77,197,026	2,769,484	3·58	1841	792,209,685	29,462,030	3·72
1761	114,294,987	4,148,999	3·63	1851	782,869,382	27,907,068	3·56
1771	128,986,012	4,733,694	3·67	1859	805,078,554	28,204,299	3·50

We shall perceive that from 1691, when the debt proper took its rise up to 1711, the rate of interest payable upon the whole funded and unfunded debt, increased from $7\frac{1}{2}$ to 10 o/o, showing that the amount of floating capital or wealth was not equal to the demand, while at the time Hargreaves and Arkwright took out their patents (1769-70) it had declined to a rate no higher than that of the present day; but then the amount raised comparatively was so insignificant,—being only *one hundred and twenty-nine millions* in *eighty years*,—while in the next *forty years* it was augmented by *seven hundred and thirty-two millions*, the result of the American war and French revolutions. That this burden has been much mitigated by the astonishing development of trade since the improvements in the cotton manufacture, is evidenced by the comparatively trifling increase in the rate at which it was supplied, even with the tendency to the destruction of confidence in such a lavish expenditure; may we even find cause for congratulation in the beneficial effects the burden has exercised, but certainly cannot fail to observe the critical nature of the period in which the cotton trade took its birth.

As a criterion of wealth, the national debt serves more to show the resources of the conntry at the period in which it was raised, or up to about the year 1815, since which it has continued steadily, though slowly, to be paid off; up to that period, marking the opening of a new era in our export trade, when the foreign trade was permanently opened up, the enormous amount of *eight hundred and sixty-one million pounds sterling* had been subscribed to the wants of the government, as the surplus wealth over and above the wants of trade; since that period the exigencies of the state have not necessitated any permanent addition, but, on the contrary, a reduction of the debt, so that the wealth, since accumulated, has been forced to seek employment in other and happily more fruitful channels, in works of improvement in place of the execrable work of destruction; for all this burden is the result of War. For the purpose of comparison we may glance at the comparative amount of the national debt of the several states of Europe, which appear thus :—

Great Britain	£805,078,554	Belgium	£30,000,000
France	400,000,000	Sardinia	30,000,000
Austria	280,000,000	Portugal	20,000,000
Spain	140,000,000	Turkey	20,000,000
Russia	132,000,000	Denmark	13,000,000
Holland	90,000,000	Hamburg	5,000,000
Prussia	35,000,000	Sweden	500,000

making the debt of this country nearly *forty-two per cent.*, of the entire European debt of *two thousand million pounds sterling*. The immense accumulation of wealth which has taken place since 1815 in this country, has come to be embarked in railways, canals, docks, harbours, bridges, mines, banking, gas, insurance, steam, and shipping companies, and a host of other joint stock undertakings, which have assisted and promoted the development of industry; in colonial and foreign stocks and shares, and landed and household property, as well as the immense amount of the circulating medium; and though unable at present to present any accurate statement of the capital embarked in these multifarious undertakings, we may find that in the one item of railways alone, the enormous amount of £308,824,851 is so embarked. As evidence of the comparative extent of our wealth as compared with other countries, while all other nations have difficulty in raising the amount of their requirements in cases of emergency, and the invariable necessity which arises for an application to this country for a part or the whole; it is our happy fortune, and the result of developed trade, that though the mass of the people cannot think so lightly of our burden as a late Chancellor of the Exchequer essayed to do, we have an abundant surplus to meet those demands whenever a sufficient guarantee can be offered.

The table No. 11 amply indicates the one great cause of this immense drain of £28,204,299 annually on our national resources—war in all its stern reality! And if any means has been ordained by which the curse shall some day be effaced from the earth, civilization and trade will assuredly be the means. The community of interest which trade promotes and fosters, must be working towards that end, the artificial and arbitrary boundaries which nations or sections have raised up, are yielding to a system of mutual confidence and reciprocity; and all find that the acme of comfort, wealth, and prosperity, is more surely and effectually obtained by the peaceful interchange of the fruits of industry. And how large a proportion does the delicate fibre cotton afford in this bond of amity? What more grateful intercourse can be imagined than the trade between this country and all the cotton growing and consuming countries, offering as we do a market for the raw material produced, whence it can be manufactured and distributed to other countries in the shape and quantity required? We return to the producer the articles of luxury and necessity he requires, obtained from every quarter of the globe, enjoying ourselves alike a compatible share in these luxuries the incentive of our labours. It must ever exert a large influence in preserving a state of peace, which, when it can be maintained with honour, it is the true glory and interest of every nation to maintain; few stronger ties of interest can be interposed, few better securities for continued good-will can be devised than the mutual benefits the cotton trade affords.

BOOK III.

Having thus shown the importance of the cotton trade, and the bearing it exerts upon our national industry, we may now proceed to analyse the two most important elements of demand and supply, the collateral circumstances which have aided or retarded their mutual progress, and the consequent wealth it should yield.

The progress up to the present time may be best delineated by considering their advance together, since the changes in one inevitably produce corresponding alterations in the other, the scale of prices in the greater degree forming the index of the relative conditions of the two. The Table No. 1. will illustrate the progress year by year, but our purpose will be met by taking the quinquennial averages of the period embraced from the commencement of the century to the present time; while the Diagram will serve further to illustrate the features it presents. In the earlier years of the century the statistics do not attain the completeness which we find in the later years; indeed, up to 1820, I am told it is impossible to obtain from official sources the quantity of cotton consumed in the country, owing to the system of bonded warehouses not having been then established; previous to that date, therefore, we cannot form an idea of the comparative progress of supply and demand, except in so far as prices assist us to a conclusion :—

	Supply. lbs.	Per cent of excess over demand.	Demand. lbs.	Per cent of excess over supply.
1800-4	57,608,050	....	....	....
1805-9	65,840,452	....	....	....
1810-4	86,787,911	....	....	....
1815-9	130,438,507	....	....	....
1820-4	153,565,906	....	164,502,068	7
1825-9	225,717,931	....	227,324,998	$0\frac{7}{10}$
1830-4	294,000,218	....	297,918,941	$1\frac{3}{10}$
1835-9	415,039,188	$1\frac{8}{10}$	407,839,645	....
1840-4	586,306,974	$5\frac{3}{10}$	556,630,623	....
1845-9	626,606,603	....	645,102,940	3
1850-4	826,670,191	$0\frac{3}{10}$	824,386,045	....
1855-9	1,029,057,680	....	1,033,281,872	$\frac{4}{10}$

But here let me guard against an error sometimes committed among men immediately concerned in forming a correct idea of the extent of either of the two great elements, demand and supply; I allude to that of considering the rate of demand to be expressed by the quantity consumed, without making allowance for the increased price required to be paid for the article in a time of inadequate supply, which necessarily checks consumption. In reality, both consumption and supply, looking at the matter through a period of time, is limited by the extent of the other, since the necessity in one case causes a countervailing effect on prices, which, with the extent of accumulated stocks, forms perhaps the fairest criterion of their relative proportions.

The continued decline in prices in the first few years of the century would indicate that supply was then equal to, if not in excess of, demand, until 1804, when the commencement of the second French revolutionary war, the orders in council, and the non-intercourse and various embargoes on the part of the United States caused the available supply of American cotton to diminish, and prices consequently to advance; for in 1807 the import was 74,925,306 lbs., and the price 17½d. per lb., while in the following year, 1808, it was 43,605,982 lbs., and the price 25½d. per lb. Neither was this the only case in which the blind policy of the United States had injured our trade, and, consequently, the demand for their own produce. In 1814, the value of American cotton had risen more than 100 per cent in this market, from the effect of the American war, which had lasted throughout that and the two previous years. Throughout the portion of the century up to 1819, the excess of supply over demand, and *vice versa*, occurred at almost certain intervals. In 1816, however, the growth of cotton received a permanent stimulus; the demand, which under a state of war of nearly twenty years' duration, had continued oppressed, assisted by the opening up of the foreign trade of the country, and the close of the war in 1815, exhibited a great tendency to increase, which became firmly established, and as a result in the year 1817 we received a greatly increased supply, followed in the next by a still greater import, which, in 1819, brought about a corresponding decline in prices, which has, until lately, continued with but few intermissions. Tooke, in his "History of Prices," remarked on the great fall in prices which took place at the period, "that the error usual in such case was committed, the stocks on the spot had been greatly reduced in 1816, and a rise in price on this reduced stock was justified, but then, as in more recent instances, the advance in price was not confined to the small stocks on the spot, but was paid for a large quantity in the country of growth to be shipped hither. Could it be imagined that the importation at the close of 1818, being within a trifle of double of what it was in 1816, could be sold at near the price to which the scarcity had raised it, or what more natural, according to the ordinary rules which govern markets, than that the price of Bowed Georgia cotton should have fallen from 1s. 10d., which it had reached between 1816-8, to 1s. in 1819? The result of over trading on a large scale was felt in numerous and extensive failures." But the extended cultivation which gave rise to this decline also tended to economy and improved cultivation, and to so vast an extent that, notwithstanding the immensely increased demand, the great fall in price became not a temporary but a settled and permanent one.

From 1820 to 1825 the demand continued largely in excess of supply, and up to 1834 continued more or less so, as a glance at the Diagram will evidence. In that year, the stocks had become smaller than they had been for sixteen years before, or have ever been since, and prices consequently fluttered upwards. From that period, however, up to 1846, the supply was more than equal to demand, and prices continued to decline until 1846, when United States Uplands cotton reached 4¼d. per lb.; fortunately, though low prices had stimulated demand, there yet accumulated a considerable stock, and in the three years to 1845, the stock increased at the rate of seventy million pounds a year. At the end of that year, it was four hundred and fifty-three million pounds,—a larger stock than had ever before or has since been accumulated; and but for this providence, the failure of the two succeeding American crops must have been much more severely felt among the manufacturing districts of this country.

The great falling off in the rate of supply at this period, the result of the low prices and failure of the crops, appears thus : —

	lbs.
1845	721,979,953
1846	467,856,274
1847	474,707,615
1848	713,020,161

showing a decline in 1846 of two hundred and sixty-four million pounds, of which two hundred and eight millions were supplied from the accumulated stocks—the price, nevertheless, rising disproportionately from 4½d. to 7⅜d. per lb. It however proved fortunate that this immense augmentation of the price took place, seeing that there subsequently proved to be an equally short supply in 1847, or a deficiency as compared with 1845 of two hundred and forty-seven million pounds, of which the stock made up only sixty-one millions—the price fluctuating about the same range as in the previous year. The prospect of increased energy on the part of the planters, with hopes of a fair yield in America, caused prices to fall in six weeks from 7⅜d. to 5⅜d. per lb. The greatly increased cost of the article, occurring as it did at the time of the potato failure in Ireland—which caused the monthly average price of wheat to rise from 42s. 6d. to 92s. 6d.,—must have added much to the commercial and financial difficulties of the period.

A glance at the Diagram renders the movements at this critical period very transparent ; the green colour will show the period and extent of the demand where it exceeded the supply ; and the red the period and extent of the supply where it exceeded demand ; we have since experienced alternate periods of a preponderance of supply and demand. The stocks, however, which up to 1853 had again slowly but steadily increased, have since as steadily declined, till it now becomes a cause of great uneasiness ; for in the event of another cotton dearth similar to that of 1846 and 1847, and without the advantage of the stocks then on hand, it is difficult to surmise the extent of mischief to which it will give rise. In place of the stocks increasing with the increased demand and rate of supply, we see they have since 1853 continued to decline ; and the rise in prices in 1851 and 1857 apparent in the Diagram A. sufficiently attests the feeling of anxiety with which the subject is regarded.

Table No. 12. will furnish the sources whence the supply of the raw material is obtained, but our purpose will be again better served by condensing the matter into annual averages of quinquennial periods. The rate of progression evident in some, and the absolute decline in others, indicate local or constitutional advantages or disadvantages for its production. Thus the average quantities annually received from each source, since 1815, have been—

Years.	United States	Brazil.	Mediterranean.	British East Indies.	B.W.Indies and British Guiana.	Other Parts.	Grand Total.
1815-9	59,404,980	19,084,711	322,362	34,293,655	11,223,446	6,109,353	130,438,507
1820-4	103,844,292	24,360,668	2,463,078	13,553,256	7,515,002	1,829,610	153,565,906
1825-9	159,326,280	24,357,882	10,293,685	23,793,450	6,129,023	1,817,611	225,717,931
1830-4	231,337,114	26,530,522	4,750,988	27,828,314	2,450,003	1,103,277	294,000,218
1835-9	327,551,781	22,972,862	7,768,755	51,260,320	1,580,566	3,904,904	415,039,188
1840-4	470,417,078	17,286,643	8,798,307	84,344,421	1,192,119	4,268,406	586.306,974
1845-9	525.590,127	21,116,077	11,661,824	66,370,532	994,996	873,047	626,606,603
1850-4	647,205,152	24,007,892	27,159,431	125,621,264	427,735	2,248,717	826,670,191
1855-9	782,274,506	23,483,264	33,751,470	180,213,488	666,974	8,667.978	1029,057,680

The relative proportions, therefore, would appear to have been—

Years.	United States	Brazil.	Mediterranean.	British East Indies.	BW. Indies and British Guiana.	Other Parts.	Grand Total.
1815-9	·46	·15	....	·26	·08	·05	1·00
1820-4	·68	·15	·02	·09	·05	·01	1·00
1825-9	·70	·11	·05	·10	·03	·01	1·00
1830-4	·79	·09	·02	·09	·01	....	1·00
1835-9	·79	·06	·02	·12	....	·01	1·00
1840-4	·81	·03	·01	·14	....	·01	1·00
1845-9	·84	·03	·02	·11	....	....	1·00
1850-4	·78	·03	·03	·16	....	....	1·00
1855-9	·76	·02	·03	·18	....	·01	1·00

and the considerations presented are—the wonderfully overpowering supply received from the United states as compared with all other countries, having at one period reached 84 per cent of the whole ; that the supply from the Brazils has been almost stationary during the forty-five years embraced, not showing any symptom of a proportional increase with the aggregate ; that the supply from the West Indies has continued steadily to decline, until it is now almost insignificant, and ceases to be regarded ; the miscellaneous supply from other parts, which had also steadily declined until the last few years, has, through the exertions of the Manchester Cotton Supply Association and several private individuals, again received an impetus, and gives hopes of opening up new and independent sources of supply; the supply from the Mediterranean has slowly but steadily declined ; and that of the East Indies, which had threatened almost to be extinguished under the low prices of 1846, has at length made an effort to respond to the wants of the times in a considerable, and it is to be hoped permanent increase. No one would regret that the cultivation should be transferred to those countries having facilities for its cheap production, since it would simply become an act of *felo de se* to bolster up prices in order that the production should be sustained in our own colonies ; and yet, when a field presents itself in them which can successfully compete with our foreign supplies, undoubtedly it should receive every legitimate encouragement that a well wisher to the colonies could desire.

The proportion of our imports which come from foreign sources may be thus shown :

	From Foreign Countries.		From British Possessions.	
	lbs.	Proportion.	lbs.	Proportion.
1815-9	78,812,053	·60 o/o	51,626,454	·40 o/o
1820-4	130,668,038	·85 ,,	22,897,868	·15 ,,
1825-9	193,977,847	·86 ,,	31,740,084	·14 ,,
1830-4	262,618,624	·89 ,,	31,381,594	·11 ,,
1835-9	358,293,398	·86 ,,	56,745,790	·14 ,,
1840-4	496,502,028	·85 ,,	89,804,946	·15 ,,
1845-9	558,368,028	·89 ,,	68,238,575	·11 ,,
1850-4	698,372,475	·84 ,,	128,297,716	·16 ,,
1855-9	839,509,240	·82 ,,	189,548,440	·18 ,,

And reflecting that in the last century the larger proportion was supplied by our own colonies, the present diminutive proportion so supplied evidences, one would think, a palpable superiority in foreign countries in this respect, or gross mismanagement in our own colonies, which are abundantly equal to the production for our requirements. Upon this subject we will however hereafter discourse, and consider the relative abilities of each cotton producing country, as shown by their past and present rate of progress.

UNITED STATES.

The immense strides made in the cultivation of cotton in the United States; the comparatively cheapened supply, since it entered into competition in our market; and the power its effect on prices exerts on the supply from other sources, gives to it an importance second to none in the world. Anything which may throw light on the subject of the cultivation and prospects of supply, therefore becomes of general interest, forming, as it does, the mainspring of the most important manufacture of our country.

Our knowledge of the production of cotton in North America is comparatively recent; indeed it seems probable it was very insignificant until the close of last century; but whatever may have been the proportion, it was confined entirely to the supply of a domestic manufacture which could not have been of any extent. In 1748, seven small bags of cotton were exported from Charleston, and again a few in 1754. In 1770 ten bags were shipped to Liverpool; and eight bags imported into the latter port in 1784 were seized by the Customs officers, on the ground that so much cotton could not have been produced in the States. The export of American cotton to Europe was thereafter as follows:—

1785	14 bags.	1788	389 bags.
1786	6 ,,	1789	842 ,,
1787	100 ,,	1790	81 ,,

The progression of the trade since the last date has been prodigious. The Table No. 4. furnishes the detail, from which we extract the following, showing the progress of the exports from the United States:—

	lbs.		lbs.
1791	189,316	1831	270,979,784
1801	20,911,201	1841	530,204,100
1811	62,186,081	1851	927,237,089
1821	124,893,405	1858	1,118,624,012

The falling off apparent in the rate of increase in the last few years, under a greatly increased rate of demand, has suggested the idea that the productive power of the country is not equal to the growing demand. It will be our aim in the following remarks, to analyse the resources at command to meet these wants, and discover, if possible, what causes do or may stand in the way of the needful extension of production.

Glancing at Table No. 13, we shall see that the proportion yielded by each of the several States of the Union has been as follows, in bales:—

Years.	New Orleans, Louisiana, Arkansas and Tennessee.	Texas, &c.	Georgia.	S. Carolina.	N. Carolina and Virginia.	Florida.	Alabama.	Total.
1824 ..	126,481	....	152,735	134,518	46,000	4,500	44,924	509,158
1834 ..	454.719	....	258 665	227,359	77,945	36,738	149,978	1,205,394
1844 ..	832,171	....	255,597	304,870	23,118	145,562	467,990	2,030,409
1854 ..	1,346,925	122,755	316,005	416,754	33,460	155,444	538,684	2,930,027
1859 ..	1,669,274	277,283	475,788	480,653	70,593	173,484	704,406	3,851,481

The inequalities thus apparent in the relative progress of the cultivation in the several States, arises from a combination of various causes, as the over working and impoverishment of the soil, want of labour, the more profitable employment of the land in other branches of agriculture, the working of more fertile soils rendering that on poorer soils unprofitable, and other varied circumstances without number.

The port whence comes our greatest supply of cotton is *New Orleans,* the chief city and port of Louisiana, situated on the Mississippi, at its outlet into the Gulf of Mexico. The mighty Mississippi, of which it thus forms the terminal port, and which gives to New Orleans its immediate advantages, greater than any other in the Union, presents, with its tributary rivers and their branches, a total of 16,674 miles navigable for steamers, delivering at New Orleans the principal part of the produce of the States through which it and all its many tributaries flow,—Mississippi, Louisiana, Arkansas, Tennessee, and North Alabama, or nearly one half the total crops of the United States. We will, however, proceed to notice the peculiar features of each of the cotton growing states.

Mississippi, one of the western States, lies west from Alabama to the Mississippi River, and contains 23,895,628 acres, of which 344,358 are cultivated. The soil presents great variety. In North Mississippi it varies from sandy plains to rich dark productive alluvial soils. On the northern and eastern sections from Mississippi down along the Alabama boundary lie the *prairie lands;* in these the soil is a dark heavy loam of great strength and fertility, and strongly impregnated with lime. The Tombigbee River flows through this section, and delivers its cotton to Mobile, another of the Gulf ports. East Mississippi has a mixed soil, some poor and some rich land ; cotton is not, however, extensively grown in it. In the west and south-west the soil is very rich. From fifty miles below the mouth of the Yazoo River, extending one hundred miles into the interior from the Mississippi River, and stretching north with a sweep to Memphis, lie the *swamp lands;* these are the most productive in the State, having all the strength of the prairie lands without their corrosive nature. But on the whole the soil and climate of Mississippi are admirably adapted to the cultivation of cotton.

The chief rivers in the State which flow into the Mississippi are the Yazoo and Big Black Rivers, the Pearl River runs into the Gulf of Mexico, and the Tombigbee, as before stated at Mobile; there are as yet but few railways, the one between Jackson Brandon and Vicksburg, on the mouth of the Yazoo River at its junction with the Mississippi, sixty miles in length, is the chief one which assists in the delivery of cotton, but several other lines are in progress. Mississippi was admitted into the union in 1817 ; the statistics are included with its neighbour state Louisiana. The increase of population has been as follows :—

	1820.	1830.	Per cent of increase.	1840.	Per cent of increase.	1850.	℔ cent of increase.
Slave population	32,814	65,648	100	192,986	195	300,419	57
Free population	42,634	71,158	60	182,665	157	306,136	68
Total	75,448	136,806	81	375,651	183	606,555	61½

Louisiana, one of the western States, lies south and west of Mississippi, containing 29,715,840 acres, of which only 1,590,000 are cultivated. It is very flat and level; the *swamp* and *prairie lands* in the south-west are only ten to fifty feet above the level of high tide; generally the land is of a rich alluvial character and highly productive; that bordering on the Red River and the Mississippi is of extraordinary fertility, but its crops are liable occasionally to almost total destruction by inundation, as in 1849 and 1850. The cultivation of the sugar cane has lately greatly interfered with the more rapid development of cotton cultivation in this State. The chief rivers running through Louisiana are the Red, Wachita, Saline, and Tensas Rivers, affording ample means of conveyance, through the Mississippi, to New Orleans. The increase in the population has been as follows:—

	1810.	1820.	℔ cent of increase.	1830.	℔ cent of increase.	1840.	℔ cent of increase.	1850.	℔ cent of increase.
Slave population....	34,660	69,114	100	109,588	58	168,350	54	244,786	45¼
Free population	41,896	87,293	108	105,987	21	184,061	74	272,953	48
Total	76,556	156,407	104	215,575	40½	352,411	64	517,739	47

The progress of the cotton crops of Louisiana and Mississippi have been as follows:—

	1839.	1849.	Per cent of increase.	1859.	Per cent of increase.
Crop, bales	469,000	811,000	72⅛	1,232,000	51⅞
Average of three years ending..	492,000	716,000	45½	1,167,000	63

Arkansas, another of the western States, lying north of Louisiana and west of Mississippi, containing 33,406,720 acres, of which only 781,531 are cultivated. The land in the southern portion is best calculated for the growth of cotton; there is much swamp and prairie. On the margin of the rivers the lands are very rich and yield heavy crops; the resources of the State are however, comparatively undeveloped, having been admitted into the Union so lately as 1836. The means of conveyance are very ample, the Arkansas River is navigable 650 miles from the Mississippi, the Red River crosses the south-west corner of the State, and the St. Francis, White, and Wachita Rivers also afford excellent facilities of transport. The increase in the population has been as follows:—

	1830.	1840.	Per cent of increase.	1850.	Per cent of increase.
Slave population.........	4,572	10,918	140	46,982	135½
Free population	25,816	85,656	234	162,657	88
Total	30,388	97,574	223	209,639	115

The increase in the crops of cotton have been as follows:—

	1839.	1849.	Per cent of increase.	1859.	Per cent of increase.
Crop, bales	7,000	47,000	571¼	105,000	123¼
Average of three years ending	8,000	48,000	500	97,100	100

Tennessee, another of the western States, lying north of Mississippi and Alabama, containing 28,160,000 acres of which only 5,175,173 are cultivated. The soil in Western Tennessee is black, rich, and fertile; in Eastern Tennessee the valleys from five to ten miles in width, lying between the mountain ridges, are very rich land, impregnated with lime. This is the largest Indian corn growing State in the Union. Admitted into the Union in 1796; its population has increased as follows:—

	1800.	1810.	Per cent of increase.	1820.	Per cent of increase.	1830.	Per cent of increase.	1840.	Per cent of increase.	1850.	Per cent of increase.
Slave population	13,584	44,525	238½	80,185	82	141,603	76¼	183,059	36¾	239,461	30½
Free population	92,018	217,202	136	342,628	58	540,301	58	646,151	19	763,164	18
Total	105,602	261,727	148½	422,813	61½	681,904	61¼	829,210	21¾	1,002,625	20¾

With the cotton crops of this State are included those of North Alabama, the increase appears as follows:—

	1839.	1849.	Per cent of increase.	1859.	Per cent of increase.
Crop, bales	69,000	217,000	214½	317,000	46
Average of three years ending.	108,000	218,000	101⅞	284,000	30¼

The growth of Tennessee is collected by the Tenessee River navigable for 1,000 miles, and the Cumberland River navigable 500 miles, both emptying into the Mississippi, through the Ohio River. The Tennessee River also flows through North Alabama and forwards the cotton of that district to New Orleans. A railway has recently been opened from Nashville to Chattanooga, 150 miles, which may divert some portion of the cotton grown in Tennessee to Charleston and Savannah, thus apparently increasing the crop at those points. There was on the 1st January, 1852, about 200 miles of railroad in operation in Tennessee, and about 600 miles in course of construction.

Texas is the newest and most western of the cotton growing States, containing about 300,000,000 acres, of which about 640,000 only are cultivated. The lands so far as known are rich, alluvial, and prairie, yielding heavy crops. The population in 1850 was 187,403, of whom 53,346 were slaves; the population, however, must have much increased since by immigration from the other states which is said to continue on a large scale.

The cotton crop of Texas in 1847 was 8,000 bales, and in 1859, 192,000 bales, showing an increase of 2,300 per cent in twelve years. Galveston is the chief port of Texas; a considerable portion, however, of the Texas cotton is forwarded direct to New Orleans by way of the Red River, and thus comes into the Louisiana receipts.

Georgia, one of the Atlantic States, lies east of Alabama, north of Florida, and west of South Carolina, containing 37,120,000 acres, of which about 6,500,000 acres are cultivated. It presents great diversity of soil. The islands and shores produce the famous Sea Island cotton. Extending inland 90 to 120 miles from the coast are pine barrens, and tide swamps, on which but little cotton is grown. The middle region of the State has a red loamy soil, once very productive, but now much impoverished by the exhaustive system of growing cotton year after year, without rotation of crops or sufficient manure. The lands in the south-west portion of the State are of a light sandy nature, and soon wear out under such treatment. Northern Georgia does not produce largely of cotton. Georgia was one of the States which originally formed the Union, and the increase in the population is thus shown :—

	1800.	1810.	Per cent of increase.	1820.	Per cent of increase.	1830.	Per cent of increase.	1840.	Per cent of increase.	1850.	Per cent of increase.
Slave population ..	59,404	105,218	78	149,656	42	217,461	45½	280,546	29	381,681	36
Free population ..	102,697	147,215	43	199,333	35	299,362	51	410,846	37	524,318	27
Total	162,101	252,433	55½	348,989	38½	516,823	48	691,392	34	905,999	31

The increase in the cotton crops has been has follows :—

	1829.	1839.	Per cent of increase.	1849.	Per cent of increase.	1859.	Per cent of increase.
Crop, ... bales	246,000	205,000	24	391,000	90¼	476,000	21¾
Average of three years ending..	211,000	257,000	21¾	296,000	15¼	360,000	21½

The chief city and port of Georgia is Savannah, situate at the mouth of the Savannah River; the principal rivers are the Savannah, Ogeechee, and Altamaha Rivers flowing into the Atlantic Ocean, and the Flint and Chattahoochee Rivers, which join to form the Apalachicola River, emptying at the port of that name in Florida into the Gulf of Mexico; a considerable portion of the cotton, the growth of Georgia, finds its way thus to Apalachicola, and is included in the Florida receipts. The principal transport of cotton, however, is effected by means of railroads of which no cotton growing state has so complete and efficient a system as Georgia. The railroads are Savannah to Macon, Augusta to Atlanta, Macon to Atlanta, Atlanta to Chattanooga, Macon to Oglethorpe, Columbus to Port Valley, Macon to Eatonton, Augusta to Erinsonville; there are also branch lines, making a total of about 900 miles of railroad in operation, besides additional lines now in course of construction.

South Carolina, another of the Atlantic States, lies north-east of Georgia, containing 17,920,000 acres, of which 4,073,000 acres are cultivated; the soil of this State is very similar to that of Georgia. Sea Island cotton grows on the coast and islands; pine barrens, marshes, and swamps extend from 80 to 100 miles inland from the coast, producing chiefly rice. Cotton is grown on the banks of the rivers and creeks, but is chiefly the produce of the interior and northern portion; the soil there is of the same red loamy description as that of Middle Georgia, the upper portion is generally fertile. South Carolina was another of the original states of the Union. The increase of population has been as follows :—

	1800.	·1810.	Per cent of increase.	1820.	Per cent of increase.	1830.	Per cent of increase.	1840.	Per cent of increase.	1850.	Per cent of increase.
Slave population ..	146,151	196,365	34¼	258,475	31½	315,401	22	327.038	3¾	384,925	17¾
Free population ..	199,440	218,750	10	244,266	12	265,784	09	267,360	1	283,544	6
Total........	345,591	415,115	20¼	502,741	21	581,185	15¾	594,398	2¼	668,469	12½

The progress of the cotton crops appear as follows :—

	1829.	1839.	Per cent of increase.	1849.	Per cent of increase.	1859.	Per cent of increase.
Crop, ... bales	195,000	210,000	12¾	458,000	118	481,000	5
Average of three years ending..	161,000	233,000	44¼	356,000	52¾	428,000	20

The chief city and port is Charleston. The principal rivers are the Pee, Dee, Santee, and Edisto, but more than three-fourths of the cotton crop is conveyed to Charleston by railroad. In 1848 there were 274,000 bales; in 1849, 340,000; and in 1850, 285,000 bales thus conveyed. On the 1st January, 1852, there were 340 miles in operation in South Carolina, and 298 miles in course of construction, much of which must have been since completed. The means of early delivery at Charleston is thus secured.

North Carolina and Virginia contribute only comparatively a trifling proportion of the total cotton crop; the soil of these States is sandy and poor, and the cultivation of cotton has in a great measure been abandoned for that of tobacco and other crops; the crops of cotton now yielded by them is less than thirty years ago. The decrease will be observed from the following statement :—
thirty years ago.

	1829.	1839.	1849.	1859.
Crop, ... bales	72,000	33,000	27,000	71,000
Average of three years ending ..	87,900	45,000	19,000	57,000

Neither has the slave population increased as in the other cotton growing states; the progress may be seen thus :—

	1820.	1830.	Per cent of increase.	1840.	Per cent of increase.	1850.	Per cent of increase.
Slave population, Virginia	425,183	479,757	12¾	448,886	7	473,026	5½
Ditto South Carolina	205,017	245,701	19½	245,331	..	288,412	17½

The very low rate of increase of late years is due to the fact that numbers of slaves have been removed to the more fertile lands in the south and west, and also to their having been largely superseded in these states by free labourers.

Florida lies south of the Atlantic States, and of part of Alabama, and forms the tongue of land, or as it were the breakwater of the Gulf of Mexico, containing 37,931,000 acres, of which only 349,000 are under cultivation. Cotton is grown almost solely in the north-west portion; the State was ceded to the United States in 1821; but owing to the Indian war, which was only terminated in 1842, its progress has been materially checked. The population has increased as follows :—

	1830.	1840.	Per cent of increase.	1850.	Per cent of increase.
Slave population	15,500	25,800	66½	39,341	52
Free population	19,230	28,647	49	48,046	68
Total	34,730	45,447	59	87,387	63

The progress in the cotton crops may be thus seen. It will be observed that the increase, which between 1839 and 1849 was very considerable, has been considerably lost in the last ten years.

	1839.	1849.	Per cent of increase.	1859.	Per cent of increase.
Cotton Crop, bales	75,000	200,000	166¾	173,000	13½
Average of three years, ending	88,000	160,000	81¾	144,000	10

Apalachicola is the chief port of Florida, and situate at the mouth of the river of that name. A considerable quantity of cotton, the growth of Alabama and Georgia, comes down the Chattahoochee and Flint rivers into the Apalachicola river, and thence to the port, thereby swelling the receipts which are returned as from Florida.

Alabama lies west of the Atlantic States, and contains 32,027,690 acres (or nearly equal to the entire area of England and Wales), of which 4,435,614 acres are cultivated. The soil in the south and east is sandy and poor, but that in the north and west is more fertile. Alabama was admitted into the Union in 1810. The progress in the population has been as follows:—

	1820.	1830.	Per cent of increase.	1840.	Per cent of increase.	1850.	Per cent of increase.
Slave population	41,879	117,549	180¾	253,425	116½	342,894	35½
Free population	86,022	191,978	123	337,331	76	428,777	27
Total	127,901	309,527	142	590,756	90¾	771,671	30½

The crops of cotton appear as follows:—

	1829.	1839.	Per cent of increase.	1849.	Per cent of increase.	1859.	Per cent of increase.
Cotton Crop, bales	80,000	252,000	215	519,000	106	704,000	35¾
Average of 3 years, ending	80,000	264,000	230	426,000	61¼	576,000	35¼

The chief city and port of Alabama is Mobile, situate at the mouth of the Mobile River, which is formed by the confluence of the principal rivers of the State, and thus delivers nearly all its produce to Mobile. The river navigation of Alabama is very complete. The Tombigbee River, navigable for 540 miles, rises in North Mississippi, and by its junction with the Alabama River, 60 miles above Mobile, forms the Mobile River, contributing to the receipts of cotton at Mobile from 80,000 to 100,000 bales annually of cotton grown in Mississippi, together with a considerable quantity from Western Alabama. The Black Warrior River, navigable for 150 miles, flows through the north-west of Alabama and delivers into the Alabama River.

The Alabama River, navigable for 450 miles, gathers the cotton from East and Central Alabama, and, joining the Tombigbee, forms the Mobile River. So complete is this magnificent system of river navigation, 1,370 miles in extent, that but a very small proportion arrives by land carriage at Mobile, though the quantity brought in by that means has lately considerably increased.

The following statement shows the proportions in which these different sources supply the receipts of cotton at Mobile:—

	1853.	1854.	1855.	1856.	1857.	1858.	1859.
	Bales.	Bales.	Bales.	Bales.	Bales.	Bales.	Bales.
Receipts from Alabama River	240,608	254,990	223,907	260,000	214,000	226,000	346,000
,, Tombigbee ,,	234,522	214,415	154,598	300,000	148,000	121,000	116,000
,, Black Warrior ,,	64,666	62,191	36,907	59,000	61,000	66,000	84,000
,, Wagons, rail, &c...	6,094	7,058	21,292	40,000	80,000	109,000	139,000
Bales..........	545,890	538,654	436,704	659,000	503,000	522,000	685,000

Railway communication in Alabama is comparatively in its infancy; there is, however, considerable railway enterprise now existing. The Mobile and Ohio Railway, of which about 232 miles are already in operation, will extend north 520 miles, and connect Mobile with the mouth of the Ohio, opening up a rich field for the extension of cotton cultivation throughout the entire length of Eastern Mississippi and Western Tennessee, which will, no doubt, largely increase the trade of Mobile, and improve the character of its cotton. Other important lines are also projected.

The cotton statistics of the United States are generally treated of in bales, though that standard is very vague and undefined. Apart from the different form and weight of the bale adopted by the various States, the weight is perpetually altering, as may be seen from the figures given in Table No. 14; there is a decided tendency to an increase, particularly in the bales from the United States, from the circumstance of inland transit charges, in that country, being charged on the bale or package, and not on the weight; from the East Indies and other places likewise, where the homeward freight is charged on the measurement, there exists, also, an inducement to press the bales as far as practicable. Thus the average weight of all kinds imported into this country has been at different periods:—

1820 .... 249 lbs. per bale.   1850 .... 392 lbs. per bale.
1830 300   ,,   1859 421   ,,
1840 365   ,,

In considering the statistics therefore so presented, we must take into consideration this increase.

To glance at the cotton crops of the United States, as given in Table No. 13, and taking the quinquennial averages, we shall discover that the rate of increase has been as follows:—

	Aggregate. Bales.	Average. Bales.	Rate of Increase. Bales.
1825-9	3,837,565	767,513	....
1830-4	5,279,001	1,055,800	288,287
1835-9	7,200,012	1,440,002	384,202
1840-4	9,905,638	1,981,128	541,126
1845-9	11,349,921	2,269,984	288,856
1850-4	13,659,901	2,731,980	461,996
1855-9	16,280,146	3,256,029	524,049

If we were to adopt the theory of trade running in certain fixed grooves, we should be justified, by the marked regularity in the rate of increase between 1830 and 1844, and 1845 and 1859, in predicting, ere long, a return to the low prices of 1846, and another great fall in the production; and though it might guide our prognostications if it were possible to divine all the attendant circumstances, we must bear in mind that the relative position and extent of the demand in 1845 and 1860 are very dissimilar; and, moreover, that the system of quinquennial averages is not always reliable, from its embracing more or less good or bad seasons (as the case may be) at one time than another; thus, next year the rate of progression will be more equal, and the quinquennial periods ending then would, perhaps, give a fairer average, from their embracing two good, two bad seasons, and one fair one. But, taking the figures as they stand, what was a source of much uneasiness, or the signs of a diminished rate of increase of supply from this source, upon which we have so long learned to depend, at the very time when requirements were greater than usual, has been somewhat meliorated by the great increase in the past two crops, as well as the anticipations as to that now being harvested. To render the decline more apparent we will take decennial in place of quinquennial averages, and the annual rate of increase in the crops will then appear:—

	Bales.		Average Price decennially of United States Uplands.
1830-9	336,244	78,747	$7\frac{3}{4}$
1840-9	414,991		$5\frac{1}{4}$
1850-9	493,022	78,031	$6\frac{1}{8}$

In these figures at first sight we discover little valid reason for so much anxiety, since the decline apparent is only $\frac{716}{78747}$ or about *one per cent*. But looking at the comparative prices, it will be remarked that apart from the small decline apparent in the extent of the crops, the years 1840-9 were years of low prices succeeding higher prices than those now existing; and that, therefore, the rate of increase should have been *much greater* in 1850-9, which were years of comparatively high prices following low ones; and that while the spur of high prices has been maintained throughout the last decennial period, by reason of the inadequacy of the supply to meet the demand, the increased production in the States induced by it has neither been equal to that in the former period, nor adequate to the growing demand.

Although these facts tend to support the reason for the prevailing uneasiness, it is not to be supposed that the United States have reached the climax of their producing power, as some people seek to essay. There is not a question but that many circumstances, apart from the decline in the relative rate of progression in production to that of demand, tend to show a reason for a prospective declension of the power of increased production—simply that circumstances which formerly existed in favour of a development of that power, are working out to their fullest extent. Thus it is stated, the most eligible lands have been put under cultivation, although as communication further opens up, lands equally so will be brought into cultivation; that where new lands have been opened up and wrought without manuring, (and upon which system the cheap prices were maintained), the land has become impoverished, and been ultimately abandoned; that to make of it a permanent cultivation, there must be a rotation of crops and the application of manure, in which case it necessitates a higher value being obtained for the produce; and lastly, and most important, that the amount of available labour is quickly being employed.

A cursory perusal of the review which I have given of each of the cotton producing States, (the data for which I have obtained from the annual statement of Messrs. Neill Brothers and Co., Cotton Merchants of New Orleans, Mobile, and New York, through the kind permission of J. C. Ollerenshaw, Esq. of Manchester,) will suffice to show that the power of these States to increase their production of cotton is not limited by any lack of lands adapted to its growth — scarcity of labour and capital are the only restrictions to their producing power, so long as cotton continues a remunerative crop.

The nature and scarcity of the labour employed is, however, a serious obstacle to the progress of the cultivation. The capital, which should find its sphere of action in agricultural extension and improvement, is locked up in the purchase of slaves to work the land ; and the number of these is limited, so that any greatly increased demand for them, raises the price so high as to neutralise in a great measure the profit of extending the cultivation by means of newly purchased hands, — thus preventing the planters and the world from deriving that advantage which ought to accrue to all parties from an increase of consumption, and forcing English spinners to seek for supplies from countries less fitted for the growth of cotton. That there has, however, been a considerable diversion of labour out of its old channels into the cotton fields, in consequence of the profitable nature of the cotton culture, is shown by the following aggregate summary of the slave population in the principal cotton states, the increase in which in the decennial periods ending 1830, 1840, and 1850, amounted to the annual averages respectively of $5\frac{5}{8}$, $4\frac{3}{4}$, and $3\frac{5}{8}$ per cent. In effecting this transfer of labour to the cultivation of cotton, which has only been done in periods of high prices like the present, the price of a good field hand, which in ordinary seasons did not exceed 500 to 700 dollars, is occasionally raised, as is now the case, to from 1,200 to 1,500 dollars.

	1820.	1830.	Per cent of increase.	1840.	Per cent of increase.	1850.	Per cent of increase.
Slave population in cotton States, excluding North Carolina & Texas	632,600	987,000	$56\frac{3}{4}$	1,451,000	47	1,979,000	$36\frac{1}{4}$
Or an annual increase of..	..	..	$5\frac{5}{8}$	..	$4\frac{3}{4}$	..	$3\frac{5}{8}$

But, while presenting these figures, which, showing a slight increase in the actual rate of progress, exhibit a decline in the per cent of increase, if we glance at the relative increase made in the other and non-cotton producing States, we shall discover that, while in the former in the twenty years 1830 to 1850, the slave population has more than *doubled* itself, in the latter the increase has been only equal to *twenty per cent*, illustrating the amount of drain which has taken place from them to supply the wants of the cotton cultivation. Thus the slave population of the—

	1830.	1850.	Rate of increase.	Per cent of increase.
Cotton producing States with the exceptions named above	987,000	1,979,000	992,000	100
Non-cotton producing States and including exceptions above	1,022,043	1,225,313	203,270	20
Total slave population of United States	2,009,043	3,204,313	1,195,270	

If we look at the yield of cotton per acre in the several States, as returned by the Marshalls in 1850, we shall discover that in those States which have been longest worked the yield is much less than in the comparatively new cotton producing States; but, since the employment of manures on the older lands, I am informed the yield per acre has largely increased.

	Yield of Seed Cotton per acre. lbs.	Clean Cotton. lbs.
Florida	250	112
Tennessee	300	135
South Carolina	320	144
Georgia	500	225
Alabama	525	236
Louisiana	550	247
Mississippi	650	292
Arkansas	700	315
Texas	750	337

So far as price is concerned, the great discrepancy apparent in the yield of the several States, is considerably mitigated and equalised by the additional cost and uncertainty of carriage with which the new and more distant lands are burdened, as compared with the older lands with their organised means of conveyance. The comparatively smaller yield of the older States, which may be ascribed to the overworking of inferior soils, we may take to show the falling off in the yield in them; and, as the new and more fertile lands have larger costs of carriage to bear, we may infer that the cost of production has increased, apart from the increased price required to be paid for slave labour, which has been greatly neutralised by the improvements in cultivation and the economy of labour. But it is sometimes asserted that the system is arriving at perfection,—that we cannot look for much further improvement to compensate for the continued decrease in the yield exhibited,—that we cannot hope for a return of the low prices of 1845 and 1848, and that, admitting the United States can supply the increasing demand, it must be effected by a corresponding increase in the price of cotton.

As already stated, the extent of land really in cultivation, as compared with that which is capable of it, is yet very small. From a table compiled by the American Government, it appears the present crops could be easily quintupled were the necessary labour and capital forthcoming. The paper purports to give the extent of land capable of producing cotton in the States, the extent in cultivation, and the hands employed thereon in 1852, thus—

	Acres under Cotton Cultivaton.	People Employed.	Acres adapted to Cotton Cultivation.	People necessary to its Cultivation.	Probable Produce in Bales of 400 lbs. each.
Florida	160,000	20,000	6,000,000	750,000	3,000,000
Texas	200,000	25,000	10,000,000	1,250,000	5,000,000
Arkansas	200,000	25,000	3,000,000	375,000	1,500,000
Louisiana	400,000	50,000	3,000,000	375,000	1,500,000
Tennessee	440,000	55,009	2,000,000	250,050	1,000.000
South Carolina	620,000	77,500	200,000	25,000	100.000
Mississippi	1,300,000	162,500	6,000,000	750,000	3,000,000
Georgia	1,480,000	185,000	3,000,000	375,000	1,500,000
Alabama	1,500,000	187,500	6,000,000	750,000	3,000,000

The question of the extent of future supplies resolves itself almost exclusively into that of the extent of available labour and of cost. There is reason to believe that formerly, during the period of low prices, the cultivation was carried on without sufficient attention to rotation of crops or manuring—partly the cause, and partly the effect of those low prices; but now, manures are being extensively used in the older States, with excellent results. The rate of increase of the slave population in the cotton growing States, we have seen advanced with regularity, except in North Carolina and Virginia, where it has remained almost unaltered during the last thirty years; and it is amply proved that there is still a very large reserve of labour in the sugar, rice, and tobacco plantations transferable, and indeed, being transferred to cotton cultivation, which at present prices pays better than other produce. An immense extension of production is now taking place and will continue so long as the prices hold up. The stimulus, however, of increased prices would increase it still more and produce for us the surplus stock we require to give us again a range of low prices, while any disaster which may check consumption, as war, or famine, or crisis in monetary matters, though undesirable contingencies may assist the increased production in restoring the low price range.

The extent to which the want of labour can be supplied is a question peculiarly deserving a few remarks. The total number of slaves in the cotton States was, in 1850, 1,979,000; and by the Government table already quoted only 787,500 of these were employed in the cotton cultivation. The planters state that on rich bottom lands seven bales to the hand are picked, and half the number of slaves on the plantations are employed in picking; with the uplands six bales to the hand is a fair proportion, which gives 350,000 slaves to pick the crop of 1850, and 700,000 of all kinds on the plantations, which, as the crop was a small one, is not far from the mark, and tallies with the official statement for the next crop of 1851. The past crop by this rule employed 640,000 to pick it, and there must have been 1,280,000 slaves on the cotton plantations, an increase of over *ten per cent* per annum in the slaves employed in cotton cultivation; thus, the slave labour in the United States in 1850 was equal to pick *six million bales* if all were employed in the cotton cultivation. But at present there are no spare hands in the United States, that is, those who are not employed in cotton cultivation are employed in some other; and no more than a very few could be added to the regular available force, for the reason that there are no spare hands anywhere, except the domestic slaves, and the planters will not spare these while they can afford to keep them in their service at home, and they are now almost always working in the fields where owned by small farmers. Not more, however, than one half the slave population in the cotton States is now employed in picking the crop. The increase in the slave population in the United States has varied but little during the last sixty years, having, during that time, always ranged within $2\frac{1}{2}$ to $3\frac{1}{2}$ per cent per annum; it is therefore quite clear that the immense requirements of the cotton cultivation can only be met by a proportionate declension in other branches of agriculture, and at the present time the cultivation of sugar, which had sprung up in Louisiana, is yielding to this more profitable cultivation. Slavery is at present working its extension by its profitable employment, so far as cotton is concerned. Ruinously low prices of cotton would extinguish slavery, but in **the Southern States of America it is now more prosperous than ever.** How long this can continue is a question which must arise in every mind, and one as difficult to find a reply to. While acknowledging its terrible strength from its deep rooted vitality, we must all dread the severity of the revulsion which must sooner or later arrive, and of which we have even lately received practical and unmistakeable warning; though, thus extending its sphere, it must ere long work its own extinction. The increasing value or cost of that labour, unless it can be fed by the return of the execrable external trade, will inevitably force on the planters the advantage of a free labouring class. All the world are daily yielding to a Christian repugnance of such an institution, and justly so, for allowing for all the wild exaggerations of the misery it entails, it is unquestionably an inhuman law. In truth it is an expensive luxury, a dangerous and artificial state, and even in a worldly point of view, an error. The cost of a first-class negro in the United States is about £300, and the interest on the capital invested in, and the wear and tear of this human chattel is equal to ten per cent, which, with the cost of maintaining, clothing, and doctoring him, or another five per cent, gives an annual cost of £45 or 17s. 4d. per week; and the pampered Coolies in the best paying of all the tropical settlements, Trinidad, receive wages that do not exceed, on an average all the year round, 6s. per week, or about *two-fifths*, while in the East Indies, with perquisites, they do not receive so much as *one-third* even of this. In Cuba the Chinese immigrants receive not more than 3s. to 4s. per week. Is it not then an error, the maintainance of so barbarous and loathsome an institution, which must ere long explode, or crumble beneath the weight of its own superstructure? Of the ability of Coolie, Chinese, or even European immigrants to labour in the cotton States, there does not seem much doubt; indeed, in Texas at the present day, there is some extent of cotton land in cultivation by free European settlers. But a radical change must occur in the constitution of these States before this free labour will pour in naturally. The treatment of the Coolies and Chinese in Cuba, which is far worse than that of the slaves, of whom it is the interest of the owner to take care, has already gone far to stay the tide of immigration in that direction; but the numbers of Chinese already in California may still be drawn down to the cotton fields by the inducement of high pay, though I much fear before a permanent alteration is made the accumulation of evils in the system may yet force a solution of the difficulty and even rend the constitution.

The anxiety to which the deficient supply of cotton received from the United States gives rise, is ascribable in a great measure to the increased consumption taking place in the manufactories of that country, as well as in those on the Continent of Europe, to meet which a considerable diversion of the exports takes place, thus diminishing the quantity or proportion of the crop available to meet our demand. With a view of illustrating this, we may take a summary of Table No. 15, by which we shall discern the distribution of the crops for the last thirty years in annual averages of quinquennial periods thus:—

Years.	Great Britain.	France.	Other Countries.	Total.	Consumption of United States.	Stocks, 1st September
1830-4	645,803	191,794	42,130	879,727	174,656	54,748
1835-9	861,645	268,621	61,503	1,191,769	239,648	50,667
1840-4	1,142,675	364,639	151,516	1,658.830	306,441	83,397
1845-9	1,246,950	321,595	247,029	1,815,574	457,894	149,320
1850-4	1.506,879	362,629	304,503	2,174,011	555,297	131,731
1855-9	1,745,838	431,724	439,103	2,612,666	632,172	101,785

showing the following proportions and rate of increase : —

Years.	Great Britain. Per Cent.	France. Per Cent.	Other Countries. Per Cent.	Total.	Consumption of United States, Rate of Increase.	Stocks, 1st September, Rate of Increase.
1830-4	·74	·22	·04	1·00	....	....
1835-9	·72	·23	·05	1·00	64,992	....
1840-4	·69	·22	·09	1·00	66,793	32,730
1845-9	·68	·18	·14	1·00	151,453	65,923
1850-4	·69	·17	·14	1 00	97,403	....
1855-9	·67	·16	·17	1·00	76,875	....

It must, however, be observed, that the consumption of the United States here given only includes that north of Virginia; the consumption south and west of Virginia is omitted, as well as in the totals given of the crops. The consumption south and west of Virginia is given for part of the time in Table No. 15 ; in the three last periods it would appear to have been, in annual averages of quinquennial periods, thus : —

    1845-9 .... 80,000 Bales.
    1850-4 .... 87,500 „
    1855-9 .... 117,500 „

exemplifying the fact that the manufacture is gaining ground in the cotton producing States.

The fact that other countries are now carrying off a gradually increasing proportion of the production, is a valid reason for a proportional falling off in our supply. But then, again, as this does not entirely arise from an increased demand for goods in those countries, there would be an equivalent decline in *our* rate of production of manufactures, and consequently of demand for the raw material; so that the falling off in the rate of increase of production of the raw material, as compared with the demand, is in our case still unaltered. The diversion of supplies is, however, worthy of comment. It is by the figures above adduced, unpleasantly substantiated, that some grounds of vantage must exist in favor of the manufacture rising up in the Continental countries of Europe. Thus, in the last twenty-five years, those countries, excluding France, have increased their demand wonderfully as compared with ours; and though their comparative extent is yet insignificant, should they continue their rapid advance, it is evident we shall soon have to contend with formidable rivals. But every one who has given any attention to the matter, knows full well that as to competing with us in foreign markets, excepting in one or two particular classes of goods, which it does not serve the purpose of our manufacturers to produce, we have almost every ingredient for ultimate success in our favor. That we must, however, lose some portion of the Continental markets as customers, seems rational and probable. The proportion which France has and should have borne as a consumer of the raw material, is painfully indicated in the last thirty years even, and exhibits the folly of protective duties, by impoverishing the protected manufacturers. The decline apparent at the close of the revolutionary period 1849, shows the dire effect of those internal disturbances which, while tending to destroy the national industry of that country, has also fettered the trade of our own.

The increase in the home consumption of the United States is considerable. The low prices, 1845 to 1849, greatly assisted the trade ; it has withal an appearance of steady increase throughout. The proportion of the home trade to the export demand is thus shown : —

	Export.	Home Consumption.
1830-4....	83 Per Cent.	17 Per Cent.
1835-9....	83 ,,	17 ,,
1840-4....	84 ,,	16 ,,
1845-9....	80 ,,	20 ,,
1850-4....	80 ,,	20 ,,
1855-9....	80 ,,	20 ,,

showing that the consumption keeps pace with both the growth and export; but if we add to this the quantity shown to be consumed in the cotton growing States, we shall discover that the consumption in the United States is increasing in a greater ratio than either. The home consumption usually referred to is only that in what may be termed the manufacturing portion of the Union, or north of Virginia. That south and west of Virginia, until lately, was not recorded, and even now is not included in the return of crops. The crops, as returned, are only the receipts at the ports. Taken as a whole, the consumption of the United States would appear to be—

	Consumption North of Virginia. Bales.	All other Places. Bales.	Total. Bales.
1848....	523,892	92,152	616,044
1849....	504,143	138,342	642,485
1850....	476,486	137,012	613,498
1851....	386,429	99,185	485,614
1852....	588,322	111,281	699,603
1853....	650,393	153,332	803,725
1854....	592,284	144,952	737,236
1855....	571,117	135,295	706,412
1856....	633,027	137,712	770,739
1857....	665,718	154,218	819,936
1858....	452,185	143,377	595,562
1859....	760,218	167,433	927,651

The extent of the cotton crops of the United States is perhaps more particularly dependent upon the nature of the seasons than any other crop in any part of the world. The length of the season, upon which so much depends, is but just sufficient for the full development of the plant, and a week later in the spring, or a week earlier in the fall, may be the ruin of an otherwise plentiful crop; besides which, of course, the period and extent of the rainy and dry seasons is as much important. The following table will show the features of the last ten seasons and their results :—

TABLE,

Showing date of frosts; time of cotton growing; dates of bloom and receipts of first bale; and crops and features of the last ten seasons in the United States of America.

Season.	WHITE FROSTS. Latest in Spring.	WHITE FROSTS. Earliest in Fall.	Time of Cotton Growing in Months and Days.	Date of First Bloom.	Receipt of First Bale.	Crops.
			Mths. Days.			
1849-50	April 16	Nov. 8	6 .. 22	June 6	Aug. 7	2,096,706 (a)
1850-51	,, 7	Oct 26	6 .. 19	,, 24	,, 11	2,355,257 (b)
1851-52	,, 22	Nov. 6	6 .. 14	,, 5	July 25	3,015,029 (c)
1852-53	,, 6	,, 7	7 .. 1	,, 3	Aug. 2	3,262,882 (d)
1853-54	March 15	Oct. 25	7 .. 10	,, 10	,, 9	2,930,027 (e)
1854-55	April 29	Nov. 5	6 .. 6	,, 12	July 25	2,847,339 (f)
1855-56	March 28	Oct. 25	6 .. 27	May 30	,, 26	3,527,845 (g)
1856-57	,, 3	,, 16	7 .. 13	June 4	,, 15	2,939,519 (h)
1857-58	April 23	Nov. 20	6 . 28	,, 24	Aug. 15	3,113,962 (i)
1858-59	,, 24	,, 7	6 .. 14	,, 1	July 25	3,851,481 (j)

(a) Frost in April. Great overflow of Mississippi in Spring. Fine season thereafter.

(b) Another great overflow of the Mississippi. Long drought in Summer. Open Winter.

(c) Genial Spring. Weather very dry from May to August. Fine picking season.

(d) Fine Spring. Rain till middle of July. Storms in August. Picking season prolonged.

(e) Late Spring. Drought till middle of July. Frost in October. Fine picking season.

(f) Spring late and unfavorable. June fine. July wet. Fine August. Storm in September. Fine picking season.

(g) Late Spring. Fine Midsummer. Wet July. Maturing and picking season very fine.

(h) Late cold Spring. Drought in Summer. Storms in August. Rapid maturing and picking.

(i) Very backward Spring. Frosts in April. Cold Summer. Light frosts, and fine picking season.

(j) Spring favourable. Fine Summer. Overflow of Mississippi. Extremely fine maturing and picking season.

EAST INDIES.

Apart from the reasons which point to the inadequacy of the rate of production in the United States to meet the growing demand, there are also numerous others which render it of the utmost importance that the supply of cotton from India should be encouraged to the largest possible extent. As a colony in which we have a deep interest, enjoying an abundance of labour, with almost every diversity of soil and climate, and adapted to cotton cultivation, as is unmistakeably proved in its present extent and antiquity, there is every incentive to probe the reason and endeavour to discover the means by which that desirable end may be attained.

The following figures will show the quinquennial average proportion which the annual imports of East India cotton bears to the total quantity imported from other countries, and exhibits the gradual ascendancy of American produce in our markets, thus:—

	East India. lbs.		All other kinds. lbs.
1815-9	34,293,655 or 26 per cent.	....	96,144,852 or 74 per cent.
1820-4	13,553,256 or 09 ,,	....	140,012,650 or 91 ,,
1825-9	23,793,450 or 10 ,,	....	201,924,481 or 90 ,,
1830-4	27,828,314 or 09 ,,	....	266,171,904 or 91 ,,
1835-9	51,260,320 or 12 ,,	....	363,778,868 or 88 ,,
1840-4	84,344,421 or 14 ,,	....	501,962,553 or 86 ,,
1845-9	66,370,532 or 11 ,,	....	560,236,071 or 89 ,,
1850-4	125,621,264 or 16 ,,	....	701,048,927 or 84 ,,
1855-9	180,213,488 or 18 ,,	....	848,844,192 or 82 ,,

The first recorded import of East India cotton took place in 1783, and though there is an evident and considerable rate of increase up to the present time, it is still unsatisfactory when compared with the increase shown from the United States. Up to the beginning of the present century the quantity of East India cotton imported was so fluctuating as to render it almost impossible to ascribe to it any general or rather specific ratio of increase; by taking for our basis however, the annual averages of decennial periods, we shall be able to arrive at a rate of progression and account intelligibly for the variations which are so frequent and apparently uncertain, thus:—

1789 to 1798	....	487,230 lbs.
1799 ,, 1808	....	3,661,134
1809 ,, 1818	....	19,776,975
1819 ,, 1828	....	23,058,315
1829 ,, 1838	....	38,025,505
1839 ,, 1848	....	72,990,689
1849 ,, 1858	....	140,768,139

The most novel and important feature presented is the sudden check which arrested the onward progress in the period 1819-28, as the consequence doubtless of the immense reduction in price established in the interval; and we cannot fail to observe the unpreparedness of the growers of India for this fall in price, as is evidenced by the rate of progress in the succeeding period having even increased under a still further decline, though not at so rapid a pace as that which happily characterises the two last decennial periods, arising partly from the higher prices prevailing in Liverpool, and partly from better cultivation, combined with greater facilities of internal communication, and speedier correspondence with Europe. The variations are caused principally by the fluctuations in prices in the Liverpool market; stimulating doubtless to a certain extent the industry of the native grower in times of high prices and deficient supply, but chiefly supplied from the quantity which otherwise would have been exported to China direct from India. The proportions which the several divisions of our Indian empire have furnished of these imports in the last nine years appears:—

Years.	Bombay.	Madras.	Bengal.	Ceylon.	Singapore.	Total
	lbs	lbs.	lbs.	lbs.	lbs.	lbs.
1850	112,408,140	5.571,450	85,789	807,363	....	118,872,742
1851	112 373,721	6,460,782	1,175,940	2,616,519	14	122,626,976
1852	80,492,272	3,808,224	557,088	64,848	....	84,922,432
1853	159,069,494	12,718,114	7,660,242	1,817.642	582,668	181,848,160
1854	110,179,104	5,420,576	1,144,416	3,044,135	47,778	119,836,009
1855	137,089,232	6,310,528	86,912	1,692.544	....	145,179,216
1856	168,263,536	8,696,128	1,418,928	1,966,384	151,648	180,496,624
1857	228,521,328	17,245,424	2,534,560	2,036,832	....	250,338,144
1858	123,769,408	5,438,944	190,400	3,323,824	....	132,722,576

Our statistics of the Indian export trade do not extend back sufficiently far to allow of any correct idea being formed of its earlier features. The earliest period we have any statistics to bear on the subject is of the port of Calcutta from the year 1795-6, at which date almost the whole of the cotton exported from India was made through that port; and even since that date a small quantity of the produce of India has gone direct to the United States. But save the novelty thus presented, the features of the trade were very incongruous, and in the later years when it did not present a proportion of the entire exports of India, the figures are of little value, except as instancing the decline in the one particular port, which, adopting again the averages of decennial periods, appears thus:—

1796 to 1805	3,903,738 lbs.
1806 „ 1815	16,470,990
1816 „ 1825	33,533,285
1826 „ 1834	16,934,258

In the case of Madras, the figures show the annual average to have been for the period, 1825-34 .... 5,041,713 lbs.

It is only in the year 1834-5, however, that the statistics at our command assume a complete form. The exports from the three Presidencies were respectively in annual averages of quinquennial periods.

Years.	Bombay.	Madras.	Bengal.	Total all India.
	lbs.	lbs.	lbs.	lbs.
1835-9	91,309,665	13,576,300	31,380,575	136,266,540
1840-4	141,802,690	18,992,400	13,976,820	174,771,910
1845-9	133,886,826	13,969,569	9,900,497	157,756,892
1850-4	179,838,889	18,770,256	22,663,188	221,272,333
1855-8	222,076,713	15,962,242	9,702,974	247,741,829

And we will observe the important part the Bombay Presidency has hitherto played in furnishing even these supplies: In Bengal there are evident signs of a decay in the cultivation—at all events for export, while Madras is yet quite unable to extend its sphere of production, as is amply evidenced by its sluggish response to an advance in prices. Even in the Bombay Presidency the low-priced years 1843 to 1849 produced a great decline in the export trade; but this is not surprising, considering that even in the United States it was stated the planters were at the time for the most part working their estates at a loss.

The distribution of this export has not, however, been made entirely to Great Britain, for the statistics show it to have been—

Years.	Great Britain.	China.	Other Parts.	Total.
	lbs.	lbs.		lbs.
1835-9	51,161,059	85,105,481		136,266,540
1840-4	88,868,685	85,903,225		174,771,910
1845-9	70,757,425	82,427,227	4,572,240	157,756,892
1850-4	130,557,160	84,332,450	6,382,723	221,272,333
1855-8	185,229,082	42,973,429	19,539,418	247,741,929

The steadiness apparent thus in the rate of supply to China until the last period, and the then sudden falling off is very remarkable. It will be at a glance detected that though the supply to this country has of late considerably increased, the total export from India has not proportionately done so. In short, that as the demand for and export to Europe increases, and raises the market price, that for China almost in an equal ratio declines; showing it to be subservient to and contingent on the British demand. And further, that in years of low prices, when the export from India to Europe is small, a corresponding increase takes place to the China market. By the figures adduced, we see that in the case of the export to Great Britain the increase in the last twenty years has been *two hundred and sixty-two per cent*, while the increase in the total exports to all parts was only *eighty-two per cent*. The simple fact seems to be, then, that our increased importation of raw cotton from India, attracted by a high price ruling in the home market, does not necessarily imply an enlarged growth in India itself, but a proportionate decline in the quantity exported to China from Calcutta and Bombay—the Chinese not being purchasers of the raw material at the high prices current in London and Liverpool.

And in India, as in all the cotton exporting markets of the world, we find the quantity exported to Continental Europe has wonderfully increased in the last period 1854-8; in that period the following have been the quantities so exported:—

	lbs.
1854-5	1,160,660
1855-6	2,235,916
1856-7	13,389,719
1857-8	33,846,464

Much controversy has arisen as to whether the increase apparent in the exports of raw cotton from India in the last twenty years is really the result of an increased production. If we were to consider the wants of the natives of India to have remained stationary, the greatly increased export of British cotton manufactures thence to India go far to make up for the increased exports of cotton hence. Looking at the Table No. 18. furnished in Dr. Forbes Watson's excellent paper read before the Society of Arts in the last session, the weight of cotton exported from this country to the East Indies in manufactured goods, taken in annual averages of quinquennial periods, appears to have been:—

	Weight of Cotton in Cotton Manufactures Exported to India.	Weight of Cotton Exported from India.
	lbs.	lbs.
1840-4	49,837,791	174,771,910
1845-9	59,118,201	157,756,892
1850-4	87,789,303	221,272,333
1855-7 (average 3 years.)	101,993,544	272,395,875

But the basis upon which the weight of exported goods is here calculated does not make any allowance for difference in the class of goods now exported; the exports of cotton goods to the East Indies now run much more on fine goods; the coarser kinds, which in former years were exported thither, are now scarcely ever shipped, so that the increase shown in the weight is perhaps a little overdrawn. Still making allowance for this, if we deduct also for the decline in the exports of India piece goods, the increase in the weight of cotton exported from India is very trifling. There is, however, abundant proof that the wants of the people have not remained stationary, the immense increase in the demand for and production of all East India produce cannot but have given to them the power of satisfying a wish for greater luxury, which with them displays itself in the decoration of the person. As instancing the demand for Indian produce of all kinds, the computed real value thereof imported into the United Kingdom in the last five years, the rate of increase has been, as compared with the declared real value of British manufactures exported thither, as shown in Table No. 19 thus:—

	East Indian Produce Imported, computed real Value. £	British Manufactures Exported to the East Indies. £
1854	12,973,613	10,025,969
1855	14,758,721	10,927,694
1856	19,373,524	11,807,639
1857	21,094,301	13,079,653
1858	17,407,185	18,283,852

And therefore we may infer, that there has been an increased internal demand for and consequent production of native manufactures, even though the quantity of the raw and manufactured cotton exported has not greatly increased. And there are good reasons which substantiate this view in another manner, thus: taking the effect of prices upon the Indian market, we shall see that the quantity available for export has increased, while the price has actually declined, thus in decennial averages:—

	Price per lb. of East Indian Cotton. d.	Cotton Imported from East Indies.* lbs.
1790	21	422,207
1800	14	6,629,822
1810	15½	27,783,700
1820	8½	20,294,400
1830	5	12,324,200
1840	4⅝	77,011,839
1850	5⅛	118,872,742
1857	5¾	250,338,144

If, therefore, as is here shown, the imports from India have continued to increase, notwithstanding a comparatively reduced price, it is evident that the market value of the article in the Indian market is comparatively lower, either arising from an increased production, or an improved and cheapened mode of cultivation; and applying a very commonplace rule, this fully proves that the people are permitted and will exercise a greater consumption under the cheapness, necessitating an increased production if a profitable one, and which, if it were not, would force a corresponding increase in price until it became so.

* Though figures here adopted are the *imports into the United Kingdom*, the first quantity representing the entire exports from India (nearly all the cotton then being exported to this country), the deductions drawn from them are quite correct.

We may now proceed to notice more particularly the extent of cotton cultivation in India; the districts in which this cultivation is carried on; the causes which have prevented or retarded its extension; and the means which have been pointed out as necessary to be employed in the accomplishment of this most important and national object, viz., an increased supply of Indian cotton, to do away with the present suicidal dependence on one source for the maintenance of our position as a manufacturing nation.

The extent of cotton production in India is a question which has been much canvassed of late years, and various estimates have been made, all more or less differing according to the basis upon which they have been formed. Major-General Briggs assumed that 375 millions of pounds weight are required annually by the natives for a portion of their dress weighing $2\frac{1}{2}$ lbs., and that for various domestic uses double this quantity is required, making the total consumption in native manufactures not less than 750 million pounds. Dr. Wight, on the other hand, sets down the consumption at 20 lbs. per capita, or 3,000 million pounds. This estimate in the opinion of the late Dr. Forbes Royle is too high, but others have even considered it too small. It may be remarked, that such a quantity would require for its production nearly twelve times the surface, assumed as the extent of the cotton farms, in a report made to the Government at the time. Dr. Forbes Watson estimated the total quantity grown to be 2,432,395,875 lbs., distributed thus:—

	lbs.
For Internal Consumption	2,160,000,000
Exportation	272,395,875

being nearly equivalent to double the quantity grown in the United States. He (Dr. Watson) assumed *twelve pounds* of raw cotton to be employed by each one of the native population, or 180 millions of people;* and taking Dr. Royle's average of the yield per acre to be 100 lbs., it follows necessarily that 24,300,000 acres are at present under cotton cultivation. Dr. Watson in working out his results, has adopted a mean from former estimates; but even this makes the consumption of cotton per capita *sixty per cent* greater in India than in the United Kingdom. At the date of the last census in 1851, the population of the United Kingdom was 27,724,849 persons, while in the same year the consumption of raw cotton was 205,086,622 lbs., or equal to $7\frac{1}{2}$ lbs. per capita, whereas the basis of Dr. Watson's estimate is $4\frac{1}{2}$ lbs. more for each individual consumer in India; and it as been objected that the manufacture of so large a quantity under the rude modes of manipulation existing there, would require an immense proportion of the native inhabitants to be continually and exclusively employed in it. It must be acknowledged however, that the people of India differ essentially from Europeans, in that cotton is the material employed for their almost entire clothing, whereas in this country, the additional employment of wool, flax, and silk will probably swell the total quantity of textile substances consumed per head to *sixteen pounds*, the wool and cotton alone amounting to 12 lbs. In India, in addition also to being worked into every kind of fabric, from the coarsest canvas to the finest muslin, an immense quantity of cotton is employed for stuffing and like purposes, requiring little labour in its preparation. The native custom of burning the whole of the clothing and bedding of the dead is another frequent source

* This includes the population in the native and so called independent states.

of consumption unknown in this country, and which must be taken into account. I am disposed to think, however, that Dr. Watson's estimate is rather over than under the mark.

If then it be correct that upwards of twenty-four millions of acres are at present under cotton cultivation in India, and which it may be remarked is nearly four times the area of that under cotton cultivation in the United States, it must be remembered that this immense area is scattered over, in a more or less degree, the whole of the great Peninsula, and yet hardly a single district throughout the whole extent of this magnificent territory is developed to one-third of its capabilities, or rendered sufficiently productive. The Bombay Presidency, containing 76,841,600 acres, and a population of 11,109,067, is calculated by Mr. Chapman to contain forty-three million acres of land admirably adapted to the growth of cotton, greater by nearly one-tenth than the extent of such land in the whole of the United States as estimated by their Government; but if only one-fourth of this extent were cultivated, and each acre produced on an average 100 lbs. of clean cotton (which by improvements it is reasonable to expect may be doubled), we should have 1,075 million pounds, or equal to the quantity at present imported into the United Kingdom from all countries; and it is said this quantity might be sold to a profit in Liverpool at $3\frac{1}{2}$d. per pound.

The chief cotton-growing district in the Bombay Presidency at the present day is Guzerat, which embraces under that name Surat, Broach, Kaira, Ahmedabad, and Kattywar, and in all of these there are millions of acres suited to cotton cultivation lying utterly waste and unproductive; nevertheless this district is said to yield 56 per cent of the whole cotton crop of the country available for export. Its average exports of cotton to Bombay from 1834 to 1846 alone was sixty million pounds, but in 1840-41 they were better than ninety-six millions. The yield per acre of cotton in Guzerat is said to vary from 250 lbs. to 2,000 lbs., one-third of this nearly being clean cotton, or from 80 lbs. to 600 lbs., the average yield to good cultivators being 150 lbs. per acre; and this fact furnishes irrefragable proof and illustration of the immense capability of the soil of India for cotton cultivation when properly conducted. Experiments in Broach have demonstrated, that on moist (not damp) land, of which there is abundance, 600 lbs. of clean cotton can be produced per acre; indeed, Mr. Landon stated the average yield of irrigated land there to be from 350 lbs. to 400 lbs. per acre, and this while the entire produce in the United States ranges from 150 lbs. to 400 lbs. The collectorate of Kandeish, after 2,306 square miles are deducted for roads, rivers, mountains, villages, and unarable lands, is said still to possess 6,058,640 acres every way suited to the growth of cotton; and this is only one of the sixteen collectorates in the Presidency, which is again only one-sixth of the vast territory even subject to British rule in India. Scinde, again, as attached to this Presidency, embraces a large tract of land adapted to the purpose, with all the advantages of a considerable system of internal navigation, and the means of cheap freightage and a thriving commerce; at present it labours under the disadvantages of a spare population, which will, however, doubtless eventually be attracted from other, and in this respect, more favoured spots. In the Bombay Presidency it is stated 2,890,279 acres, or one-twenty-sixth of the entire area, is under cotton farm cultivation; and that, in 1854, 52,313 acres were reported as being planted with American cotton, and the extent of the latter may now be said to be three times as great. In old times the Presidency supplied Bengal with considerable quantities of the raw and manufactured material, and continues still to be by far the most enterprising in the matter of production; indeed, it is alone in this Presidency that the quantity available for export has shown any signs of increase.

The Madras Presidency, containing 84,537,600 acres, and a population of 22,301,697, has made little progress in the cultivation, either for home consumption or export. In the year 1854-5, it contained only 917,374 acres of land under cotton farm cultivation. At that date there were 2,320 acres under the American kind. Dr. Wight reported that the four southern provinces of Coimbatore, Salem, Madura, and Tinnevelly, contained an area of 28,500 square miles, of which 2,480,000 acres were readily susceptible of cotton cultivation, and certainly capable, with a proper application of skill and capital, of yielding 100 lbs. per acre of clean cotton, or, in other words, an aggregate of 200 millions annually. The export cotton trade of Madras has hitherto been comparatively insignificant, though we may reasonably hope that ere long it will become a source of considerable supply.

The Bengal Presidency, containing 185,502,720 acres, and a population of 49,855,137, consumes in its native manufactures nearly the entire cotton crop, yet it possesses the excellent cotton growing district of Berar, perhaps the best field in India, were the means of transport and other matters developed. The export trade in cotton has been very small; the largest quantity ever exported was in 1817-8, in which year from the port of Calcutta there were shipped 75,252,225 lbs., and, excepting one or two attempts at an increase in times of high prices, it has since that date continued to decline; by far the larger portion of that exported being to China. It is to be hoped, however, that the opening up of the Grand Canal in the Doab will prove to be attended with a considerable increase in the growth of cotton for the British market; the extent of land it is said to be capable of irrigating is 5,400,000 acres, which had become utterly waste for want of moisture; if one-third of this quantity only were under cotton cultivation, we might have an increased export from this source alone of 180 million pounds, that is, if the opinions are correct as to its adaptability to the cultivation. The great cotton field of Berar, however, presents perhaps the largest scope for action; were *it* but put on the same footing with the seaboard districts in regard to means of transport, there is little doubt but that a breadth of land would then become available, adequate to supply the full demands of Great Britain. There are, however, political considerations connected with the question of a railroad into the dominions of the Nizam which perhaps weigh against its expediency. The North-Western Provinces and the Punjaub contain 105,022,720 acres, and a population of 40,025,975, showing it to be the most densely populated district of India; and here again there is reported to be thousands of miles of good land free to a great extent from jungle and timber and adapted to the cultivation of cotton; and yet this great area does little or nothing in an export trade, though the fact of its lying out of the reach of the monsoons, abounding with streams and rivers fed by the waters springing from the mountains of Cashmere and Kunawar, renders it certainly fitted to become a future source of supplies. There is further attached to this presidency the kingdom of Oude, containing 15,192,320 acres, and a population of 2,970,000, and the Eastern Settlements, including Pegu, estimated to contain 55,492,480 acres, but very thinly inhabited, the number being estimated at 1,639,493; making the total area of the presidency to be 361,210,240 acres, and the population 94,490,605.

Looking back through this meagre and scattered data, and comparing the facts with those presented on the subject of the United States, they appear very startling. India containing in its three presidencies (exclusive of the native, or so-called Independent States) 522,589,440 acres of land, and a population of 127,901,369, or about one person to every four acres. The southern and cotton growing States of America (including Texas), containing about 530,000,000 acres, with a population of about 5,718,925, or one to every ninety acres; it is astonishing that while from the latter the average export of cotton in the four years ending 1858, has been 1,131,690,697 lbs., that from India, during the same period, did not exceed 247,741,929 lbs., and this arising from the fact that the present means and system of cultivation there does not admit of a successful competition in regard to price. The soil of India having been worked during thousands of years, while that of the United States is comparatively new, is a valid reason for a discrepancy existing, inasmuch as that it requires *twice as much* land in India (taken throughout) to produce 100 lbs. of clean cotton as in the United States. The cost of the land is about the same; but then the important item of labour is about 80 per cent cheaper than in the United States. Again, the States have their Mississippi and magnificent rivers; our Indus and Ganges avail us little in the matter of cotton supply. What the former may do remains to be demonstrated; one point is certainly proved, and that is, that with a yield of 100 lbs. per acre, under facilities of cheap transit, India can, even under the present system of cultivation, sell cotton in Liverpool at a price, which, making allowance for inferiority of quality, is more advantageous to the manufacturer than other kinds for employment in about 70 per cent of his business. But we must not conclude that because throughout the length and breadth of the peninsula there is 2,400,000,000 lbs. of clean cotton now produced, that, therefore, any large portion of it can compete on those terms,—much of it is grown at a great distance from a shipping port, and though railroads may in some measure meet this objection, the yield obtainable, though sufficient to maintain the production for consumption at the spot, would not be able to sustain itself in a competition in our markets. A large portion of it is grown in inaccessible spots for native use, and would not therefore enjoy those advantages, to fit it to compete with America; the future increase must rather come from its systematic cultivation in soils chosen as favourable to its growth, and places having ready means of transit to the selling markets.

The question of the relative abilities of the United States and India to compete for the supply of our great staple manufacture, is in the main contingent on the facilities of cheap labour and transit. For the immeasurable superiority of the soil of Texas, with its 300,000,000 acres, as compared with our Indian possessions, which do not seem to be capable of producing a greater average yield, under the present careless system of cultivation, than 100 lbs. of clean cotton per acre (although as before said, where care has been employed, and particularly by the application of judicious irrigation, greatly increased results have been obtained), is only counterbalanced by the relative scarcity of labour in the former, and perhaps an almost equal rate of charges for transit as compared with that of our Indian supply, which is now for the most part obtained from the coasts and spots having facilities of easy and comparatively cheap communication; and as instancing the importance of this *transit* on the abilities of India to supply our wants, a table furnished by Mr. A. C. Brice to the India House, and quoted by Dr. Watson, will serve to show, that while in those parts contributing to the exports from Bombay having means of easy transit, the production for export has increased, other parts with long coast navigation and at a distance in the interior have even declined,—

	1852-3.	1853-4.	1854-5.	1855-6.	1856-7.
	lbs.	lbs.	lbs.	lbs.	lbs.
Surat, Cutch, Broach, and Ahmedabad	99,923,544	106,888,992	58,119,096	143,656,534	196,809,872
Candeish, Ahmednuggur, Poonah, Sattara, Sholapore, and Berar	75,488,224	63,066,136	40,537,504	59,440,528	65,243,304
Belgaum, Dharwar, Raichoor, Bellary (west side), and Kurnool	39,200,000	17,640,000	13,284,096	13,565,160	29,008,000

Thus hope may exist from this fact alone, that with the development of the means of conveyance, a steady and considerable increase will take place in the exports of cotton.

The causes which have prevented or retarded the cultivation of cotton in India for the British and other markets, is a subject of great importance, and may be shortly touched upon here. The discussion or analysis of the several deterrent causes of social and industrial progress, either in detail or generally, point out incidentally the remedies and the means necessary to be employed for the regeneration of India, and the proper development of her vast capabilities as a cotton growing country. The extreme poverty of the native growers is acknowledged by all who have had the opportunity of observing them, and among the Government officials, from the Governor-General to the Revenue collector, it is an admitted fact; hence the secret of the "social despotism" excercised by the exorbitant money-lenders, who in reality grasp the fruits of the grower's industry. The want in India of purchasers on the spot, with improved modes of cultivation, and of cleaning and packing the cotton for the market is an equally admitted evil. The system of advances to cultivators of whatever description of produce is of general practice in India, and if it were conducted on proper principles would be of great advantage; it might be adopted by English capitalists to a large extent, and be productive of mutual advantage and profit. As it is, it is well known that the "middlemen" exact exorbitant interest for their advances, and when the cotton is received by them from the ryot, it is and always has been carelessly treated, adulterated, exposed to the weather and to dirt, to the great deterioration of its value. Hence much of its present inferiority in price to the American produce in the English market, and an extended demand for it only in case of a dearth of cotton from the United States. Under the present order of things the systematic adulteration of Indian cotton will always exist; the poverty of the native growers and the absence of English agents to make reasonable advances to them on the spot, compels them to borrow money at a ruinous rate of interest, and to sell their cotton much below its real value; the consequence is, they become indifferent as to its quality or condition, in fact as to everything pertaining to it except *mere quantity*. Ignorant, and a prey to the native money lenders, improvement with them in the art of cultivation is entirely out of the question; they are unassisted, incapable of progress, and bound, as in fetters of iron, to the imperfect modes of culture pursued by themselves and their forefathers. Under more favourable circumstances, however, they would make greater advances in improvement, and by the aid of knowledge, and implements and machines of European or American construction, speedily and successfully compete in favoured localities with their rivals on the banks of the Mississippi.

The want of a regular rotation of crops in many districts, and the almost universal mismanagement in the cultivation itself, or especially in the gathering of the produce and the cleaning and packing processes, tend to depreciate the cotton at least *fifteen per cent* in value, and at the same time to render it (except at intervals) almost unmarketable in the Liverpool market, because the buyer there expects a dirty article in exchange for his money.

The absence of a regular or steady demand for the article, and the fact of the prices always fluctuating according to a sanguine or gloomy prospect of the coming crop in the Southern States of America, regardless of the condition of that in the East, operates as an effectual bar to the steady progression of shipments of Indian cotton to this market; and this because it is well-known that American cotton will command the preference, and that the Indian varieties will only realize remunerative prices readily when the English manufacturers are threatened with a real or fancied scarcity in the supply from New Orleans. One great reason, therefore, of cotton not being extensively grown in India for export must be palpably evident. It is because the merchant is never sure of the produce he might purchase realizing in the English market a sufficiently remunerative price—it becomes a speculation entirely, and he cannot afford to trade on contingencies; and this is particularly the case with the cultivator, because he is ever at the mercy of his insatiable creditor, the money lender of his village, and should he be disappointed in the price actually obtained, he would find it difficult to provide for himself and family the bare necessaries with which he is compelled from his position to rest satisfied. I do not mean to insinuate, nor do I think, that fault lies in any quarter, for it is the natural result of circumstances. The course now adopted by the Government of aiding the march of civilization and enlightenment by the means of intercommunication and transit, will do more than any other thing towards its eradication; and until this is effected, the natives of India will never increase their growth of cotton for export to the extent of its capabilities.

As the Indian cultivator shall be freed from this unnatural incubus the production will increase—he will be able to cope with his American competitor, and his position will be then doubly improved, when the success or failure of his own crops shall impart the tone to the market, and influence our prices accordingly. That it is possible for them, with facilities of cheap transit, to compete with the Americans as cotton growers, cannot I think, admit of a reasonable doubt, but in order to do so they must have immunity from the tyranny of the "middlemen"; in short they must be so elevated and enlightened as to be able to triumph over or resist the machinations or impositions of the money lender; and there is every probability that ere long European houses, one and all, will find it to their advantage to advance to the grower all his requirements on a moderate charge, and furnish machines and instruct him in their use. Raw cotton can be purchased in most of the cotton districts at from 1½d. to 2d. per lb., which price leaves the ryot a fair rate of profit, considerably higher than he can ever expect from the grasping middleman. It is further found that, notwithstanding the enormous cost of carriage to the coast, and of freightage, insurance, and charges to England, it can be sold in the Liverpool market at from 3½d. to 4d. per lb. As before said, much of the present inferiority of the East India cotton arises from the systematic adulteration, and carelessness of the picking and cleaning, all of which is susceptible of amelioration or entire removal, and the disparity, therefore, between the price of American and East India cotton must diminish. That the produce of India can be considerably improved, and brought at least to the standard of "American uplands" with an increased yield is a fact of great interest; and if we look at some of the samples of East Indian Egyptian seed cotton in the Industrial Museum at the India House, yielding even a greater quantity of produce per acre than the indigenous kind, and worth upwards of 60 per cent more, we may reasonably conclude that there is every room for improvement, and for our Indian possessions becoming the first cotton growing country of the world.

It is universally acknowledged that means of cheap transit are essential to the development of India's industrial resources and its onward march in the path of civilization and material improvement, and that without such means the culture of cotton by the natives will always be on a limited scale for export; for we have it on the best official authority, that transport charges have more to do with the cotton movement in India than perhaps any one single deterrent cause, and the reduction of even a halfpenny per pound or so would give such an impetus to it as would lead to a supply equal to a large portion of our wants as a manufacturing nation from this source alone. "The cost of conveyance" says Mr. Ashworth, in his admirable lecture before the Society of Arts, "of a bale of 400 to 500 lbs. of cotton a distance of a thousand miles on the Mississippi river has been as low as one dollar, and ranges from that sum to one-and-a-half dollars, or 6s. 3d., and it is therefore in commodious and cheap conveyance more than in cost of growth that the present advantage of America over India as a cotton growing country is to be accounted for." Looking at the expenses of land and coast carriage in India, we find it interferes considerably with the extension of the export cotton trade; for instance, the cotton producing districts south of the Nerbudda, and those of Oomrawutty and Nagpore, in Berar, situated remote from Mirzapore on the Ganges, lying between Benares and Allahabad, where if we take their average distance to the entrepôt in question, each pound of cotton costs in transit 2¼d. per lb. This heavy charge arises from the fact that the cotton is exported on the backs of oxen, each carrying 160 lbs., at the extreme rate in fine weather of seven miles a day. But this is not all; it has then to be borne by water carriage little short of five hundred miles further, viz., to Calcutta, from which port, if conveyed to England, any idea of profit is absolutely out of the question, unless a much higher range of prices should exist at Liverpool than is consistent with the rates usually current. Writing of these cotton districts and on this point, General Briggs informs us "that in the absence of a defined and good road, a drove of several hundred head of cattle requires to be constantly watched and prevented from straying on the march, and this leads to the necessity of travelling by day in the hot weather, when the thermometer is seldom less than 100 deg. and frequently 130 deg. of Farenheit. These droves are seldom so few as a hundred and often exceed a thousand; every morning after daylight each has to be laden, and before the operation is over the sun is already high above the horizon. The cattle have then to proceed at the slow rate of two miles an hour, and seldom perform a journey of more than eight or nine miles a day. The horde generally halts one day in seven. If the caravan is overtaken by rain, the cotton becoming saturated with moisture, is so heavy as to prevent its transport on the cattle ; and the roads, if lying through the cotton-ground, are such that men even sink to the ankles at every step, and cattle to their knees. It may easily be supposed that under such a calamity the merchant and the carrier are both ruined."

It is impossible to deny that the subject of internal communication in India had not received that attention which its vast importance demanded, until—chiefly in consequence of the facts elucidated by Mr. Bright's Committee—the pressure of public opinion in this country had been brought to bear upon the Home Government of India. There is, however, good reason for believing that such matters now receive the anxious attention of the authorities, and it is gratifying to think that within probably three years nearly five thousand miles of railway will have been stretched through most important divisions of that vast and hitherto commercially inaccessible country. The means, however, by which further transit facilities shall be afforded involve a grave subject of consideration. Every one concurs in the assertion that the greatest civilizer and improver is the means of cheap and rapid transit, and latterly the Government has readily given its support to the projects set on foot with that view. It has sanctioned railroads, which involve an expenditure of capital of near £40,000,000, and on which an annual charge of nearly two millons sterling will accrue, and it is certain that a long period must elapse before taken as a whole these will pay the guaranteed rate of interest. No one would attempt to deny the prospective importance of the railroads now in progress, but, perhaps excepting some seaboard districts which might be advantageously opened up by such means, it is probable enough has been done for the present in this direction ; and the general feeling now exists that sufficient pecuniary aid has been granted to this description of transit, and that attention ought to be directed to the formation of canals and to measures calculated to render as far as possible the different rivers navigable. The climate of India is such that the means of irrigation is as much a matter of importance as transit; it is equally the interest of the cultivator to produce good crops as to have the means of conveying them to a better market. Moreover, many kinds of produce which can ill afford the cost of carriage by railway *could* be borne by this means without the uncertainty and deterioration which is entailed by the present bullock carriage. It is asserted, and with much force of argument, that canals, unlike railways, will, with the improvement of agricultural knowledge there, very soon defray their cost out of the income from irrigation, while the expense of transit by that means is immeasurably less. The labour too employed in the construction of canals is for the major part mere hand labour, which in India is cheap and comparatively abundant, while in the case of railways the European civil engineers and mechanics all receive far higher wages than in this country, while they at the same time, from the greater temperature, are fitted to perform but half the work. Throughout the larger portion of India, if we except the Western Ghauts, the nature of the country is admirably adapted to the formation of canals. The Government has extended a helping hand to at least one such enterprise, and will doubtless in like manner do so towards others where required. We understand that there is now the prospect of every effort being made to open up the Godavery, the great highway into the cotton field of Berar; and we have the opinion of Colonel Cotton that the navigation of the Godavery alone would do much to restore a large district in India to a state of agricultural prosperity, and to raise its inhabitants in the scale of social well-being.

So far, then, Government is affording evidence of its willingness to promote works calculated to assist in opening up the country, and in affording those means of irrigation so essential to the development of its resources. Thoroughly to accomplish this much, will nevertheless depend on private enterprise directed on the spot. In addition, however, to the transit and other difficulties now in course of removal, two causes especially preventive of efforts on the part of both the British and native capitalist to expend on schemes for such a purpose have been in operation, namely—the uncertain tenure of land, and the imperfect administration of justice. With regard to the latter, the majority of those examined on the point before the Colonization (India) Committee, were agreed as to the great room for improvement in this department; one involving the rights of property and other questions of great moment. With respect to land tenure, public opinion both in this country and in India has gradually arrived at the conclusion, that not only should lands now in the hands of Government be finally sold in fee simple, but that the redemption of the land tax in all parts of India cannot be too soon effected. For a number of years in a few remote parts of India, Government has granted land in what has been so far entitled to be called "fee simple," but attached to the transfer were certain privileges which have tended to nullify the advantage. In December, 1858, the Home Government sent orders to India, which we believe are now being acted upon, and which do so far facilitate the transfer of land in the manner wished for. Much, however, in this way still remains to be done, and it is to be hoped that the subject will at an early date receive the attention of the authorities, both here and in India.

With reference to the legislative enactments affecting the Cotton Trade of India, a few words may be ventured upon, as well as upon the question of the currency as having an important bearing on the general welfare of that country.

The course to be pursued by the Government of India in the matter of the Cotton Trade has not been clearly defined, and though the unquestioned policy of free and unfettered trade in this as in every other article may be said to meet the question, it does not in fact do so. The expenses of Government in India must be defrayed, and legislation in the matter, therefore, resolves itself into a question of to what extent, if any, the article among others shall subscribe to the revenue. We, as a manufacturing, rather than as a producing nation in England, have come to recognise the benefit of exempting the raw material from taxation, on the ground that the employment of the people in the trade to which it indirectly ministers, more than compensates for the loss, and further that as an article almost of necessity, and certainly conducive to the comfort and happiness of the people, it does not form so fit a subject of taxation as articles of luxury, which, in like manner, can better bear such an imposition. It may be remarked, that no special legislation becomes necessary, and moreover that it is an undeniable advantage to the country to find a consumer for its surplus produce, the growth and export of which, therefore, should not be checked by the imposition of any duty. This is generally admitted, I think, but India must not be viewed solely as a producing nation. India may and does produce twice the weight of cotton exported by the whole of the United States; the question arises—is it India's advantage to export the whole of this immense quantity, and thereby become a customer to Lancashire of an almost equivalent extent? It is, of course, the interest of this country that it should do so. Or, should India retain her raw cotton, and clothe her people unaided and independent? The whole difficulty is one of figures and cost. In the ordinary course of events the river will find its own bed adjusted by the law of supply and demand, but to predict the future course of the Government becomes a matter of considerable difficulty, for in this is also involved the troublesome consideration of the occupation of the people.

It is a fact that cotton can be carried from the producing districts often 200 or 300 miles inland to the seaboard, thence to Bombay and to Lancashire, and there be spun and woven, and travels back in its manufactured state to the very places whence the raw material first came, and still enters into competition with, and is in fact displacing the twist, not to say the cloth, which is spun in the very cotton-field itself. This tends to show that Indian labour is at present unprofitably and disadvantageously employed in spinning and weaving, and by imposing a duty on raw cotton, or an import duty on British twist and cloths, we are giving a premium to the maintenance of an unwholesome condition of trade. Here, however, the question arises, why then has not more raw cotton been drawn out from the country? A number of circumstances, some natural, some artificial, are the reasons, and these cannot be overcome but by time. First and foremost, the great difficulty of inefficient means of transit and communication, and the poverty and ignorance of the larger part of the producers and consumers, who in selling the cotton obtain but a tithe of that we pay for it, and, in purchasing the English manufactured article, in a similar way become the sufferers by the craftiness of the middlemen or native merchants; until it is clear, the poor ryot finds it more to his advantage to retain it for his wants, and during the hot season, when little labour in agriculture is required, convert the raw material by hand into coarse and heavy manufactures. But the means of transit, which are undergoing great improvement and extension, will afford the surest guarantee of the removal of this unnatural incubus on the native and the country, and while enriching both, form a source of great advantage to our trade. Meantime it may be questioned, whether it is the proper policy to be pursued by the Government to levy a tax on imported British cotton manufactures, which tends to foster the native hand manufacture. And so far from the labour not being required, it is on the contrary greatly needed, the cry has lately been—the want of labour in the cotton fields for picking and cleaning. The cotton districts are among the most thinly peopled of India, and when we remember that it requires 750 adults, working ten hours, to free from seed one ton of cotton, we can comprehend how the diversion of part of this labour has effected an already deficient supply. It is chiefly in the cotton districts that cotton spinning and weaving maintain their position, and interfere with cotton picking and cleaning. It is better that native manufacture should die out, unless it can sustain itself without protection. Let

Government do all in its power to disenthral the poorer native from the vicious influence of the middlemen, and the people will devote themselves to such occupations as will be most to their own interests, which will, I imagine, at present be in the proper production of the raw material Great Britain so much needs; and reaping from it a fair mede of profit, will, with the cheaper and better adapted cloths of Europe, be placed in a position to enjoy greater luxuries of life. India should on no account be governed for the English. I would deprecate the course now advocated, if it simply tended to help British shipping and Lancashire mills; but if the import duty on twist and calicoes imported into India is continued, or even raised to a very great extent, hand spinning and weaving must die out, and we merely prolong the struggle to make the cotton yield the grower in India less money, or to make it cost the spinner in Lancashire more; while a tax is thereby levied on the consumer of either native or British fabrics in India, which is paid to the native manufacturer to protect him in his unprofitable business. The case is different with mills conducted on English principles and with English machinery; if Government decides that it will be a national object to foster such, most of the objections to an import duty on twist and cloths vanish. I believe, however, the true policy of government is primarily to legislate so as to drain the raw cotton out of the country, and create a demand for our manufactured goods in lieu of those now manufactured in India. To acquire an increased interchange of products with other countries is the aim of every aspiring nation; to sell as much of its produce, and receive in return foreign articles to please the taste or fancy of the people, is one of the greatest incentives of trade; though it must be admitted that if the ingredients of manufacturing success exist, India acquires more wealth by itself manufacturing either for its own wants or for export.

We have heretofore considered the native cotton manufacture of India only as that conducted under the old and rude hand processes; but we must now regard the matter from another and distinct point of view. We will look at the advantages accruing to India from adopting our more improved processes for her own benefit, and consider its seeming practicability. We hear that the quantity of the raw material employed in the Indian native manufacture, is more than double that imported into this country, and this under all the disadvantages of the present expensive and wasteful mode of cultivation and manufacture there. How much the demand might expand were the processes economised more in accordance with those we employ, may be judged by the great development we have seen as having occurred in our own trade in the past century. That there is abundant room for economy is amply proved in the successful competition of British manufactures in all those parts of India into which they have gained access; and this economy must in part come from the substitution of machine for hand labour. The cry of there being no other occupation for the native population, is certain to be raised against the destruction of the native trade; but its fallacy was never more palpably evident than in this particular case. Taking India as a whole, it is the consumer of its entire production; what advantage then can it enjoy in spending one week in the manufacture of a piece of cloth which can be as well made in one day? It is argued, that throughout the dry season, when vegetation is checked, there is no occupation for the people in agriculture, and that it is then they are employed in spinning and weaving for the wants of the coming active season. If this applied in its full sense each family would work for itself, and British manufactures would probably never force their way against the hand-wove fabrics, so long as it existed; and if, on the other hand, it is merely a class trade followed only by a limited number, it is clear that the number of consumers must pay so much more, which is an additional burden upon them for the advantage of the manufacturing few. These are, however, exploded objections, and it is unnecessary further to dwell upon them; every one now acknowledges that India's advance must be attained by aiding, and if need be, forcing its forward progress by the economical employment of science and art, to material and useful purposes. Whether Great Britain or Bombay can supply some of India's wants cheaper than heretofore has yet to be decided; but it is clearly the consumer's interest to buy from the cheapest market. Granted, labour is cheap there (that it is not over abundant however, is proved by its being too dear to compete with machinery even at this great distance); but it follows, that if assisted by science and art, it may become as valuable and comparatively as scarce as with us. There is the soil, the climate, all the natural facilities of production; knowledge is all that is required to render it advantageous to more fully employ it; and if we should throw the native weaver out of that employment, we, in doing so, only lead him to a more profitable one, and advance his own condition.

The question mainly resolves itself into whether Lancashire shall manufacture the material to supply the place of the native fabrics; or India manufacture for itself on the same economical principles, instead of sending the raw material several thousands of miles for that purpose, to be returned charged with all the immense attendant expenses which apparently might be saved? In looking at the subject—the advantages to the capitalist, the people, and the country, all command attention. Unless there is a clear benefit to be gained by the capitalist, it is fruitless for us to hope that the manufacture by machinery will ever be established in India; except that Government, regarding the advantages to the people and the country, should extend a helping, or rather protective, hand; and this is always a questioned, if not condemned, policy. Whether it will be advantageous to the capitalist in India, when all the difficulties shall have been cleared away, to admit of a fair competition, is likely to remain an open point until some further practical solution shall have been effected. The disadvantages under which Great Britain labours in competing with any properly organised Indian mills, in having to carry the material backwards and forwards, are so great as apparently to more than counterbalance the disadvantages under which India labours. There are, however, so many contingent circumstances which enter into the calculation, and the pros and cons are so numerous, and withal so prodigious, that the whole question seems to hinge on those very contingencies.

The *first cost of mills* will in India be double what it is with us, arising from the large freight and charges which would have to be incurred in the transport of the machinery, &c., and greatly increased cost of European superintendence in erection, as in all the attendant circumstances.

Wear and tear of buildings and machinery in India, is stated certainly not to be less than 10 per cent, while in this country it is about 5: thus—the machinery requires renewal every 15 years, buildings every 45 years; say, as value of buildings are one-fourth of that of machinery, every 20 years or 5 per cent.

Wages: the proportion of "skilled" to the "mere hand labour" is in this country not much more than 1 in 10; but it is estimated by those well acquainted with the subject that it would in India amount to 3 in 10.

Operatives in India would be paid at the rate of 2s. per week, while in England the extreme average would give 15s. per week; but as in India the day's work effected is much less per man, besides other drawbacks, the amount of work done is 15 to 20 per cent less than in England, while in the rate of wages they have an advantage equal to 87 per cent.

Skilled labour, or that which would have to be supplied by Europeans, will be increased by 150 per cent.

Raw material will cost the manufacurer in India less by all the transit, and home merchants' charges; and Manchester, London, transit, and Bombay selling charges on British manufactures, which would in like manner be saved.

Let us then, from this data, endeavour to work out the relative cost of manufacturing the material employed in our trade in the year 1856, the date at which the last return was made by the Factory Inspectors; and it will better answer our purpose to deal only with the operations of spinning and weaving. We may suppose, that out of the entire manufacture, the value of which in that year was £57,000,000, £40,000,000 was the value of the produce of those two primary operations, made up as follows:—

	£
Labour	10,000,000
Cotton actually consumed, 856,700,000 lbs.	22,000,000
Wear and tear of machinery, valued by Mr. Ellison at £40,250,000, at 5 per cent	2,012,500
Interest on capital employed, as estimated by Mr. Ellison at £64,750,000, at 4 per cent	2,590,000
Profit and incidental expenses	3,397,500
	40,000,000

This would in India stand thus:—

Labour, *skilled*, say 30 per cent, or £3,000,000, would be increased 150 per cent	7,500,000
Operatives, 70 per cent, or £7,000,000, would do, say 17½ per cent less work, say increased to £8,225,000, on which there would be a saving of 87 per cent	1,069,250
	8,569,250
Cotton is charged to us with 12 per cent merchants' charges in Bombay, of which say 8 per cent would be saved to Indian manufacturer; exchange 6 per cent; and with freight, insurance, home merchant, and sale charges, and loss of weight, &c., equal to another 22 per cent, makes up a total of 36 per cent; but as instead of using Indian cotton we use better qualities from other countries, upon which the charges are not near so severe, we may safely say 30 per cent may be allowed for these on £22,000,000, less 30 per cent; say on £15,400,000	17,380,000
Wear and tear of machinery and buildings, being on £80,500,000 at the increased rate of 10 per cent	8,050,000
Interest on capital employed, being £105,000,000 at 7 per cent	7,350,000
Profit and incidental expenses	6,795,000
	48,144,250
From which deduct Manchester, London, transit, insurance, and Bombay charges, allowing for advantage in exchange, or 30 per cent on £40,000,000, the value of our manufacture	12,000,000
	36,144,250
And if we take from off this 10 per cent, which is charged in addition (as duty) on the British manufactures imported into India, or £40,000,000	4,000,000
	£32,144,250

These figures would appear to show the startling fact, that India could manufacture by machinery at a cost 20 per cent less than Great Britain can sell British manufactures in the Bombay market; and when we regard the results of Mr. Landon's efforts at Broach, and the good repute in which the projected companies are held in Bombay, as is shown by the shares of the "Spinning and Weaving Company," being quoted 58 per cent premium (having paid a dividend equal to 16 per cent); the "Oriental Weaving and Spinning Company" at 39 per cent; the "Throstle Mill Company" at 5 per cent; and the "East India Spinning and Weaving Company, Limited, at par;"* we might be disposed to condone any fostering spirit Government might display for the new branch of industry there. But these circumstances which we regard as showing in favour of India, are not of the great weight we might at first sight be disposed to think them. The present experimental manufacture, which we may take to be embraced in the before-mentioned mills, extend only to the manufacture of yarns of no higher number than No. 40's (or 40 hanks, of 850 yards each, to the pound), while in this country we spin up to 700's for useful purposes. This is in a great measure accounted for from the fact of the indigenous cotton which is used being so very inferior, for in Lancashire it is not spun into higher numbers than 16's. But supposing the exotic cotton to be grown of the finest quality, of which there seems every probability, would it then become possible to spin the finer counts to compete with the British yarn? For that purpose the machinery becomes much more complicated and expensive, and the immense charge for interest greatly accumulates against India. The manufacture of the coarser counts must first be fully established before the latter can be attempted; and this will take some time. That machinery can be successfully employed there in particular localities in the manufacture of low counts, cannot be doubted; it is merely a question of time and of first cost. One of the greatest drawbacks to the enterprise, is the high rate of interest paid for money there; but ere a very few years have rolled by, this must yield considerably to the necessities of the times. As confidence is imparted, the immense stores of wealth which must be locked up, the ill-got gains of the despised middleman, all will come out for employment in the development of the resources of the country, the increase in the value of property will yield a capital which will more than equal demand. As the people learn to bring science to bear upon their pursuits their wealth must vastly increase, and *pari passu*, despite the demand, the present exorbitant rate will be lowered nearer to our standard. As this development is going forward too, the demand for labour will increase, and so far from its being necessary to maintain an expensive and fruitless occupation for a part of the population, the application of machinery will be fully required to maintain the advantages of a cheap labouring class to aid and feed it.

Although we find that the Companies before named have erected or are erecting in Bombay altogether 60,000 spindles and 300 looms, and adding to these 18,000 spindles in the Broach mills and 30,000 in the Fort Glo'ster Mills in Calcutta, we have a total number of 108,000 spindles and 300 looms, which evidences some considerable enterprise in the matter;† I still believe, however, that the policy of the

---

* Since this was written the position of the shares of these companies has again further improved upon the announcement of Mr. Wilson's policy in regard to the Indian machine manufacture.

† Several other companies, with the same objects, have been formed since this was written, and have, or are about, to send home orders for the necessary machinery.

Government should be to drain out the raw produce from the country, and allow the native hand manufacture to expire. India is not yet prepared to invest to the full extent in cotton mills, and so long as English capital is employed, there is little advantage gained by the people of India from the change. The present tax will bring in little revenue, being collected on only about one-twentieth of the entire Indian consumption, while the other *ninety-five* per cent, or the native manufacture, is increased in cost to the native consumer to nearly an equivalent extent; doing certain harm to the consumer, and perhaps under present circumstances fostering more the *hand* than *machine* manufacture.

I have already alluded to the currency of India, and it forms a subject of such importance to the effectual development of its trade and commerce, that I cannot conclude without a few remarks on the subject, though it scarcely comes within the scope of our present object. During the last three years of which we have accounts, the import of bullion into the three Presidencies has been upwards of 41 millions sterling, or equal to the entire value of imported merchandise, while the exports have not exceeded two millions, leaving to have been employed in the country 39 million pounds sterling during the period cited; of course some part has been employed in the manufacture of ornaments and jewellery, but the Indian Mint Returns show that an immense proportion was converted into coin. By the increase in the trade with the East in the last few years, there has been an immense drain of bullion to pay for the produce we have imported from that source. In 1856 and 1857 alone, nearly £30,000,000 sterling was exported from this country, though some portion of this was of course on Government account; and in the year just closed it reached £15,000,000. It is not the immense proportions of this drain that is most startling, but that it consists almost entirely of silver, and this is caused, or greatly increased, from silver being the only legal tender in our Indian Colonies. To illustrate the effects of this drain upon our reserves of silver; the price of the article in our market, which in 1850 ranged about 5s. per ounce, has, within the past year, reached the enormous sum of 5s. 2¾d. per ounce; to this country, this is a matter of great importance. The yield of silver in the world has steadily increased from six millions in the commencement of the century up to £8,000,000 per annum at the present time, and this supply does not appear capable of extension : while that of gold, which ranged about four to five millions up to 1840, has increased to about £35,000,000, at which it has stood since 1853. It is obvious, therefore, that, should this condition of circumstances continue with the extension of our trade with the East, there are difficulties in store which must ultimately seriously affect the position of our own coin; but hoping, as we must do, that the difficulty will be met by the Government of India as far as lays in their power, the rest cannot be provided against, and the law of supply and demand must work out the solution. The cumbersome and expensive form of silver, as the sole circulating medium and only legal tender in India, entails great expense and waste on trade conducted on such a basis; the leading transactions between 180 million people involves an immense use of the coin; the wear and tear, and the restricted employment which is necessitated by its bulky form, imposes on the Government and the trader alike a heavy tax, and cripples the capabilities of the country. There does not appear any reason why the trade of the country should not be relieved of this heavy encumbrance by the partial substistution of a more easy form of media, such as the issue of Government notes, or at all events gold coin, and the nation relieved of the immense cost of maintaining one so expensive as the present, while we on our part would be relieved of the dread of seeing our silver coin reach an unpleasant premium, and of the enormous gold discoveries of America and Australia forcing on our gold a rate of depreciation in value equally undesirable. As indicating the feeling in the matter, for several mails past, merchants have been shipping fine gold in bars of 12 oz., which, being worth 84s. per oz., cost about £50 sterling each. These are shipped to Bombay, then stamped after assay, when they pass for 500 rupees. The novelty may be the beginning of an important movement. If these 500-rupee gold bars are so convenient, some considerable relief may be thus granted. There are unquestionably some reforms called for in this respect; the necessity for a gold coinage must force itself upon public opinion, and sooner or later be followed by the issue of some readily convertible form of paper or credit, for which there exists a great want, which, along with other financial arrangements, it is to be hoped the Government will not delay the consideration of, and that the adoption of some comprehensive scheme may be the result.*

In conclusion, we have shown, I think, that India embodies all the constituent qualities necessary to enable her to become the first cotton producing country in the world. We have seen that means are being vigorously employed to assist her onward progress in this and other respects, and there is great hope that before long she will rival America both in the quality and quantity of produce in the English market. The cloud which has so long o'ershadowed the vast Asiatic Continent is quickly dissipating before the dawn of civilization, and in opening up the country, and developing its resources, our legislators will have followed the most certain road for securing its emancipation and forward march in the sure path of moral and material development.

WEST INDIES AND BRITISH GUIANA.

Our West India Colonies have now almost ceased to be regarded as a source of cotton supply, and, were it not that the quality of the cotton imported from them is very good, and well suited to the finer phases of our manufacture, it would long since have been erased from commercial notice. In 1787, we have seen that, the quantity imported from this source formed nearly *thirty-eight per cent* of the total import into the United Kingdom; but in the present day there is barely a sixteenth part of the quantity imported, while it forms but $\frac{1}{2000}$ part of the entire imports. The causes which have brought about this decline are totally dissimilar from those which have affected the other cotton growing countries; the main cause being the scarcity of labour, hastened on perhaps by the greater adaptibility of the principal part of the soil to the cultivation of sugar and other products, and the greater decline which has taken place in the price of cotton as compared with sugar. Thus, looking at the period 1817 to 1822, we find the relative decline to have been :—

---

* Since this paper was delivered to the Royal Asiatic Society, it has been resolved by the Government of India to issue Government Notes.

	Value of Cotton per lb.	Value of Sugar per cwt.
1817	20⅙d.	49s. 8d.
1818	20d.	50s. 0d.
1819	13½d.	41s. 4d.
1820	11¼d.	36s. 2d.
1821	9½d.	33s. 2d.

Which exhibits a decline in the case of cotton of *fifty-five per cent*, and in sugar of only *thirty-three per cent*, while the last prices may be said to represent very nearly their present position. But, added to this, we have also another and very plausible reason for the decline—in the great reduction of the duty formerly charged on foreign as compared with West India cotton, which was effected in 1833, at the very time the Emancipation Act was working the ruin of the planters.

At the time of the discovery of the West Indies by the Europeans, we know that large quantities of the cotton plant were cultivated, and the material itself manufactured by the native Indians; and we may suppose that the 6,600,000 lbs. imported by us in 1787 formed but a mere tithe of their then exporting power. Indeed, we know that in 1803 Essequibo and Demerara together exported 46,435 bales, and that at that date it was rather a cotton than sugar producing country. At the close of the war in 1815 it had, however, declined to 30,315 bales, and in 1832, the year immediately following upon the passing of the great Emancipation Act, it had fallen to 5,000 bales; and, though Demerara and Berbice continue to export a small quantity received from Surinam, there has not been a single pound produced in either since 1841. Formerly, it is stated, the yield per acre, under the great care bestowed on the cultivation there, was 300 lbs.; but, at the time of its final extinction, there is reason to believe it was under 150 lbs. That the quantity produced might now under favourable circumstances be greatly increased, there does not appear a doubt, for the quality and yield are very favourable; yet these circumstances, as compared with the abundant facilities enjoyed by other more favoured colonies, are not likely to occur within the time of the present generation, for it does not appear probable that anything short of an abundant population can ever cause an extension of the cultivation there sufficient to exert any perceptible effect on the question of cotton supply. When the West Indies took rank as one of the supplying countries, the major portion of that imported was from the Mainland or British Guiana, and there is abundance of soil suited to its cultivation there, as well as in many of the Windward and Leeward Islands; and, if ever it should enjoy an abundant population, there is no doubt but it will form a colony well fitted to supply all the finer qualities of cotton—that at present imported being equal to Egyptian, and only surpassed by the fine Sea Island cotton of the islands and shores of the United States.

The proportion which the West India cotton has formed of our total imports since 1815 is shown in Table No. 12, as well as at page 42; from those figures the great decline which has taken place will be apparent, and it will be seen how much it was accelerated by the emancipation of the negroes, notwithstanding that a decided falling off was apparent prior thereto—the result of the great decline taking place in the price of the raw material from the greatly extended production opening up in the United States, as well as in other parts, destroying the monopoly which was theretofore vouchsafed to our colonies. We have the detail of the quantity received from each of the British West India possessions during the last twenty-eight years; and it will be found in Table No. 20. The main features it presents are in the imports from—

Years.	Demerara.	Berbice.	Grenada.	St. Vincent.	Barbadoes.	The Bahamas.
	lbs.	lbs.	lbs.	lbs.	lbs.	lbs.
1831	979,720	554,083	141,038	49,576	333,405	183,794
1836	818,648	262,049	117,935	71,864	121,752	157,118
1841	83,285	3,154	61,776	49,622	99,032	925,751
1846	275,901	113,638	9,335	53,382	380,248	257,507
1851	157,596	....	24,715	42,687	86,948	8,532
1856	210,560	....	67,760	35,616	51,632	....
1857	112,224	....	42,336	69,328	28,000	1,113,392
1858	227,696	....	57,476	57,120	3,472	....

The effect of slavery abolition is here very marked. But the Table also illustrates the fact that it was not only the want of labour which caused the decline in the cultivation, since, prior to the passing of the Emancipation Act the falling off in the cultivation had been very great. In Barbadoes, an island still abundantly supplied with labour, the cultivation has continued steadily to decline, and to give place to the more profitable one of the sugar cane; and other places, in which the traces of cultivation are still maintained, happen to be those where the scarcity of labour most exists; from Union Island, a dependency of St. Vincents, and Carriacou, of Grenada, low, rocky, sandy islands, comes the principal part of that grown on the islands, and this only on account of their comparative unfitness for the more profitable sugar cultivation. From the Bahamas the quantity is very fluctuating; for, while the import in 1857 was 1,113,392 lbs., in 1856 and 1858 there was not a single pound imported thence.

In British Guiana, as I have before said, there exist large wastes of land admirably adapted to the cultivation, and with labour, in every probability it could compete with the United States of America—but it is useless indulging in bootless lamentations; As regards the schemes that are being put forward to promote the cultivation in Jamaica and other islands, I am almost of opinion that the energy and abilities so employed might select numberless better fields, both as regards soil, climate, and the most important item of labour. While expressing this opinion, it is not because there is not land adapted, but that the scarcity of labour must render any success but very partial. In British Guiana the extent and quality of the land for the purpose is infinitely superior; six million acres are said to be admirably adapted, which might produce a prodigious quantity; but equally with the islands, the scarcity of labour is there a certain stop to progress; there is not sufficient for the purposes of the more profitable sugar crop, and so there cannot be for any extended cotton cultivation. Labour is so scarce, that a good hand is paid 1s. to 1s. 4d. per day, with perquisites; and at this price the colonists would gladly employ large numbers of immigrants. Government have at length conceded greater scope to the Colonial Governments; and for the sake of the colonists, it is to be hoped the present tide of immigration may continue, for they are at present helplessly at the mercy of the independent and capricious creoles, who want some steady competition in the market, as in

Barbadoes, to rouse their dormant energies. The success attending the immigrants is amply proved by the large sums they carry away in savings on their return to their native country, which they have the power of doing at the end of five years, at the expense of the planter or employer. The system of immigration, however, is a heavy burden on the West India planter, and clogs his action very materially — the only countervailing circumstance in his favour being the comparative proximity to Great Britain, which admits of the produce reaching market early.

AFRICA

Is and ever has been properly the home of the cotton plant. In America the cotton plant and labour is exotic ; and, in fact, both were transplanted from African soil. Through a series of ages Africa has grown in darkness, and its capabilities, therefore, are yet unknown and unopened up, and though our commercial relations with the West Coast have long existed, hitherto or until quite recently there has been no trade in cotton ; indeed, the efforts of a merchant of Manchester, twenty years since, to produce cotton on the Gold Coast for this market signally failed, and entailed on him considerable loss. The efforts of Mr. Clegg, with the assistance of the missionaries out there, have, however, now imparted a new life to the subject, and assisted by the inducement of high prices here, there is great hope of its becoming a source of large supplies. Cotton is now and could be procured there to any extent, cheaper than from the United States. In the States the supply of cotton fluctuates, no two years giving an equally good crop. In Africa the supply might be furnished both regularly and abundantly.

Egypt, the source whence we have up to the present time almost wholly received our supplies of African cotton, grew no cotton until 1823 ; and Tooke, in his History of Prices, remarked that the "quantity, which previously to 1824, had been imported from Egypt into this country, was perfectly insignificant, reached in 1826, 21,000,000 lbs., and the effect of this sudden increase, (which was not thereafter maintained), was greater than the mere quantity relatively to the total supply, inasmuch as it operated on the minds of the buyers as opening a great and indefinite source of supply, at a reduced cost." The quantity exported from Alexandria during the last ten years has been :—

	lbs.		lbs.
1850	46,059,965	1855	56,874,300
1851	30,347,338	1856	54,419,904
1852	66,424,960	1857	49,489,552
1853	43,885,201	1858	52,369,408
1854	43,546,500	1859	49,259,210

The quality of its cotton is second only to the *Sea Island*, or *long staple American.* The Pasha of Egypt, with true sagacity, introduced the cultivation as a means of increasing his revenue, and he has largely benefited by its introduction. At this moment, steps are being taken to render the Delta of the Nile more extensively available for cotton culture. The average exports from Alexandria during the last ten years has been about 49,000,000 lbs., while in 1823 it was only 5,623 bales, or two to three million pounds. Besides the quantity now exported, there are 50 to 60,000 bales annually consumed in the factories established by the Pasha.

The imports into the United Kingdom of cotton from Egypt have been:—

	lbs.		lbs.
1852	45,823,568	1856	34,399,008
1853	28,067,984	1857	24,532,256
1854	23,353,120	1858	38,232,320
1855	32,622,688		

Algeria, under Napoleon III., has become a cotton growing colony. In 1850 the Emperor set operations on foot for the purpose, and last year some nine or ten thousand acres were under cultivation. Samples worth 12½d. per lb. have been shown here. The people entered so enthusiastically upon the cultivation for the first year as to exceed their means of carrying on the farms successfully, and in 1856-7 their energies languished so much as to render a bounty necessary from the Government to-keep them at work; but no doubt, eventually, there will be a large growth of cotton in Algeria. With such ready means of transit to the manufacturing market, with all the advantages of climate and labour, the French colonists have all the elements of success in their favour. As yet none of their produce has reached our markets, and except in the event of some great dearth in America forcing prices up to a high pitch here, it is not probable it will do so for some time.

Morocco and Tunis are both well suited to the growth of the staple, and efforts are being made in both countries to promote its growth. The Bey of Tunis, having witnessed the success attending the exertions of the Pasha of Egypt, is most anxious to encourage his people to take up cotton growing. A Tunisian cotton company was formed two or three years since, but their experiments have not resulted in anything worthy of report.

In **Loanda and Angola** cotton is attracting some attention. The Portuguese merchants, and others, are endeavouring to create a trade in cotton, and, from the reports furnished by Portuguese papers, there is expectation of a considerable export this next year—it is a question of freight merely. The cotton can be bought to advantage, but the expenses of shipment are heavy, otherwise an immense quantity might be obtained from the interior of the country, which has been reported upon by Dr. Livingstone as abounding with it; and it seems really only a question of time now that attention has been awakened in these quarters by the Cotton Supply Association.

On the east coast, or rather along the banks of the **Zambesi** which empties itself into the Mozambique Channel, cotton already grows wild, and Dr. Livingstone states in a recent letter to James Aspinall Turner, Esq., Member for Manchester, that he bought a rove of this cotton at the cost of about 1d. It seems probable that if a company were formed with capital to send out a flat bottomed steamer of small draught to traverse this river, a large quantity of cotton could be collected at a fraction of 1d. per lb. Machinery for cleaning, with a station and agent upon the coast, would enable this cotton to reach Liverpool at 3d. to 4d. per lb., and there is no doubt that a profit of £35,000 would be realised on every 10,000 bales sent home. Indeed, seldom has any opening of so profitable a character occurred as s here presented.

The West Coast, embracing Sierra Leone, Liberia, the Gold Coast, and the Yoruba country, having its outlet at Lagos, and at the mouths of the Niger, is that **part of Africa** to which we must look for immediate results—merchants and traders have had their attention earnestly directed to the question of cotton exportation throughout these districts by the Cotton Supply Association. At Sierra Leone persons have been furnished with the necessary gins for cleaning cotton, and steps are being taken both for its growth and purchase from the natives, but here the success has not been so complete. At Elmina a native proprietor and merchant, the owner of about 160 square miles of land, is about to enter largely into the trade; he is raising capital for the purpose, and can control the labour of *half a million* of the natives in the interior and along the coast; this gentleman (who, by the way, speaks five or six European languages) has an establishment at Accra and another at Lagos; at the latter place he has erected an extensive ginning and packing establishment within the last year. By the letters of a mail or two back the Cotton Supply Association received an interesting letter from Accra, stating that a district had just been discovered, not far inland, where 70,000 Africans were engaged growing and spinning and weaving cotton. An enterprising firm has offered to the Gold Coast Agricultural Society to purchase all the cotton they can procure, and has given *carte blanche* for the price. From the newly-discovered district just referred to 1,085 bags of 30 lbs. each were immediately purchased, and are on the point of shipment to this order. Numerous firms have expressed their determination of going into the trade, and constant shipments are now being made to Liverpool. Prizes have been offered, and various kinds of machinery have been sent by the Cotton Supply Association to each of the districts just named, and there is at this time considerable activity along the coast to induce the natives to become traders in cotton instead of slave. A movement is also on foot in the United States to send out, as colonists to the West Coast, a number of *free negroes*, acquainted with cotton cultivation, in order that they may take with them those mechanical and agricultural arts of which the rude natives are not yet masters. By these means the people will become attracted to industrial pursuits for the sake of profit, and the inducement to sell the negro will diminish in the same ratio; they are eager for our manufactures, and while elevating their condition by commerce, we shall extend our own trade very considerably.

Dr. Baikie has just tendered his services to the Cotton Supply Association in the region where he is stationed, viz., at Rabba, some 4 to 500 miles up the Niger; he is in the heart of a cotton country. It is to be hoped that steamers will soon traffic up the Niger until it shall become the Mississippi of Africa, and the great outlet for cotton.

Lagos is the most considerable cotton port at present. The operations of Mr. Thomas Clegg, at Lagos, Abbeokuta, and the interior, gave the first great impulse in this quarter, and now there are many merchants endeavouring to establish the cotton trade on a firm and extensive basis.

Lagos, until very recently, was the seat of a great slave mart. The first efforts for promoting the trade in cotton were made at Badagry in the Bight of Benin, which, however, was not well suited to the purpose, and was furthermore continually threatened with destruction, so that it was well nigh abandoned, when the efforts of Commodore Bruce finally dispersed the nest of slave traders, and Lagos became an open port for legitimate commerce, since which the trade has gradually increased. The Yoruba nation of this district is famous for enterprise and skill in trade; the country is well adapted to the growth of cotton; and water communication connects Lagos with a native town of 100,000 inhabitants, called Abbeokuta, about sixty miles in the interior. The receipts from Abbeokuta and Lagos may be thus summarised:—

lbs.	lbs.
1852 1,810	1855 1,651
1853 4,617	1856 11,492
1854 1,588	1857 35,419

And since 1857 the cotton has come home through several channels, but principally through the Abbeokuta Institution, which, for the last two years, has transmitted monthly more than 100 bags or 150,000 lbs. annually. The quality of the cotton is found to be of the most serviceable kind, very similar to Middling Orleans cotton. During the year 1857, the relative price was:—

                                          d.
African .... 7.15 per lb.
Middling, New Orleans .... 7.25 ,,

The fractional advantage in favour of the latter arising from the superior process by which it was cleaned.

The President of Liberia, as well as the Gold Coast Agricultural Society, has sent out messengers among the tribes, calling attention to cotton as an article of trade, and in a very few years there can be no doubt but that cotton will become the leading article of growth; thus taking its stand upon its own ground, as that fibre which was especially designed to grow and be cultivated in Africa above all other countries in the world. Africa is the proper home of the cotton plant, and will, eventually, supply the world. Slavery in America will, no doubt, sooner or later come to an end, and where must we then look for supplies but to Africa and India. The population along the West Coast is ample to ensure cheap labour. The towns in the interior, not far from the coast, are numerous and well populated, ranging from 10,000 to 100,000 inhabitants. The colony of Natal has taken up the cultivation of cotton, and a correspondent reports that he has fifteen tons of cotton ready for shipment. The Governor of the colony is also anxious to introduce the culture among the Zulus and native tribes, and has proposed to the Home Government that the *hut tax* paid by the Aborigines should be allowed to be paid for in cotton as an incentive to its growth. The value of a sample bale of native cotton just received is 9d. per lb., and it is well adapted to the trade of Lancashire, and superior to average New Orleans.

The opening of the African cotton trade, which thus bids fair to become of large dimensions, must ever be considered as having been greatly assisted by the Cotton Supply Association. There is no question but that Africa is the most hopeful source of future supply, and it is to be hoped the Association will receive the support it deserves, and persevere in its very successful efforts. As an Association, working out a far more noble destiny than that of a mere trading company, it is deservedly popular. Had the twenty million pounds sterling allowed for the abolition of slavery, or one tithe of that now spent annually in the maintainance of war steamers for the control of the slave trade, been applied to its objects, a far more sure and effectual settlement of the question would have been effected than is now presented by the Southern States of America and Cuba.

BRAZIL

Is the only other source of cotton supply of note which remains to be particularly noticed. It was among those countries which furnished our earlier supplies of the raw material; but the quantity has not increased since the beginning of the century. Our imports from this source are given in Table No. 12; by that we shall see the largest import into this country was in the year 1825, and that since that period it has even declined. Mr. Ellison, in his hand-book, stated the exports from Brazil to have been:—

1840	22,335,520 lbs.	1848	20,457,116 lbs.
1841	22,140,030	1849	27,181,312
1842	20,466,566	1850	35,498,048
1843	22,324,718	1851	28,270,080
1844	26,056,160	1852	28,744,000
1845	26,446,240	1853	31,933,056
1846	20,651,040	1854	28,551,584
1847	19,419,224	1855	27,838,720

There is a diversity of opinion as to the capabilities of Brazil as a source of cotton supply; but it seems to be admitted that there are almost boundless tracts of suitable land. The quality of the cotton now produced is excellent; the means of transit are good and improving; the San Francisco River has an uninterrupted internal navigation of upwards of 1,000 miles, furnishing the means of transport, which, with the Pernambuco, and other railways to be completed, will give great facility to the extension of the cultivation but then there is the same want felt which ruined the West Indies as producers, viz., the want of labour; since the abolition of the external slave trade in Brazil, in 1850, caused an extension of the available supply impossible, the slaves have increased in demand and value, the labour being almost wholly employed in the more profitable cultivations to the detriment of the cotton planters. Although the decline in the rate of production has not been so severe as in the West Indies, the causes are about the same, save the advantage of abundant and fertile lands enjoyed by the former. If Brazil could command the needful labour, there is no question but that she would become a large supplier of our wants in the finer class of staple; but until some change occurs favourable to that end, we must not look for any considerable increase in the supply.

Among other places we must not omit to note **Australia.** At present efforts are making in our Australian Colonies, and strong hopes are entertained of great success. Samples have been received of excellent quality from the neighbourhood of Moreton's Bay. The great distance causes a considerable drawback to our being thus supplied, and, with a scanty population, it seems at present ill fitted to compete with other cotton producing colonies. Labour can, doubtless, be obtained from China, and even India, and it may not be long before, in the progress of the Australian world, cotton is both largely grown and manufactured there, sufficient not only for its own immediate wants, but for export.

Looking then to these remarks, our hopes for the future are somewhat gloomy as regards supply. It is amply substantiated that available land in everyway suited to the production of unlimited quantities is readily obtainable; each quarter of the globe enjoying land of different degrees of fertility, producing from 100 to 400 lbs. of clean cotton per acre, and quality ranging in market value from 3d. to 2s. 6d. per lb., with different distances of sea and land transit, and of available labour. Thus, America has abundance of new and suitable land, adequate to yield on an average 300 lbs. per acre, and of a quality worth 7d. per lb. ; but then the want of labour prevents any extensive addition to the present growth, and where it can be effected it is only with a charge for labour equal to about 3d. per lb. In India, with a very slight increase in the rate of freight as compared with America, there is also abundance of land, producing 80 to 100 lbs., but which, it seems fair to essay, will produce, with ordinary improvements, 150 lbs. per acre, worth about 5d. per lb., and a redundance of labour to be had at less than 1d. per lb., but, with a large additional charge, however, for inland transit, at present equal to $\frac{1}{2}$d. to $1\frac{1}{2}$d. per lb. In Africa the data is not obtainable as to the yield per acre, but land is so abundant and fertile, and labour so cheap, that cotton can, it is stated, be obtained in almost unlimited quantities at $\frac{3}{4}$d. to $1\frac{1}{4}$d. per lb., and this for a quality worth from 6d. to 7d. per lb.; so that allowing for an increase in price by virtue of a created demand, it seems likely to undersell even the Americans themselves in our markets. But this success is contingent to a large extent on the demand continuing as active as at present, that the extraordinary expenses incurred by the promoters in starting the new trade may be returned to them, else, like the French colonists in Algeria, they may yet turn away from it in disgust. For my own part I am almost inclined to expect that, except in case of a failure of the next or future American crops, the present large crop in America, with a steady prospective increase from all other sources, will cause a fall in price sufficiently inimical to this advance, to retard in a great measure the relief which otherwise would be afforded. Everyone must agree, that it is decidedly a matter of national interest, apart from any bias, that we should be relieved of our present critical dependence on America ; that we should also have supplies from other sources to compensate for deficient crops, which recur at certain cycles of time there : moreover, it is a matter of philanthropic as well as Christian feeling that we should withdraw our support from raising the value of slave labour, as our present demand for the raw material does in the States, and doing this we should be following the surest road to the erasure of the blot of slavery from our time.

Having thus glanced at the prospects of supply, we now draw to the close of our subject ; but we may say a few words on some of the more salient points in the phases of demand in this country. First we have the demand for the raw material which we import, to be exported again to other manufacturing countries or consumed in our own manufactories. The proportion will be seen in Table No. 1, which furnishes the data since 1781, and, taking decennial averages, it appears thus :—

	Quantity Imported.	Re-exported.	Taken for Consumption
1789-1798	28,480,000 lbs.	861,131 lbs.	27,618,869 lbs.
1799-1808	56,786,950	1,819,478	54,967,472
1809-1818	104,555,923	6,625,417	97,930,506
1819-1828	182,480,492	15,613,500	171,976,732
1829-1838	337,856,788	25,587,242	311,656,814
1839-1848	569,849,543	50,500,006	516,561,275
1849-1858	880,811,929	124,968,995	761,570,000
The year 1859	1,225,989,072	175,143,136	976,600,000

It will not, however, be inferred that these figures form any index to the progress of the Continental manufactories during the same last-mentioned period. All those nations possessing a mercantile navy have prodigiously increased their demand and *imports direct from the places of growth*, as we have already before shown.

The Table No. 21 furnishes in detail the destination of cotton re-exported from this country; the features it presents generally are not very striking, except in the slow but steady rate of progression of the exports to each of the manufacturing countries up to within the last few years. The increase in the exports to France since 1848 is very great. The effect of the Russian war upon the Continental markets is strikingly pourtrayed in these tables. Previous to the commencement of the war, Russia took away twenty-five per cent of the whole quantity re-exported by us, and the closing of the ports for nearly two years naturally gave an impetus to the trade of other countries; one-half the deficiency was made up to Russia, by indirect receipts through Prussia; thus we find our exports thence were with that object. The Russian demand has not yet recovered itself, though some portion of the deficiency is compensated for by direct shipments from America and other producing countries.

A considerable and increasing proportion of the East India cotton is thus taken for export. Looking at the statistics of the last ten years, in bales, as returned by the trade, it appears thus:—

	East India.	Other Kinds.	Total Exported.
1850	96,300	176,100	272,400
1851	103,450	165,050	268,500
1852	100,740	182,060	282,800
1853	151,500	198,100	349,600
1854	168,050	147,780	315,830
1855	188,600	128,300	316,900
1856	216,200	140,500	356,700
1857	226,540	110,710	337,250
1858	173,900	174,800	348,700
1859	272,500	163,400	435,990

And the only tangible reason for this apparent partiality is the comparative cheapness of the article, and perhaps from the merchants receiving orders with prices limited, which precludes other and cleaner qualities being purchased by them; it cannot surely be that our manufacturers are so blinded as to undervalue the Indian qualities to such an extent as to benefit their Continental neighbours and competitors?

The quantity retained by our own manufacturers may be seen in the same table, No. 1; and the columns 25 and 27 in Table No. 8, furnishes the relative proportions employed in the fabrication of manufactures for the home and export trades. Taking them in quinquennial averages they appear thus:—

	Home Trade. lbs.	Export Trade. lbs.
1834-1838	136,180,152 = 38 per cent	222,461,722 = 62 per cent
1839-1843	171,678,178 = 36 „	302,645,053 = 64 „
1844-1848	193,631,389 = 34 „	367,827,931 = 66 „
1849-1853	221,207,238 = 33 „	450,152,762 = 67 „
1854-1858	245,226,342 = 29 „	606,493,658 = 71 „

Showing that the larger proportion of our increased manufacture has gone to meet the foreign demand.

It must, however, be observed, that the quantities of the raw material thus given are not necessarily a criterion of value ; it will be seen that the qualities of cotton goods exported, as compared with those for the home trade, are mostly plain goods, and to the new markets opened up of a coarser grade and heavier make, it being generally estimated by the trade that the relative value of the two classes of fabrics is one-third less in the former than in the latter. Columns 26 and 28 in the same table furnish the value of both ; thus, in quinquennial averages, they appear :—

	Home Trade.	Export Trade.
1834-1838	£18,291,029	£22,403,559
1839-1843	17,701,738	23,569,158
1844-1848	17,288,000	24,707,786
1849-1853	19,336,990	29,542,472
1854-1858	20,123,535	37,406,496

Showing that though the relative *value* of the manufactures, which furnish the home, is greater than that for the foreign trade, *as compared with the quantity*, yet the increase in the value, or improvement in quality, is greater in the case of the latter ; which is accounted for by the improved quality of the manufactures taken by the Indian and other markets, which have been some time opened up.

A very able writer on the subject of the cotton manufacture, in the Companion to the British Almanac, remarks that the quantity of cotton used in the mills does not always show the amount of work done. The quantity thus consumed was enormously greater in 1848 than in 1847, in 1852 than in 1851, but the quantities of work done and wages paid did not increase in a similar ratio. The latter two elements depend in a great measure on the *weight* of cotton used in making a particular *size* of cloth or yarn. In some states of the market heavy goods pay the manufacturer better than those of lighter texture; and at such a time the consumption of cotton is increased, though neither the manufacturers' profits, nor the workman's wages, may have reached a higher aggregate. In some cotton fabrics the material is worth *two-thirds* of the whole value, in others it amounts to only *one-fiftieth ;* these are extreme cases, and between them every kind of ratio is observable in some or other of the numerous varieties of manufacture. In the case of yarns the material is worth *three-fourths* of the whole price in some specimens, and only *one-twentieth* in others. A given number of spindles employed in making cotton twist of the thickness called No. 20, would use up 1,340 lbs. of cotton, in the time which would elapse in producing No. 30's out of 840 lbs., No. 40's out of 525 lbs., and No. 60's out of 224 lbs., in the high numbers the relative value of the material is lower than in the low numbers. In some of the gigantic cotton mills 30,000 or 40,000 lbs. less of cotton will be used in some weeks than in others, although all the machinery and all the hands may be employed at both the periods ; the difference arising from fine light goods being made at one time, and coarse heavy goods at another. When the demand for printed "muslins" and other light goods, is relatively brisker than that for "domestics" or coarser cotton goods, the consumption of cotton in England is found to lessen. An advance in the price of cotton is much more strongly felt in respect to coarse goods and yarns, than in fine, so much so, indeed, that the demand from many foreign markets almost ceases, if the price fluctuates beyond its usual limits; whereas, in lighter goods wherein labour forms a larger ratio of the cost, the manufacturer has an inducement to produce light goods instead of heavy; and for a like reason, when the demand is slack, there is less dead weight, in a stock of light goods, than of heavy goods of equal market value.

The nature of our export trade in cotton manufactures may be seen from the Table No. 3, which furnishes from the year 1820 (the earliest date at which we have official or complete statistical records), the total official and declared real value of both goods and yarns; but the Tables No. 22 and 23 will furnish the detail which our purpose requires. Looking at their declared real value and reducing the data again for brevity sake into quinquennial averages, it will appear—

	GOODS.		YARNS.		TOTAL.
Years.	Quantity.	Value.	Quantity.	Value.	Value.
	Yds.	£	lbs.	£	£
1820-4	293,266,567	14,203,493	21,427,732	2,718,277	16,921,770
1825-9	346,970,665	13,410,712	46,331,408	3,563,185	16,973,897
1830-4	475,817,439	14,067,538	70,247,712	4,549,312	18,616,850
1835-9	629,616,947	16,596,325	99,028,685	6,614,592	23,210,917
1840-4	848,233,492	16,555,693	131,604,978	7,264,459	23,820,152
1845-9	1,106,794,951	18,214,707	140,568,360	7,687,037	24,901,744
1850-4	1,539,199,542	23,884,743	143,096,515	6,651.874	30,536,617
1855-9	2,168,112,850	32,064,065	183,233,832	8,594,948	40,659,013

The relatively retrogressive aspect of the demand for our yarns attracts attention; this is not the result of any lack of energy on the part of our manufacturers or spinners, but of the progress making in the process of spinning on the Continent. Where formerly an immense proportion of yarn was received hence for weaving abroad, new spinning factories have been established, and the entire process of manufacture is oftentimes performed independent of our aid. But this, of course, applies only to the European demand, particularly that of Russia and Sweden, which have latterly taken but a tithe of what they were formerly wont to do. The demand for our Colonial Possessions and of other countries out of Europe is that to which we must look for the increased consumption and demand necessary to maintain our position as a manufacturing nation.

The proportion of our exported cotton manufactures, taken by our British Possessions and Dependencies, and by foreign countries, may be seen by Table No. 20, and taking annual averages of quinquennial periods, the relative rate of progression of the declared real value of such exports appears thus:—

	British Possessions and Dependencies.	Foreign Countries.
1820-4	£3,471,282	£13,450,288
1825-9	3,547,685	13,426,211
1830-4	3,449,589	15,167,260
1835-9	3,462,495	17,748,422
1840-4	6,710,755	17,109,397
1845-9	6,522,680	18,379,063
1850-4	9,100,895	21,435,722
(4 years.) 1855-8	11,451,071	27,320,585

Another point which the Table No. 8 illustrates is the relatively prodigious increase in the quantity as compared with the value, or decrease in the value as compared with the quantity of the raw material worked up; the result of the diminished price of the material and improvements in the process of manufacture, and, perhaps, in the diminished rate of profit taken by our manufacturers as the result of competition. The first two reasons admit, I think, of little doubt, but the last, which formed the subject of remark at page 28, may be deserving of a little closer scrutiny; and the Table No. 8 will assist us in the investigation. Admitting the correctness of those figures, the following will show the price per lb. left to the manufacturers, merchants, &c. in each of the last twenty-six years thus: —

Years.	Total Value of Manufactures.	Cost of the Raw Material Employed.	Leaving Surplus for Cost of Manufacture.	Upon the Quantity Worked up.	Equal to in Pence Per Pound.
1834	£38,304,409	£11,550,553	£26,753,856	lbs. 311,335,657	20·62
1835	40,257,875	14,518,058	25,739,817	329,207,692	18·76
1836	43,691,658	15,081,011	28,610,647	355,684,232	19·31
1837	36,101,141	10,777,351	25,323,790	359,245,035	16·91
1838	45,117,859	13,132,102	31,985,757	437,736,755	17·54
1839	36,502,318	12,692,165	23,810,153	375,500,277	15 22
1840	49,616,655	13,243,773	36,372,882	511,342,743	17·07
1841	39,744,285	12,089,309	27,654,976	451,093,631	14·71
1842	37,220,311	10,664,723	26,555,588	461,676,400	13·80
1843	43,270,911	11,382,861	31,888,050	572,003,105	13·37
1844	42,865,638	11,621,328	31,244,310	553,396,602	13·55
1845	46,988,094	11,400,319	35,587,775	606,400,000	14 09
1846	44,574,592	13,018,609	31,555,983	622,900,000	12·16
1847	36,446,714	13,004,679	23,442,035	462,800,000	12 16
1848	39,103,893	10,280,939	28,822,954	561,800,000	12·31
1849	43,441,576	13,859,999	29,581,577	630,000,000	11·27
1850	45,826,992	17,937,100	27,889,892	588,100,000	11·38
1851	48,299,356	16,225,429	32,073,927	656,900,000	11·72
1852	51,256,194	16,641,239	34,614,955	720,400,000	11·53
1853	55,573,195	18,425,879	37,147,316	761,400,000	11·71
1854	55,094,047	18,251,081	36,842,966	802,700,000	11·11
1855	54,736,520	19,619,888	35,116,632	839,200,000	10·04
1856	57,074,852	22,129,599	34,945,253	856,700,000	9·79
1857	60,157,703	25,925,228	34,232,475	858,000,000	9·57
1858	60,387,034	26,254,800	34,132,234	902,000,000	9·08
1859	71,373,214	27,530,774	44,842,440	966,643,000	10·77

The figures here presented show that in those years of abundant supplies, and consequent cheap prices of the raw material, the margin for labour and expenses of manufacture gives way, on account of a larger proportion of a heavier and consequently less expensive description of goods being manufactured; but apart from this fact, there has been a steady decline in the item of margin for expenses, even while these expenses have actually increased. The more marked decline, however, of 1855-56-57-58, the result of over competition, leaves but one impression, convinced as we must be, that neither the price of food, labour, or material, nor the improvements in manufacture have been such as to account for it. We cannot but infer that this over-competition has resulted in great loss to the manufacturers; and, if such is really the case—and it is almost admitted—the sooner it is destroyed the better; indeed, looking at the figures for 1859, the difficulty would seem to have found its own solution, mayhap in connection with the late crisis. It may be supposed that competition cannot be overdone, but this is a delusion ; whenever it occurs in such extremes it cannot but end in harm to trade and loss to the manufacturers, and prevent those salutary effects which a legitimate competition would produce. If the manufacturer has made losses or disproportionately diminished profits without an adequate consideration, then there must necessarily follow a check to improvement in the trade—a retrogressive movement to compensate for them—and capital is withdrawn in distrust until the cause is satiated in its results ; indeed, work whichever way it will, it cannot but result in a paralization and weakening of the manufacturing interest especially to compete with foreign countries.

A feature in the subject of cotton cultivation, and the uses of the products of the plant, may be noted before finally closing. The cotton seed, which until lately, was not employed to any considerable extent, is found to yield a valuable oil and cake. The oil is well fitted for burning, lubricating, and perhaps painting, while the cake is employed to feed cattle and hogs, and for manure, and as material for the manufacture of gas for illuminating ; while the waste cotton fibre is employed for the manufacture of paper, and the bark stripped off the plant yields a good and useful fibre.

TABLE No. 1.

Showing the Quantity of Raw Cotton Imported into, Exported from, and Consumed in the United Kingdom;* with the Rates of Duty Imposed, and Amount of Revenue Collected therefrom, since 1781.

Years.	Imported.	Consumed.†	Exported.	Revenue.	Duty.
	lbs.	lbs.	lbs.	£	
1781	5,198,778	5,101,990	96,788	....	free
1782	11,828,039	11,406,810	421,229	....	free
1783	9,735,663	9,558,037	177,626	....	free
1784	11,482,083	11,280,238	201,845	....	free
1785	18,400,384	17,992.888	407,496	....	free
1786	19,475,020	19,151,867	323,153	....	free
1787	23,250,268	22,176,887	1,073,381	....	free
1788	20,467,436	19,614,290	853.146	....	free
1789	32,576,023	32,278.186	297,837	....	free
1790	31,447,605	30,603,451	844,154	....	free
1791	28,706.675	28,343,233	363,442	....	free
1792	34,907,497	33,422,032	1,485.465	....	free
1793	19,040.929	17.869.363	1,171,566	....	free
1794	24,358.567	23,008,617	1,349,950	....	free
1795	26,401,340	25,207,603	1,193,737	....	free
1796	32,126,357	31,431,395	694,962	....	free
1797	23,354,371	22,745,313	609,058	....	Duty first imposed in 1798.
1798	31,880,641	31,279,502	601,139	71,810	West India, 8/9; Bowed Georgia, 6/6, and Pernambuco 12/6 per 100lbs.; East India 4o/o ad val.
1799	43,379,278	42,534,607	844,671	207,158	same
1800	56,010,732	51,594,122	4,416,610	240,822	same
1801	56,064,305	54,203,433	1,860,872	176,976	same
1802	60,345,600	56,615,120	3,730,480	176,058	East India, £4 16s. o/o ad val.; Turkey and United States, 7/10; British Possessions 10/6; other parts, 15/0 per 100 lbs.
1803	53,812,284	52,251,231	1,561,053	365,518	Pernams, 25/0; all other kinds, 16/8 per 100 lbs
1804	61,867,329	61,364,158	503,171	599,486	same
1805	59,682,406	58,878,163	804,243	568,102	Pernams 25/3¾; all other kinds, 16/10½ per 100 lbs.
1806	58,176,283	57,524,416	651,867	543,526	same
1807	74,925,306	72,748,363	2,176,943	676,975	same
1808	‡43,605,982	41,961,115	1,644,867	425.384	same
1809	92,812,282	88,461,177	4,351.105	867,694	All kinds, 16/11 per 100 lbs.
1810	132.488,935	123,701,826	8,787,109	1,032,029	same
1811	91,576,535	90,309,668	1,266,867	796,753	same
1812	‖63,025,936	61,285,024	1,740,912	731,063	same
1813	....	Records destroyed by fire.		....	
1814	‖60,060.239	53,777,802	6,282,437	584.227	same
1815	100.709,146	93,928,754	6,780,392	780,199	All kinds, 8/7 per 100 lbs.
1816	95,280,965	88,175,931	7,105,034	379,125	same
1817	126.303,689	118,148,247	8,155,442	501,749	same
1818	178,745,577	163,586,124	15,159,453	484,683	same
1819	151,153,154	134,530,185	16,622,969	407,099	West India 6/3; all other kinds 8/7 per 100 lbs.
1820	151,672,655	152,829,633	6,024,038	426,957	Foreign, 6 o/o ad val.; West India, 6/3 per 100 lbs.; E. India and other B. P., 6 o/o ad val.
1821	132,536,620	137,401,549	14,589,497	287,349	11 March: West India, free; other kinds as before.
1822	142,837,628	143,428,127	18,269,776	258,614	same

* For Great Britain *only* prior to 1815, and for the United Kingdom thereafter.
† The quantities given as Consumed previous to 1820, are the calculated differences between the quantities imported and those exported.
‡ 1808 was the year of the American embargo on foreign trade.
‖ The years 1812-14 were those of the American War.

TABLE No. 1.—Continued.

SHOWING THE QUANTITY OF RAW COTTON IMPORTED INTO, EXPORTED FROM, AND CONSUMED IN THE UNITED KINGDOM; WITH THE RATES OF DUTY IMPOSED, AND AMOUNT OF REVENUE COLLECTED THEREFROM.

Years.	Imported.	Consumed.	Exported.	Revenue.	Duty.
	lbs.	lbs.	lbs.	£	
1823	191,402,503	186,311,070	9,318,402	327,700	West India, free; foreign, 6 o/o ad val.; East India and other British Possessions, 6 o/o ad valorum.
1824	149,380,122	141,038,743	13,299,505	255,258	same
1825	228,005,291	202,546,869	18,004,953	526,651	same
1826	177,607,401	162,889,012	24,474,920	228,916	same
1827	272,448,909	249,804,396	18,134,170	332,355	same
1828	227,760,642	208,987,744	17,396,776	281,178	Aug. 10th: Foreign, 6 o/o ad val.; British Possesions, 4d. per cwt.
1829	222,767,411	204,097,037	30,289,115	238,378	same
1830	263,961,452	269,616,640	8,534,976	359,988	same
1831	288,674,853	273,249,653	22,308,555	363,538	Foreign, 5/10 per cwt.; all British Possessions, 4d. per cwt.
1832	286,832,525	259,412,463	18,027,940	626,687	same
1833	303,656,837	293,682,976	17,363,882	473,011	June 1st: Foreign, 2/11; British Possessions, 4d. per cwt.
1834	326,875,425	302,935,657	24,461,963	373,812	same
1835	363,702,963	326,407,692	32,779,734	399,262	same
1836	406,959,057	363,684,232	31,739,763	430,006	same
1837	407,286,783	368,445,035	39,722,031	450,658	same
1838	507,850,577	455,036,755	30,644,469	557,892	same
1839	389,396,559	352,000,277	38,738,238	416,257	same
1840	592,488,010	528,142,743	38,673,229	648,937	5 o/o additional on former duties.
1841	487,992,355	437,093,631	37,673,585	528,508	same
1842	531,750,086	473,976,400	45,251,302	567,156	July 9th: Foreign, 2/11; British Possessions, 4d. per cwt.
1843	673,193,116	581,303,105	39,619,979	742,491	same
1844	646,111,304	554,196,602	47,222,541	682,042	same
1845	721,979,953	606,600,000	42,916,332	....	March 19th; Duty finally repealed.
1846	467,856,274	614,300,000	65,930,732	....	free
1847	474,707,615	441,400,000	74,954,336	....	free
1848	713,020,161	576,600,000	74,019,790	....	free
1849	755,469,012	629,900,000	98,893,508	....	free
1850	663,576,861	588,200,000	102,469,717	....	free
1851	757,379,749	658,900,000	111,980,394	....	free
1852	929,782,448	739,600,000	111,884,321	....	free
1853	895,278,749	760,900,000	148,569,680	....	free
1854	887,333,149	776,100,000	123,326,112	....	free
1855	891,751,952	839,100,000	124,368,160	...	free
1856	1,023,886,304	891,400,000	146,660,864	....	free
1857	969,318,896	826,000,000	131,927,600	....	free
1858	1,034,342,176	905,600,000	149,609,600	....	free
1859	1,225,989,072	976,600,000	175,143,136	....	free

All the figures in this Table are from official sources, excepting of the quantity Consumed since 1845, in which year the Duty was finally repealed, and consequently no official record has since been kept; the figures given in the Table are furnished by Messrs. George Holt and Co., of Liverpool, and are those adopted by the trade

TABLE No. 2.

Showing the Annual Average Price of Wheat; of United States Uplands, Brazils and Pernambuco, and East India Surat Cotton; and of 100's and 40's Best Seconds Mule, and 30's Water Twist of Common Quality.

WHEAT.						COTTON.			COTTON YARN.		
						United States Uplands	Brazil & Pernambuco.	East India Surat.	No. 100's Mule.	No. 40's Mule.	No. 30's Water.
Years.	Per Qr. s. d.	Years.	Per Qr. s. d.	Years.	Per Qr. s. d.	Per lb. d.	Per lb. d.	Per lb. d.	Per lb. s. d.	Per lb. s. d.	Per lb. s. d.
1664	..	1744	20/0	1786	38/10	..	..	..	38/0	..	..
1665	..	1745	22/0	1787	41/2	..	..	..	38/0	..	..
1666	..	1746	30/0	1788	45/0	..	24	..	35/0	..	..
1667	..	1747	25/0	1789	51/2	..	18	..	34/0	..	..
1668	..	1748	33/0	1790	53/2	..	21	9	30/0	..	..
1669	..	1749	30/0	1791	47/2	..	24	11	29/9	..	..
1670	..	1750	30/0	1792	41/9	..	26	13	16/1	..	..
1671	..	1751	33/0	1793	47/10	17	24	13	15/1	..	..
1672	..	1752	32/0	1794	50/8	15	22	10	15/1	..	..
1673	..	1753	35/0	1795	72/11	21	25	17	19/0*	..	..
1674	..	1754	23/0	1796	76/3	21	26	17	19/0	..	..
1675	..	1755	26/0	1797	52/2	24	31	16	19/0	..	.
1676	..	1756	37/0	1798	50/4	33	39	23	9/10†	..	..
1677	..	1757	40/0	1799	66/11	38	42	19	10/11	..	..
1678	..	1758	36/0	1800	110/5	26	32½	14	9/5	..	..
1679	..	1759	26/0	1801	115/11	27½	34	16	8/9	..	..
1680	..	1760	28/0	1802	67/9	26	29½	14	8/4	..	..
1681	..	1761	22/0	1803	57/1	12½	26½	11½	8/4	..	..
1682	..	1762	32/0	1804	60/5	14	25¼	11½	7/10	..	..
1683	..	1763	32/0	1805	87/1	16½	26½	14½	7/10	..	..
1684	..	1764	36/0	1806	76/9	18	22	14½	7/2	..	..
1685	..	1765	42/0	1807	73/1	17½	22	13	6/9	..	..
1686	..	1766	36/0	1808	78/11	25½	24½	19½	..	..	..
1687	24/0	1767	48/0	1809	94/5	24	30¼	18½	..	..	..
1689	30/0	1768	44/0	1810	103/3	18½	26	15½	..	..	..
1727	32/0	1769	37/0	1811	92/5	14	20½	11½	..	..	..
1728	48/0	1770	41/4	1812	122/8	18	23	14	..	..	..
1729	42/0	1771	47/2	1813	106/6	25½	29	17½	..	..	..
1730	26/0	1772	50/8	1814	72/1	30	31½	21½	..	..	..
1731	23/0	1773	51/0	1815	63/8	21½	31	17½	..	3/0½	..
1732	20/0	1774	52/8	1816	76/2	18¼	26	15⅛	..	2/7½	..
1733	24/0	1775	48/4	1817	94/0	20⅛	25	17	..	2/6	..
1734	32/0	1776	38/2	1818	83/8	20	25	15¾	..	2/6	2/9
1735	34/0	1777	45/6	1819	72/3	13½	18⅜	9⅝	..	1/10½	2/1
1736	30/0	1778	42/0	1820	65/10	11½	15½	8½	..	1/7¼	1/10½
1737	30/0	1779	33/8	1821	54/5	9½	12⅝	9⅞	..	1/5¼	1/6½
1738	27/0	1780	35/8	1822	43/3	8¼	11⅛	6⅞	..	1/4¾	1/5½
1739	34/0	1781	44/8	1823	51/9	8¼	12	6¾	..	1/4¾	1/6¾
1740	40/0	1782	47/10	1824	62/0	8½	11⅜	6⅝	..	1/3½	1/7¼
1741	34/0	1783	52/8	1825	66/6	11⅝	15⅛	6⅞	..	1/5½	1/7¼
1742	20/0	1784	48/10	1826	56/11	6¾	10½	5½	..	1/1	1/1
1743	20/0	1785	51/10	1827	56/9	6½	9¾	5⅛	..	1/0½	1/0½

* The 100's Mule Yarn in 1795 was spun from Bourbon Cotton.

† The 100's Mule Yarn in 1798 was spun from Sea Island Cotton.

TABLE No. 2.—Continued.

SHOWING THE ANNUAL AVERAGE PRICE OF WHEAT; OF UNITED STATES UPLANDS, BRAZIL AND PERNAMBUCO, AND EAST INDIA SURAT COTTON; AND OF 100'S AND 40'S BEST SECONDS MULE, AND 30'S WATER TWIST OF COMMON QUALITY.

Years.	WHEAT.	COTTON.			COTTON YARN.		
		U. S. Uplands.	Brazil and Pernams.	East India Surat.	No. 100's. Mule.	No. 40's. Mule.	No. 30's. Water.
	Per Quarter. s. d.	Per lb. d.	Per lb. d.	Per lb. d.	Per lb. s. d.	Per lb. s. d.	Per lb. s. d.
1828	60/5	6⅜	8⅜	4⅝	..	1/2¼	1/0⅛
1829	66/3	5¾	7¼	4	3/2	1/2	1/0½
1830	64/3	6⅛	8¼	5	2/11	1/2	1/0¼
1831	66/4	6	7¾	4⅝	..	1/1½	10½
1832	58/8	6⅝	9	5	2/11	1/0½	11¾
1833	52/11	8½	10¾	6⅛	3/3	1/1¼	11½
1834	46/2	8⅝	11⅞	6⅝	3/6	1/2	..
1835	39/4	10¼	14⅛	7½	4/3	1/4½	..
1836	48/9	9⅞	12⅞	6¾	5/6	1/4	..
1837	55/10	7	9¼	4⅞	3/6	1/6	..
1838	64/4	7	9⅜	5	3/9	1/2	..
1839	70/6	7⅞	10	5¾	4/1	1/1½	11
1840	66/4	6	9¼	4⅝	3/7	1/0½	10¼
1841	64/4	6¼	8¾	4⅝	3/0	11½	9½
1842	57/3	5⅜	7¼	4	2/9	10¼	9¼
1843	50/1	4⅝	6⅜	3⅝	2/11	11¼	9
1844	51/3	4⅞	6⅜	3⅝	3/2	10	9
1845	50/10	4⅜	6⅜	3	3/2	10⅜	8⅞
1846	54/8	4⅞	7⅜	3⅜	3/2	11¾	10⅝
1847	69/9	6⅜	7⅜	4½	1/8	9	8
1848	50/6	4¼	6	3¼	1/6¼	7½	7¼
1849	44/3	5⅛	5½	3⅞	2/0	* 8⅛	8
1850	40/3	7¼	7⅞	5⅛	2/6½	10⅞	11
1851	38/6	5¾	7½	4	1/9	9¼	9¾
1852	40/9	5⅜	7	3¾	2/1½	9⅛	9¾
1853	53/3	5⅝	7	3½	2/5	9⅜	9¾
1854	72/5	5⅜	7	3½	2/3	8⅝	8¾
1855	74/8	5¾	7	3⅞	2/5	8⅝	9
1856	69/2	6	7⅛	4⅜	2/8	9½	9⅝
1857	56/4	7¼	8¾	5⅜	2/1	11⅛	11
1858	44/2	6¼	8¼	4¾	2/4	10¾	10⅞
1859	43/9	6¼	8⅜	4¾	2/4	11¾	11⅜

* The price of No. 40's Mule Yarn, previous to 1849, is the market price at the close of each year; from that year it is the average of twelve monthly averages, furnished by Messrs. Du Fay & Co.

TABLE No. 3.

Showing the Official and Declared Real Value of Cotton Goods and Yarns Exported from the United Kingdom* since 1785.

Years.	OFFICIAL VALUE. Manufactures.	Yarns & Twist.	Total.	DECLARED REAL VALUE. Manufactures.	Yarns & Twist.	Total.
	£	£	£	£	£	£
1785	....	....	864,710			
1786	....	....	915,046			
1787	....	....	1,101,457			
1788	....	....	1,252,240			
1789	....	....	1,231,537			
1790	....	....	1,662,369			
1791	....	....	1,875,046			
1792	....	....	2,024,368			
1793	....	....	1,733,807			
1794	....	....	2,376,077			
1795	....	....	2,433,331			
1796	....	....	3,214,020			
1797	....	....	2,580,568			
1798	3,572,217	30,271	3,602,488	These particulars cannot be rendered,		
1799	5,593,407	204,602	5,808,009	the records having been destroyed by fire.		
1800	5,406,501	447,556	5,854,057			
1801	6,606,368	444,441	7,050,809			
1802	7,195,900	428,605	7,624,505			
1803	6,442,237	639,404	7,081,641			
1804	7,834,564	902,208	8,736,772			
1805	8,610,990	914,475	9,525,465			
1806	9,753,824	736,225	10,490,049			
1807	9,708,046	601,719	10,309,765			
1808	12,503,918	472,078	12,975,996			
1809	18,425,614	1,020,352	19,445,966			
1810	17,898,519	1,053,475	18,951,994			
1811	11,529,551	483,598	12,013,149			
1812	15,723,225	794,465	16,517,690			
1813	Records destroyed by fire.					
1814	16,535,528	1,119,850	17,655,378	17,279,576	2,791,248	20,070,824
1815	21,480,792	808,853	22,289,645	19,038,206	1,674,021	20,712,227
1816	16,183,975	1,380,486	17,564,461	13,055,713	2,628,448	15,684,161
1817	20,133,966	1,125,258	21,259,224	14,047,049	2,014,181	16,061,230
1818	21,292,354	1,296,776	22,589,130	16,400,319	2,395,304	18,795,623
1819	16,696,539	1,585,753	18,282,292	12,189,475	2,519,783	14,709,258
1820	20,509,926	2,022,153	22,532,079	13,707,111	2,826,643	16,533,754
1821	21,642,936	1,898,679	23,541,615	13,816,707	2,305,830	16,122,537
1822	24,559,272	2,351,771	26,911,043	14,581,666	2,697,590	17,279,256
1823	24,119,359	2,425,411	26,544,770	13,698,768	2,625,947	16,324,715
1824	27,171,556	2,984,345	30,155,901	15,315,141	3,135,396	18,450,537
1825	26,597,575	2,897,706	29,495,281	15,153,270	3,206,729	18,359,999
1826	21,445,743	3,748,527	25,194,270	10,602,414	3,491,338	14,093,752
1827	29,203,138	3,979,760	33,182,898	14,095,023	3,545,578	17,640,601
1828	28,981,575	4,485,842	33,467,417	13,639,695	3,595,368	17,235,063
1829	31,810,474	5,458,958	37,269,432	13,549,916	3,976,787	17,526,703
1830	35,649,805	5,657,624	41,307,429	15,285,222	4,133,663	19,418,885
1831	33,903,249	5,674,617	39,577,866	13,274,957	3,974,951	17,249,908
1832	37,206,430	6,726,563	43,932,993	12,670,255	4,722,652	17,392,907
1833	40,133,344	6,279,076	46,412,420	13,777,277	4,703,962	18,481,239
1834	44,278,035	6,802,238	51,080,273	15,293,991	5,210,939	20,504,930
1835	44,915,901	7,399,879	52,315,780	16,413,420	5,706,476	22,119,896
1836	50,733,587	7,844,837	58,578,424	18,501,754	6,120,282	24,622,036
1837	41,918,547	9,211,743	51,130,290	13,629,760	6,955,856	20,585,616

* The figures in this Table, prior to 1800, apply only to Great Britain, but thereafter to the United Kingdom.

TABLE No. 3.—Continued.

Showing the Official and Declared Real Value of Cotton Goods and Yarns Exported from the United Kingdom since 1785.

Years.	OFFICIAL VALUE. Manufactures.	Yarns & Twist.	Total.	DECLARED REAL VALUE. Manufactures.	Yarns & Twist.	Total.
	£	£	£	£	£	£
1838	54,610,502	10,202,027	64,812,529	16,702,022	7,431,845	24,133,867
1839	58,491,986	9,400,689	67,892,675	17,676,246	6,858,145	24,534,391
1840	62,596,791	10,532,401	73,129,192	17,553,004	7,101,289	24,654,293
1841	58,818,802	10,960,468	69,779,270	16,222,496	7,266,950	23,489,446
1842	56,448,592	12,239,280	68,687,872	13,900,794	7,771,420	21,672,214
1843	69,707,174	12,482,425	82,189,599	16,251,708	7,193,904	23,445,612
1844	78,714,981	12,324,594	91,039,575	18,814,869	6,988,580	25,803,449
1845	81,630,939	12,034,895	93,665,834	19,156,096	6,963,235	26,119,331
1846	78,966,648	14,419,171	93,385,819	17,717,778	7,882,048	25,599,826
1847	71,530,572	10,706,618	82,237,190	17,375,244	5,957,980	23,333,224
1848	81,101,212	12,083,891	93,185,103	16,753,369	5,927,831	22,681,200
1849	99,112,670	13,303,624	112,416,294	20,071,046	6,704,089	26,775,135
1850	102,087,890	11,687,490	113,775,380	21,873,697	6,383,704	28,257,401
1851	113,558,361	12,808,128	126,366,489	23,454,810	6,634,026	30,088,836
1852	112,103,349	12,937,509	125,040,858	23,223,432	6,654,655	29,878,087
1853	118,586,493	13,124,153	131,710,646	25,817,249	6,895,653	32,712,902
1854	123,075,911	13,085,063	136,160,974	25,054,527	6,691,330	31,745,857
1855	138,992,779	14,718,699	153,711,478	27,578,746	7,200,395	34,779,141
1856	147,783,412	16,138,706	163,922,118	30,204,166	8,028,575	38,232,741
1857	143,347,278	15,741,206	159,088,484	30,372,831	8,700,589	39,073,420
1858	164,442,350	17,778,831	182,221,181	33,421,843	9,579,479	43,001,322
1859	....	....	....	38,742,740	9,465,704	48,208,444

TABLE No. 4.

Showing the Quantity of Raw Cotton Exported from the United States of America; the Average Price Per Pound; and Total Value in American and Sterling Money.

Years.	Sea Island.	Other kinds.	Total Quantity Exported.	Average Price in Cts. ℔ lb.	Value.	Value Sterling.§
	lbs.	lbs.	lbs.	Cents.	Dollars.	£
1791	....	....	189,316	....	....	....
1792	....	....	138,328	....	....	....
1793	....	....	487,600	....	....	....
1794	....	....	1,601,700	....	....	....
1795	....	....	*6,276,300	....	....	....
1796	....	....	*6,106,729	....	....	....
1797	....	....	3,788,429	....	....	....
1798	....	....	9,360,005	....	....	....
1799	....	....	9,532,263	....	....	....
1800	....	....	17,789,803	....	....	....
1801	....	....	20,911,201	....	....	....
1802	....	....	27,501,075	....	....	....
1803	....	....	41,105,623	18·9	7,920,000	1,650,000
1804	....	....	38,118,041	19·0	7,404,117	1,542,524
1805	....	....	40,383,491	23·4	9,445,000	1,967,708
1806	....	....	37,491,282	22·2	8,332,000	1,735,833
1807	....	....	66,212,737	21·5	14,232,000	2,965,000
1808	....	....	†12,064,366	18·5	2,221,000	462,708
1809	....	....	53,210,225	14·1	8,515,000	1,773,958
1810	....	....	93,874,201	16·0	15,108,000	3,147,500
1811	....	....	62,186,081	15·5	9,652,000	2,010,833
1812	....	....	‡28,952,544	10·6	3,080,000	641,666
1813	....	....	‡19,399,911	11·9	2,324,000	484,166
1814	....	....	‡17,806,479	14·9	2,683,000	558,958
1815	....	....	82,998,747	21·1	17,529,000	3,651,875
1816	....	....	81,747,116	29·4	24,106,000	5,022,083
1817	....	....	85,649,328	23·6	22,628,000	4,714,166
1818	....	....	92,471,178	33·8	31,332,000	6,527,500
1819	....	....	87,997,045	23·9	21,082,000	4,392,083
1820	....	....	127,860,152	17·4	22,309,000	4,647,708
1821	11,344,066	113,549,339	124,893,405	16·2	20,157,484	4,199,475
1822	11,250,635	133,424,460	144,675,095	16·6	24,035,058	5,007,303
1823	12,136,688	161,586,582	173,723,270	11·8	20,445,520	4,259,483
1824	9,525,722	132,843,941	142,369,663	15·4	21,947,401	4,572,375
1825	9,655,278	166,784,629	176,439,907	20·9	36,346,649	7,572,218
1826	5,972,852	198,562,563	204,535,415	17·2	35,025,214	7,296,919
1827	15,140,798	279,169,317	294,310,115	10·0	29,359,545	6,116,571
1828	11,288,419	299,302,044	310,590,463	10·7	22,487,229	4,684,839
1829	12,833,307	252,003,879	264,837,186	10·0	26,574,311	5,536,314
1830	8,147,165	290,311,937	298,459,102	9·9	29,674,883	6,182,267
1831	8,311,762	268,668,022	276,979,784	9·1	25,289,492	5,268,644
1832	8,743,373	313,471,749	322,215,122	9·8	31,724,682	6,609,308
1833	11,142,987	313,555,617	324,698,604	11·1	36,191,102	7,539,812
1834	8,085,937	376,631,970	384,717,907	12·8	49,448,402	10,301,750
1835	7,752,736	379,606,256	387,458,992	16·8	64,961,302	13,533,604
1836	7,849,597	415,721,710	423,571,307	16·8	71,284,925	14,851,026
1837	5,286,971	438,964,566	444,251,537	14·2	63,240,102	13,175,021
1838	7,286,340	588,615,957	595,902,297	10·3	61,556,811	12,824,335
1839	5,107,404	408,566,808	413,674,212	14·8	61,238,982	12,758,121
1840	8,779,669	735,161,392	743,941,061	8·5	63,870,307	13,306,313

* 1795-6: The figures for these years include a quantity of Foreign Cotton in the Exports.
† 1808 was the Year of the embargo on foreign trade.
‡ 1812-13-14: These years were those of the American War.
§ The American money is converted into Sterling at 4s. 2d. per dollar.

TABLE No. 4.—Continued.

Showing the Quantity of Raw Cotton Exported from the United States of America; the Average Price Per Pound; and Total Value in American and Sterling Money.

Years.	Sea Island.	Other kinds.	Total Quantity Exported.	Average Price in Cents ℔ lb.	Value.	Value Sterling.§
	lbs.	lbs.	lbs.	Cents.	Dollars.	£
1841	6,237,424	523,966,676	530,204,100	10·2	54,330,341	11,318,821
1842	7,254,099	577,462,918	584,717,017	8·1	47,593,464	9,915,305
1843	7,515,079	784,782,027	792,297,106	6·2	49,119,806	10,233,292
1844	6,099,076	657,534,379	663,633,455	8·1	55,063,501	11,471,562
1845	9,380,625	863,516,371	872,896,996	5·92	51,739,643	10,779,092
1846	9,388,533	538,169,522	547,558,055	7·81	42,767,341	8,909,862
1847	6,293,973	520,925,985	527,219,958	10·34	53,415,848	11,128,301
1848	7,724,148	806,550,283	814,274,431	7·61	61,998,294	12,916,311
1849	11,969,259	1,014,633,010	1,026,602,269	6·4	66,396,967	13,832,701
1850	8,236,463	627,145,141	635,481,604	11·3	71,984,616	14,996,795
1851	8,299,656	918,937,433	927,237,089	12·11	112,315,317	23,399,024
1852	11,738,075	1,081,492,564	1,093,230,639	8·05	87,965,732	18,326,194
1853	11,165,165	1,100,405,205	1,111,570,370	9 85	109,456,404	22,803,417
1854	10,486,423	977,346,683	987,833,106	9·47	93,596,220	19,499,212
1855	13,058,590	995,366,011	1,008,424,601	8·74	88,143,844	18,363,300
1856	12,797,225	1,338,634,476	1,351,431,701	9·49	128,382,351	26,746,323
1857	12,940,725	1,035,341,750	1,048,282,475	12·55	131,575,859	27,411,637
1858	12,101,058	1,106,522,954	1,118,624,012	11·70	131,386,661	27,372,221

§ The American money is converted into Sterling at 4s. 2d. per dollar.

TABLES No. 5 AND 6.
SHOWING THE QUANTITY OF RAW COTTON EXPORTED FROM THE PORT OF CALCUTTA, AND THE ROADSTEAD OF MADRAS, AND DISTINGUISHING ITS DESTINATION.

TABLE No. 5.—PORT OF CALCUTTA.

Years.	Great Britain.	China.	America.	Other Parts.	Grand Total.
	lbs.	lbs.	lbs.	lbs.	lbs.
1795-96	608,256	......	864	244,800	853,920
1796-97	296,400	......	......	360,450	656,850
1797-98	517,632	314,880	68,736	80,544	981,792
1798-99	3,007,296	......	270,816	1,166,112	4,444,224
1799-1800	315,264	......	316,896	192	632,352
1800-1	146,000	......	......	750	146,750
1801-2	66,600	......	......	......	66,600
1802-3	621,600	2,405,400	......	334,200	3,361,200
1803-4	726,000	14,061,300	239,400	503,700	15,530,400
1804-5	180,600	11,658,300	120,000	404,400	12,363,300
1805-6	726,900	17,770,500	267,300	9,000	18,773,700
1806-7	2,194,500	7,159,200	1,342,200	373,500	11,069,400
1807-8	1,115,100	12,331,200	1,159,200	326,700	14,932,200
1808-9	604,800	15,288,600	......	41,400	15,934,800
1809-10	12,234,300	10,697,100	......	842,100	23,773,500
1810-11	1,043,100	8,124,000	......	1,200,900	10,368,000
1811-12	48,000	9,778,800	......	292,500	10,119,300
1812-13	......	1,659,300	......	234,000	1,893,300
1813-14	3,511,500	22,815,300	......	22,800	26,349,600
1814-15	6,476,100	24,762,000	......	258,000	31,496,100
1815-16	5,168,400	22,341,600	600	788,100	28,298,700
1816-17	23,262,238	25,651,404	1,730,200	4,908,110	55,551,952
1817-18	38,890,875	22,374,375	6,050,925	7,936,050	75,252,225
1818-19	35,721,988	15,703,246	9,306,836	7,964,168	68,696,238
1819-20	9,204,900	11,101,500	441,900	709,800	21,458,100
1820-21	3,881,700	21,119,100	......	33,300	25,034,100
1821-22	1,617,368	17,744,144	......	247,230	19,608,742
1822-23	1,951,272	5,567,554	......	291,182	7,810,008
1823-24	3,475,078	9,508,720	......	40,180	13,023,978
1824-25	3,647,688	16,344,568	......	606,554	20,598,810
1825-26	4,805,200	14,535,812	......	22,550	19,363,562
1826-27	4,149,036	25,752,264	......	81,098	29,982,398
1827-28	1,398,756	16,202,380	......	117,752	17,718,888
1828-29	1,191,952	15,172,378	......	124,476	16,488,806
1829-30	611,884	10,382,266	......	70,356	11,064,506
1830-31	2,117,158	15,517,024	......	47,888	17,682,070
1831-32	1,267,556	12,369,700	......	19,762	13,657,018
1832-33	897,080	11,424,076	......	......	12,321,156
1833-34	1,078,464	13,055,466	......	5,986	14,139,916

TABLE No. 6.—ROADSTEAD OF MADRAS.

Years.	Great Britain.	China.	Other Foreign Countries.	Internal Ports.	Grand Total.
	lbs.	lbs.	lbs.	lbs.	lbs.
1824-25	482,551	3,789,790	180,042	507,761	4,960,144
1825-26	659,478	3,101,643	114,653	2,735,586	6,611,360
1826-27	312,818	3,345,043	48,695	819,364	4,525,920
1827-28	204,200	3,713,261	113,991	154,660	4,186,112
1828-29	300,995	4,073,005	443,750	1,536,794	6,354,544
1829-30	244,551	4,154,003	35,216	2,793,926	7,227,696
1830-31	964,902	2,997,544	228,397	167,749	4,358,592
1831-32	3,684,241	675,680	123,975	329,416	4,813,312
1832-33	1,567,634	856,970	47,483	1,997,385	4,469,472
1833-34	612,051	431,413	188,042	1,678,478	2,909,984

NOTE.—In the case of the exports from Calcutta, "Other Countries" includes some small Shipments to "Internal Ports" on the Coromandel and Malabar Coasts.
For Continuation, see TABLE No, 7.

TABLE No. 7.

SHOWING THE QUANTITY OF RAW COTTON EXPORTED FROM THE THREE PRESIDENCIES OF BENGAL, MADRAS, AND BOMBAY, FROM THE YEAR 1834.

BENGAL.

Years.	Great Britain.	China.	Other Places.	Total.
	lbs.	lbs.	lbs.	lbs.
1834-35	3,051,190	25,459,994	398,622	28,909,806
1835-36	11,681,706	43,540,518	2,457,366	57,679,590
1836-37	1,586,408	33,103,486	1,442,970	36,132,864
1837-38	380,074	15,888,232	152,258	16,420,564
1838-39	293,350	17,334,105	130,597	17,758,052
1839-40	2,100,346	11,451,420	1,276,558	14,828,324
1840-41	106,434	13,316,521	1,656,919	15,079,874
1841-42	365,620	6,878,397	2,000,794	9,244,811
1842-43	158,732	12,365,300	1,659,118	14,183,150
1843-44	143,142	16,087,935	316,863	16,547,940
1844-45	109,636	16,396,944	72,240	16,578,820
1845-46	12,154	7,334,314	357,266	7,703,734
1846-47	......	8,872,801	638,013	9,510,814
1847-48	1,624,433	10,415,585	731,487	12,771,505
1848-49	30,513	2,618,227	288,871	2,937,611
1849-50	27,306	1,389,532	428,439	1,845,277
1850-51	985,026	18,248,478	3,897,662	23,131,166
1851-52	642,537	38,151,251	1,965,364	40,759,152
1852-53	6,853,728	24,848,383	1,782,028	33,484,139
1853-54	2,065,056	11,663,904	367,248	14,096,208
1854-55	59,136	7,436,128	135,968	7,631,232
1855-56	598,192	12,372,080	43,198	13,013,470
1856-57	3,434,928	12,610,864	1,181,040	17,226,832
1857-58	164,948	635,488	139,928	940,364
1858-59	296,386	30,268	25,550	352,204

MADRAS.

Years.	Great Britain.	China.	Other Places.	Total.
	lbs.	lbs.		lbs.
1834-35	3,039,500	1,712,500		4,752,000
1835-36	7,761,500	11,974,500		19,736,000
1836-37	8,316,000	18,873,500		27,189,500
1837-38	1,256,500	3,908,000		5,164,500
1838-39	2,400,500	8,569,000		10,969,500
1839-40	12,991,500	6,978,500		19,970,000
1840-41	3,888,500	3,405,920	5,244,580	12,539,000
1841-42	13,384,000	7,810,768	2,799,732	23,994,500
1842-43	2,629,000	19,484,416	1,835,084	23,948,500
1843-44	1,576,500	11,791,248	1,142,252	14,510,000
1844-45	7,166,000	17,600,688	1,307,812	26,074,500
1845-46	3,123,000	6,506,832	653,168	10,283,000
1846-47	3,466,500	8,635,872	634,128	12,736,500
1847-48	3,147,746	6,200,946	114,386	9,463,078
1848-49	3,033,728	7,801,543	455,494	11,290,765
1849-50	5,026,023	7,676,468	362,489	13,064,980
1850-51	9,037,889	9,155,350	1,245,281	19,438,520
1851-52	4,632,380	10,737,153	2,011,986	17,381,519
1852-53	16,575,197	13,026,102	2,157,948	31,759,247
1853-54	8,721,984	2,480,400	1,004,632	12,207,016
1854-55	8,006,035	1,711,500	3,208,978	12,926,513
1855-56	4,792,388	54,000	2,303,176	7,149,564
1856-57	19,597,302	1,003,200	2,952,844	23,553,346
1857-58	11,699,984	651,600	7,867,961	20,219,545
1858-59	6,432,353	3,596,400	4,023,522	14,052,275

TABLE No. 7.—Continued.
SHOWING THE QUANTITY OF RAW COTTON EXPORTED FROM THE THREE PRESIDENCIES OF BENGAL, MADRAS, AND BOMBAY, FROM THE YEAR 1834.

BOMBAY.

Years.	Great Britain.	China.	Other Places	Total.
	lbs.	lbs.		lbs.
1834-35	32,177,712	32,408,532		64,586,244
1835-36	45,795,596	32,398,996		78,194,592
1836-37	68,163,901	44,464,364	2,627,563	115,255,828
1837-38	38,100,472	56,161,928	2,901,016	97,163,416
1838-39	31,800,887	67,672,812	1,874,548	101,348,247
1839-40	59,001,134	29,168,699	5,040,453	93,210,286
1840-41	81,581,688	33,711,049	16,270,700	131,563,437
1841-42	104,795,091	47,409,464	8,812,013	161,016,568
1842-43	69,839,914	76,444,744	5,494,672	151,779,330
1843-44	91,781,824	52,318,538	27,343,466	171,443,828
1844-45	50,854,590	67,102,790	3,866,617	121,823,997
1845-46	40,042,243	63,908,435	4,340,138	108,290,816
1846-47	87,607,744	57,461,490	1,764,283	146,833,517
1847-48	89,429,561	45,579,529	3,073,622	138,082,712
1848-49	64,139,278	85,700,135	4,563,677	154,403,090
1849-50	105,637,028	43,379,222	1,738,713	150,754,963
1850-51	131,423,883	49,646,801	2,833,313	183,903,997
1851-52	75,829,306	111,829,247	7,753,607	195,412,160
1852-53	157,932,069	37,797,257	1,935,462	197,664,788
1853-54	127,396,389	41,632,704	2,429,448	171,458,541
1854-55	111,448,366	36,746,295	5,027,786	153,222,447
1855-56	165,380,930	44,265,032	7,370,953	217,016,915
1856-57	230,377,806	35,170,497	13,325,043	278,873,346
1857-58	185,356,315	19,237,031	34,600,797	239,194,143
1858-59	157,289,419	38,607,749	7,559,925	203,457,093

ALL INDIA.

Years.	Great Britain.	China.	Other Places	Grand Total.
	lbs.	lbs.		lbs.
1834-35	38,268,402	60,051,648		98,320,050
1835-36	65,238,802	90,371,380		155,610,182
1836-37	78,066,309	100,511,883		178,578,192
1837-38	39,737,046	79,011,434		118,748,480
1838-39	34,494,737	95,581,062		130,075,799
1839-40	74,092,980	53,915,630		128,008,610
1840-41	85,576,622	50,433,490	23,172,199	159,182,311
1841-42	118,544,711	62,098,629	13,612,539	194,255,879
1842-43	72,627,646	108,294,460	8,988,874	189,910,980
1843-44	93,501,466	80,197,721	28,802,581	202,501,768
1844-45	58,130,226	101,100,422	5,246,669	164,477,317
1845-46	43,177,397	77,749,581	5,350,572	126,277,550
1846-47	91,074,244	74,970,163	3,036,424	169,080,831
1847-48	94,201,740	62,196,060	3,919,495	160,317,295
1848-49	67,203,519	96,119,905	5,308,042	168,631,466
1849-50	110,690,357	52,445,222	2,529,641	165,665,220
1850-51	141,446,798	77,050,629	7,976,256	226,473,683
1851-52	81,104,223	160,717,651	11,730,957	253,552,831
1852-53	181,360,994	75,671,742	5,875,438	262,908,174
1853-54	138,183,429	55,777,008	3,801,328	197,761,765
1854-55	119,513,537	45,893,923	8,372,732	173,780,192
1855-56	170,771,510	56,691,112	9,717,327	237,179,949
1856-57	253,410,036	48,784,561	17,458,927	319,653,524
1857-58	197,221,247	20,524,119	42,608,686	260,354,052
1858-59	164,018,158	42,234,417	11,608,997	217,861,572

TABLE No. 8.

Showing the Weight in Pounds, and Value of Raw Cotton Imported, Re-exported, and Taken for Consumption in the United Kingdom; with the Annual Stocks, and Average Prices since 1834.

Years.	IMPORTED. Quantity. 1	IMPORTED. Computed Value. 2	RE-EXPORTED. Quantity. 3	RE-EXPORTED. Computed Value. 4	TAKEN FOR CONSUMPTION. Quantity. 5	TAKEN FOR CONSUMPTION. Computed Value. 6	STOCKS 31st DECEMBER. In the Ports. 7	STOCKS 31st DECEMBER. In Dealers' and Spinners' Hands. 8	ANNUAL AVERAGE PRICE. United States Uplands. 9	ANNUAL AVERAGE PRICE. East India "Surats," 10
	lbs.	£	lbs.	£	lbs.	£	lbs.	lbs.	d. Per lb.	d. Per lb.
1834	326,875,425	12,127,078	24,461,963	733,858	302,935,657	11,238,912	64,500,000	19,100,000	$8\frac{5}{8}$	$6\frac{5}{8}$
1835	363,702,963	16,039,300	32,779,734	1,166,958	326,407,692	14,394,579	73,146,000	16,300,000	$10\frac{1}{4}$	$7\frac{1}{2}$
1836	406,959,057	17,255,064	31,739,763	1,088,673	363,684,232	15,420,211	90,886,000	24,300,000	$9\frac{7}{8}$	$6\frac{3}{4}$
1837	407,286,783	12,218,603	39,722,031	965,245	368,445,035	11,053,351	85,782,000	33,500,000	7	$4\frac{7}{8}$
1838	507,850,577	15,235,517	30,644,469	744,660	455,036,755	13,651,102	110,307,000	50,800,000	7	5
1839	389,396,559	13,161,603	38,738,238	1,061,427	352,000,277	11,897,609	93,360,000	27,300,000	$7\frac{7}{8}$	$5\frac{3}{4}$
1840	592,488,010	15,345,439	38,673,229	808,270	528,142,743	13,678,897	168,450,150	44,100,000	6	$4\frac{5}{8}$
1841	487,992,355	13,078,195	37,673,585	817,516	437,093,631	11,714,109	195,926,640	30,100,000	$6\frac{1}{4}$	$4\frac{5}{8}$
1842	531,750,086	12,283,426	45,251,302	846,199	473,976,400	10,948,854	207,729,100	42,400,000	$5\frac{3}{8}$	4
1843	673,193,116	13,396,543	39,619,979	637,881	581,303,105	11,567,931	295,050,960	51,700,000	$4\frac{5}{8}$	$3\frac{5}{8}$
1844	646,111,304	13,568,337	47,222,541	798,060	554,196,602	11,638,128	338,191,620	52,500,000	$4\frac{7}{8}$	$3\frac{5}{8}$
1845	721,979,953	13,573,223	42,916,332	652,328	606,600,000	11,404,080	398,892,060	52,700,000	$4\frac{3}{8}$	3
1846	467,856,274	9,778,196	65,930,732	1,114,229	614,300,000	12,838,870	209,583,360	44,100,000	$4\frac{7}{8}$	$3\frac{3}{8}$
1847	474,707,615	13,339,283	74,954,336	1,656,490	441,400,000	12,403,340	172,189,140	22,700,000	$6\frac{3}{8}$	$4\frac{1}{2}$
1848	713,020,161	13,048,268	74,019,790	1,095,492	576,600,000	10,551,780	194,947,650	37,500,000	$4\frac{1}{4}$	$3\frac{1}{4}$
1849	755,469,012	16,620,318	98,893,508	1,760,304	629,900,000	13,857,800	220,564,050	37,400,000	$5\frac{1}{8}$	$3\frac{7}{8}$
1850	663,576,861	20,239,094	102,469,717	2,664,212	588,200,000	17,940,100	201,152,320	37,500,000	$7\frac{1}{4}$	$5\frac{1}{8}$
1851	757,379,749	18,707,279	111,980,394	2,239,607	658,900,000	16,274,830	192,894,000	39,500,000	$5\frac{3}{4}$	4
1852	929,782,448	21,477,974	111,884,321	2,092,236	739,600,000	17,084,760	258,405,360	58,700,000	$5\frac{3}{8}$	$3\frac{3}{4}$
1853	895,278,749	21,665,745	148,569,680	2,911,965	760,900,000	18,413,780	284,161,680	58,200,000	$5\frac{5}{8}$	$3\frac{1}{2}$
1854	887,333,149	20,175,395	123,326,112	2,302,197	776,100,000	17,617,470	250,404,450	31,600,000	$5\frac{3}{8}$	$3\frac{1}{2}$
1855	891,751,952	20,848,515	124,368,160	2,475,218	839,100,000	19,634,940	193,615,060	31,500,000	$5\frac{3}{4}$	$3\frac{7}{8}$
1856	1,023,886,304	26,448,224	146,660,864	3,345,770	891,400,000	22,998,120	135,425,180	66,200,000	6	$4\frac{3}{8}$
1857	969,318,896	29,288,827	131,927,600	3,430,894	826,000,000	24,945,200	181,456,510	34,200,000	$7\frac{1}{4}$	$5\frac{3}{8}$
1858	1,034,342,176	30,106,968	149,609,600	3,955,309	905,600,000	26,359,000	153,255,760	37,800,000	$6\frac{1}{4}$	$4\frac{3}{4}$
1859	1,225,989,072	34,559,636	175,143,136	4,937,142	976,600,000	28,727,000	192,500,000	37,757,000	$6\frac{1}{4}$	$4\frac{3}{4}$

Referring to the above Table, Columns 1 and 3, exhibiting the actual weight of Raw Cotton imported into and exported from Great Britain and Ireland since 1834, are compiled from the Board of Trade Returns for those years. Columns 2 and 4, exhibiting its value, are from 1853 the values given by the Board of Trade; prior to that date, they are computed as nearly as circumstances will admit upon the same basis of calculation as now adopted by the Board of Trade. Column 5, showing the pounds weight taken for Consumption, is down to 1844, the actual quantity on which duty was paid as returned by the Customs,; subsequent to that date, the figures are kindly furnished by Messrs. George Holt and Co. the Liverpool Cotton Brokers. Column 6, exhibiting the value of the Cotton taken for Consumption, is computed on the same basis of value as that applied to the imports in Column 2. Columns 7 and 8 show the pounds weight of stocks in the ports and in spinners' hands in the United Kingdom on the 31st December in each year, the figures for which are kindly furnished by Messrs. Stolterfoht Sons and Co., and Messrs. George Holt and Co., of Liverpool. Columns 9 and 10 exhibit the annual average price of "Fair American Uplands," and "East India Surat" Cotton in Liverpool, from figures also furnished by the latter firm.

TABLE No. 8.—Continued.

Showing the Weight of Yarns and Goods of British Manufacture Exported from the United Kingdom since 1834: their Value, and the Quantity of Raw Cotton used in their Manufacture.

Years.	YARNS.		GOODS.				TOTAL WEIGHT		Total Declared Value.
	Quantity.	Declared Value.	Sewing Thread.	Other Goods.	Quantity of Yarn.	Declared Value.	of Yarn.	of Raw Cotton.	
	11	12	13	14	15	16	17	18	19
	lbs.	£	lbs.	Yds.	lbs.	£	lbs.	lbs.	£
1834	76,478,468	5,211,015	1,981,736	555,705,809	90,720,535	15,302,571	169,180,739	188,636,523	20,513,586
1835	83,214,198	5,706,589	1,842,124	557,515,701	97,823,222	16,421,715	182,879,544	203,910,691	22,128,304
1836	88,191,046	6,120,366	2,020,998	637,667,627	111,644,210	18,511,692	201,856,254	225,069,723	24,632,058
1837	103,455,138	6,955,942	2,099,081	531,373,663	100,371,229	13,640,181	205,925,448	229,606,874	20,596,123
1838	114,596,602	7,431,869	2,362,983	690,077,622	120,781,629	16,715,857	237,744,214	265,084,798	24,147,726
1839	105,686,442	6,858,193	2,711,798	731,450,123	138,298,236	17,692,182	246,696,476	275,066,570	24,550,375
1840	118,470,223	7,101,308	2,876,709	790,631,997	139,446,138	17,567,310	260,793,070	290,784,273	24,668,618
1841	123,226,519	7,266,968	4,915,109	751,125,624	138,291,158	16,232,510	266,432,786	297,072,556	23,499,478
1842	137,466,892	7,771,464	1,972,632	734,098,809	129,842,680	13,907,884	269,282,204	300,249,657	21,679,348
1843	140,321,176	7,193,971	2,594,783	918,640,205	171,032,210	16,254,000	313,948,169	350,052,208	23,447,971
1844	138,540,079	6,988,584	2,731,039	1,046,670,823	190,529,858	18,816,764	331,800,976	369,958,088	25,805,348
1845	135,144,865	6,963,235	2,567,705	1,091,686,069	202,360,687	19,156,096	340,073,257	379,181,681	26,119,331
1846	161,892,750	7,882,048	2,320,335	1,065,460,589	194,841,389	17,717,778	359,054,474	400,345,738	25,599,826
1847	120,270,741	5,957,980	2,855,841	942,540,160	168,864,426	17,375,245	291,991,008	325,569,973	23,333,225
1848	135,831,162	5,927,831	3,523,642	1,096,751,823	187,178,090	16,753,369	326,532,894	364,084,176	22,681,200
1849	149,502,281	6,704,089	4,479,329	1,337,536,116	231,214,175	20,071,046	385,195,785	429,493,300	26,775,135
1850	131,370,368	6,383,704	3,062,503	1,358,182,941	225,271,266	21,873,697	359,704,137	401,070,112	28,257,401
1851	143,966,106	6,634,026	3,034,239	1,543,161,789	258,213,447	23,454,810	405,213,792	451,813,378	30,088,836
1852	145,478,302	6,654,655	4,392,176	1,524,256,914	270,593,273	23,223,432	420,463,751	468,817,082	29,878,087
1853	147,539,302	6,895,653	4,885,322	1,594,592,659	295,620,164	25,817,249	448,044,788	499,569,938	32,712,902
1854	147,128,498	6,691,830	4,622,404	1,692,899,122	312,227,202	25,054,527	463,978,104	517,335,585	31,745,857
1855	165,493,598	7,200,395	4,855,869	1,937,734,025	355,838,641	27,578,746	526,188,108	586,699,740	34,779,141
1856	181,495,805	8,028,575	5,371,643	2,035,274,969	374,120,893	30,204,166	560,988,341	625,502,000	38,232,741
1857	176,821,338	8,700,589	4,404,705	1,979,970,780	366,580,557	30,372,831	547,806,600	610,804,359	39,073,420
1858	200,016,902	9,579,479	4,517,730	2,324,139,085	416,206,718	33,421,843	620,741,350	692,126,605	43,001,322
1859	192,341,516	9,465,704	5,449,134	2,563,445,393	446,080,980	38,742,740	643,871,630	717,916,867	48,208,444

Referring to the Table above, Column 11, presenting the pounds weight of cotton yarns exported annually since 1834, is compiled from the Board of Trade Returns for those years. Columns 12, 16, and 19, showing the declared value of yarns and goods exported, are derived from the same source. Column 13, showing the pounds weight of sewing thread exported, is from 1853 extracted from the Board of Trade Returns: prior to that date, sewing thread was not officially recorded, being returned in value only, and consequently included in that of goods; the figures for the previous years, therefore, are furnished by Richard Burn, Esq. of Manchester. Column 14 exhibits the quantity in yards of cotton fabrics exported, and is compiled from the Board of Trade Returns. Column 15 gives the weight of yarn employed in the fabrication of these goods, and is also furnished by Richard Burn, Esq. Column 17, showing the pounds weight of yarn in goods and yarns exported, is derived from the addition of the figures given in Columns 11, 13, and 15. Column 18, exhibiting the pounds weight of raw cotton employed in the manufacture of the yarn thus used in the fabrication of yarns and goods of cotton exported, is derived from the addition of 11¼ per cent to the weight of yarn given in Column 17, being the allowance for waste calculated by G. F. Mandley, Esq. of Manchester, as incurred in its preparation.

TABLE NO. 8.—Continued.

Showing the Proportional Weight and Value of the Home and Export Trade in British Manufactured Cotton Goods.

Years.	RAW COTTON IMPORTED. Quantity. 20	Computed Value. 21	Taken for Home use. Quantity. 22	ACTUALLY CONSUMED. Quantity. 23	Computed Value. 24	EXPORTED IN MANUFACTURES. Quantity. 25	Declared Value. 26	HOME TRADE. Quantity. 27	Computed Value. 28	Total Value of British Cotton Manufacture 29
	lbs.	£	lbs.	lbs.	£	lbs.	£	lbs.	£	£
1834	326,875,425	12,127,078	302,935,657	311,335,657	11,550,553	188,636,523	20,513,556	122,699,134	17,790,823	38,304,409
1835	363,702,963	16,039,300	326,407,692	329,207,692	14,518,058	203,910,691	22,128,304	125,297,001	18,129,571	40,257,875
1836	406,959,057	17,255,064	363,684,232	335,684,232	15,081,011	225,069,723	24,632,058	130,614,509	19,059,600	43,691,658
1837	407,286,783	12,218,603	368,445,035	359,245,035	10,777,351	229,606,874	20,596,123	129,638,161	15,505,018	36,101,141
1838	507,850,577	15,235,517	455,036,755	437,736,755	13,132,102	265,084,798	24,147,726	172,651,957	20,970,133	45,117,859
1839	389,396,559	13,161,603	352,000,277	375,500,277	12,692,165	275,066,570	24,550,375	100,433,707	11,951,943	36,502,318
1840	592,488,010	15,345,439	528,142,743	511,342,743	13,243,773	290,784,273	24,668,618	220,558,470	24,948,037	49,616,655
1841	487,992,355	13,078,195	437,093,631	451,093,631	12,089,309	297,072,556	23,499,478	154,021,075	16,244,807	39,744,285
1842	531,750,086	12,283,426	473,976,400	451,676,400	10,664,723	300,249,657	21,679,348	161,426,743	15,540,963	37,220,311
1843	673,193,116	13,396,543	581,303,105	572,003,105	11,382,861	350,052,208	23,447,971	221,950,897	19,822,940	43,270,911
1844	646,111,304	13,568,337	554,196,602	553,396,602	11,621,328	369,958,088	25,805,348	183,438,514	17,060,290	42,865,638
1845	721,979,953	13,573,223	606,600,000	606,400,000	11,400,319	379,181,681	26,119,331	227,218,319	20,868,763	46,988,094
1846	467,856,274	9,778,196	614,300,000	622,900,000	13,018,609	400,345,738	25,599,826	222,554,262	18,974,766	44,574,592
1847	474,707,615	13,339,283	441,400,000	462,800,000	13,004,679	325,569,973	23,333,225	137,230,027	13,113,489	36,446,714
1848	713,020,161	13,048,268	576,600,000	561,800,000	10,280,939	364,084,176	22,681,200	197,715,824	16,422,693	39,103,893
1849	755,469,012	16,620,318	629,900,000	630,000,000	13,859,999	429,493,300	26,775,135	200,506,700	16,666,441	43,441,576
1850	663,576,861	20,239,094	588,200,000	588,100,000	17,937,100	401,070,112	28,257,401	187,029,888	17,569,591	45,826,992
1851	757,379,749	18,707,279	658,900,000	656,900,000	16,225,429	451,813,378	30,088,836	205,086,622	18,210,520	48,299,356
1852	929,782,448	21,477,974	739,600,000	720,400,000	16,641,239	468,817,082	29,878,087	251,582,918	21,378,107	51,256,194
1853	895,278,749	21,665,745	760,900,000	761,400,000	18,425,879	499,569,938	32,712,902	261,830,062	22,860,293	55,573,195
1854	887,333,149	20,175,395	776,100,000	802,700,000	18,251,081	517,335,585	31,745,857	285,364,415	23,348,190	55,094,047
1855	891,751,952	20,848,515	839,100,000	839,200,000	19,619,888	586,699,740	34,779,141	252,500,260	19,957,379	54,736,520
1856	1,023,886,304	26,448,224	891,400,000	856,700,000	22,129,599	625,502,000	38,232,741	231,198,000	18,842,111	57,074,852
1857	969,318,896	29,288,827	826,000,000	858,000,000	25,925,228	610,804,359	39,073,420	247,195,641	21,084,283	60,157,703
1858	1,034,342,176	30,106,968	905,600,000	902,000,000	26,254,800	692,126,605	43,001,322	209,873,395	17,385,712	60,387,034
1859	1,225,989,072	34,559,636	976,600,000	976,643,000	27,530,774	717,916,867	48,208,444	258,726,133	23,164,770	71,373,214

Referring to the above table, or resumé, columns 20, 21, 22, 25 and 26 are repetitions or transfers of columns 1, 2 and 5 in Table No. 1, and 18 and 19 in Table No. 2 respectively. Column 23 showing the weight of raw cotton annually consumed in our manufactories, is arrived at by adding to the quantity taken for consumption, as given in column 5, the stocks in dealers and spinners hands at the commencement of the year, given in column 8 (the stock at the commencement of 1834 was 27,500,000 lbs.), and deducting that at the end of the year given in same column. Column 24 showing the comparative value of the cotton actually consumed is computed on the same basis of value as that applied to the imports. Column 27 showing the quantity left for the home trade manufacture, is of course only an approximation, and includes the stock of goods at the end of each year which may be subsequently exported, and of which it is impossible to obtain any separate account: it is obtained by deducting from the weight of cotton actually consumed, the approximate weight of cotton in exported cotton goods. Column 28 exhibiting the value of the home trade manufacture, is computed upon the inference that the goods for the home trade are of one-third more value in the finish and style of manufacture, which proportion is worked out upon column 27. Column 29 showing the total value of the British cotton manufacture is computed upon the inference that the columns 26 and 28 are correct, and is obtained by adding the value of exported goods given in the former to the computed value of the home trade given in the latter.

TABLE No. 9.

Showing the Declared Real Value of British Textile and other Manufactures Exported from the United Kingdom to Foreign Countries since 1820.

Years.	COTTON. Goods.	COTTON. Yarns.	COTTON. Total.	WOOLLEN AND WORSTED. Goods.	WOOLLEN AND WORSTED. Yarns.	WOOLLEN AND WORSTED. Total.	LINEN. Goods.	LINEN. Yarns.	LINEN. Total.	SILK Manufactures of All Kinds.	TOTAL. Textile Fabrics, &c.	TOTAL. Other Manufactures	GRAND TOTAL. Value of Exports.
	£	£	£	£	£	£	£	£	£	£	£	£	£
1820	13,690,109	2,826,639	16,516,748	5,586,138	810	5,586,948	1,653,972	607	1,654,579	371,775	24,130,050	12,294,603	36,424,653
1821	13,787,964	2,305,823	16,093,787	6,462,866	1,917	6,464,783	1,978,697	2,931	1,981,628	374,473	24,914,671	11,744,960	36,659,631
1822	14,521,142	2,697,582	17,218,724	6,488,167	2,392	6,490,559	1,773,979	234	1,774,213	381,763	25,865,199	11,103,765	36,968,964
1823	13,700,658	2,625,946	16,326,604	5,636,586	1,127	5,637,713	2,094,868	774	2,095,642	351,409	24,411,368	11,046,681	35,458,049
1824	15,317,591	3,135,396	18,452,987	6,043,051	2,188	6,045,239	2,441,775	812	2,442,587	442,596	27,383,409	11,012,892	38,396,301
1825	15,152,797	3,206,729	18,359,526	6,185,648	14,467	6,200,115	2,128,962	1,735	2,130,697	296,736	26,987,074	11,890,314	38,877,388
1826	10,602,031	3,491,338	14,093,369	4,966,879	22,794	4,989,673	1,486,105	1,557	1,487,662	168,801	20,739,505	10,797,218	31,536,723
1827	14,091,587	3,545,578	17,637,165	5,245,649	37,392	5,283,041	1,894,473	714	1,895,187	236,113	25,051,506	12,131,351	37,182,857
1828	13,649,012	3,595,405	17,244,417	5,069,741	56,243	5,125,984	1,999,383	1,622	2,001,005	255,871	24,627,277	12,186,899	36,814,176
1829	13,558,132	3,976,874	17,535,006	4,587,603	73,648	4,661,251	1,885,067	774	1,885,841	267,920	24,350,028	11,480,622	35,830,650
1830	15,294,923	4,133,741	19,428,664	4,728,666	122,430	4,851,096	2,065,670	754	2,066,424	521,010	26,867,194	11,384,309	38,251,503
1831	13,282,185	3,975,019	17,257,204	5,231,013	158,111	5,389,124	2,458,320	2,384	2,460,704	578,874	25,685,906	11,477,742	37,163,648
1832	12,675,633	4,722,759	17,398,392	5,244,479	235,307	5,479,786	1,774,727	8,705	1,783,432	529,691	25,191,301	11,253,224	36,444,525
1833	13,782,377	4,704,024	18,486,401	6,294,522	246,204	6,540,726	2,167,024	72,006	2,239,030	737,404	28,003,561	11,663,786	39,667,347
1834	15,302,571	5,211,015	20,513,586	5,736,871	238,544	5,975,415	2,443,346	136,312	2,579,658	637,198	29,705,857	11,943,334	41,649,191
1835	16,421,715	5,706,589	22,128,304	7,639,354	358,690	7,998,044	3,326,325	318,772	3,645,097	917,822	37,193,021	16,100,958	53,293,979
1836	18,511,692	6,120,366	24,632,058	4,632,058	333,098	4,989,075	2,127,445	479,307	2,606,752	973,786	33,460,470	16,886,670	47,372,270
1837	13,640,181	6,955,942	20,596,123	4,665,977	333,098	4,989,075	2,127,445	479,307	2,606,752	503,673	28,695,623	13,375,121	42,070,744
1838	16,715,857	7,431,869	24,147,726	5,795,069	384,535	6,179,604	2,820,272	746,163	3,566,435	777,280	33,414,467	16,646,503	50,060,970
1839	17,692,182	6,858,193	24,550,375	6,271,645	423,320	6,694,965	3,414,967	818,455	4,233,452	868,118	36,346,910	14,958,306	51,305,216
1840	17,567,310	7,101,308	24,668,618	5,327,853	452,957	5,780,810	3,306,088	822,876	4,128,964	792,648	35,371,040	15,937,700	51,308,740
1841	16,232,510	7,266,968	23,499,478	5,748,673	552,148	6,300,821	3,347,555	972,466	4,320,021	788,894	34,909,214	16,635,902	51,545,116
1842	13,907,884	7,771,464	21,679,348	5,185,045	637,305	5,822,350	2,346,749	1,025,551	3,372,300	500,189	31,464,187	15,820,801	47,284,988
1843	16,254,000	7,193,971	23,447,971	6,790,232	742,888	7,533,120	2,803,223	898,829	3,702,052	667,952	35,351,095	16,855,352	52,206,447
1844	18,816,764	6,988,580	25,805,344	8,204,836	958,217	9,163,053	3,024,800	1,050,676	4,075,476	736,455	39,780,328	18,754,377	58,534,705
1845	19,156,096	6,963,235	26,119,331	7,693,117	1,066,925	8,760,042	3,036,370	1,060,566	4,096,936	766,405	39,742,714	20,368,368	60,111,082
1846	17,717,778	7,882,048	25,599,826	6,335,103	908,270	7,243,373	2,830,808	875,405	3,706,213	837,577	37,386,989	20,399,887	57,786,876
1847	17,375,245	5,957,980	23,333,225	6,896,038	1,001,364	7,897,402	2,958,851	649,893	3,608,744	985,426	35,824,997	23,017,380	54,842,377
1848	16,753,369	5,927,831	22,681,200	5,733,828	776,975	6,510,803	2,802,789	493,449	3,296,238	588,117	33,076,358	19,773,087	52,849,445
1849	20,071,046	6,704,089	26,775,135	7,342,723	1,090,223	8,432,946	3,493,829	732,065	4,225,894	998,334	40,432,309	23,163,716	63,596,025
1850	21,873,697	6,383,704	28,257,401	8,588,690	1,451,642	10,040,332	3,947,682	881,312	4,828,994	1,255,641	44,382,368	26,985,517	71,367,885
1851	23,454,810	6,634,026	30,088,836	8,377,183	1,484,544	9,861,727	4,107,396	951,426	5,058,822	1,326,778	46,336,163	28,112,559	74,448,722
1852	23,223,432	6,654,655	29,878,087	8,730,934	1,430,140	10,161,074	4,231,786	1,140,565	5,372,351	1,551,866	46,963,378	31,113,476	78,076,854
1853	25,817,249	6,895,653	32,712,902	10,172,182	1,456,786	11,628,968	4,758,432	1,154,977	5,913,409	2,044,361	52,299,640	46,634,141	98,933,781
1854	25,054,527	6,691,330	31,745,857	9,120,759	1,537,612	10,678,371	4,108,457	944,502	5,052,959	1,692,380	49,169,567	48,015,159	97,184,726
1855	27,378,746	7,200,395	34,779,141	7,718,374	2,025,095	9,744,469	4,118,013	632,981	4,750,994	1,524,144	51,098,947	44,589,138	95,688,085
1856	30,204,166	8,028,575	38,232,741	9,500,428	2,889,642	12,390,070	4,887,780	1,365,980	6,253,760	2,962,056	59,838,627	55,988,321	115,826,948
1857	30,372,831	8,700,589	39,073,420	10,703,376	2,941,800	13,645,176	4,516,830	1,647,953	6,164,833	2,889,829	61,773,258	60,292,849	122,066,107
1858	33,421,843	9,579,479	43,001,322	9,776,944	2,966,923	12,743,867	4,124,356	1,746,340	5,870,696	2,096,300	63,712,185	52,896,571	116,608,756
1859	38,742,740	9,465,704	48,208,444	12,032,831	3,080,306	15,113,137	4,607,245	1,684,489	6,291,734	2,351,839	71,965,154	58,475,273	130,440,427

TABLE No. 10.

Showing the Price of Beef and Mutton at St. Thomas's Hospital, Southwark, at Lady-Day and Michaelmas, in Each Year from 1688 to 1858.

Years.	BEEF Lady Day. Per Stone s. d.	BEEF Michaelmas. Per Stone s. d.	MUTTON. Lady Day Per Stone s. d.	MUTTON. Michaelmas. Per Stone s. d.	Years.	BEEF. Lady Day Per Stone s. d.	BEEF. Michaelmas. Per Stone s. d.	MUTTON. Lady Day Per Stone s. d.	MUTTON. Michaelmas. Per Stone s. d.
1688	1/10	1/9	....	....	1736	1/10	1/6	1/10	1/8
1689	1/10	1/9	....	....	1737	1/8	1/6	1/10	1/8
1690	1/10	1/8	....	....	1738	1/8	1/6	2/0	1/8
1691	1/10	1/8	....	....	1739	1/8	1/6	2/2	1/10
1692	1/10	1/9	....	....	1740	1/9	1/10	2/2	2/0
1693	2/2	1/10	....	....	1741	2/6	2/2	....	2/4
1694	2/2	2/0	....	....	1742	2/3	2/0	2/8	2/2
1695	2/2	1/11	....	....	1743	1/10	1/8	2/2	2/0
1696	2/3	1/9	....	....	1744	1/8	1/6	1/10	1/10
1697	2/1	1/11	....	....	1745	1/8	1/8	2/0	1/8
1698	2/3	1/9	....	....	1746	1/8	1/8	2/0	1/10
1699	2/2	1/9	....	....	1747	1/10	1/10	2/2	1/10
1700	1/11	1/7	....	....	1748	2/0	2/0	2/0	2/0
1701	2/0	1/7½	....	....	1749	1/10	1/8	2/4	1/10
1702	1/10	1/8	....	....	1750	1/8	1/8	1/10	1/10
1703	1/11	1/6	....	....	1751	1/8	1/8	2/0	1/10
1704	1/7	1/6	....	....	1752	1/8	1/9	2/0	1/10
1705	1/8	1/8	....	....	1753	1/9	1/10	1/10	2/0
1706	1/8½	1/6	....	....	1754	2/0	2/0	2/4	2/0
1707	1/8	1/6	....	....	1755	2/0	2/0	2/2	2/0
1708	1/9	1/6	....	....	1756	2/0	2/0	2/2	2/0
1709	1/9	1/6	....	....	1757	2/0	2/2	2/3	2/4
1710	1/9	1/9	....	....	1758	2/0	2/0	2/8	2/6
1711	1/10½	1/9½	....	....	1759	2/0	1/10	2/4	2/2
1712	1/11	1/9	....	....	1760	1/10	1/10	2/3	2/0
1713	1/10	1/9	....	....	1761	2/0	1/10	2/4	2/0
1714	1/10½	1/9½	....	....	1762	1/10	1/8	2/3	2/10
1715	1/11½	1/8	....	....	1763	1/10	2/0	2/4	2/2
1716	1/10	1/8	....	....	1764	2/2	1/10	2/8	2/2
1717	2/0	1/9	....	....	1765	2/0	2/0	2/6	2/4
1718	1/9	1/8	....	....	1766	2/0	2/4	2/8	2/8
1719	1/10	1/9	....	....	1767	2/6	2/6	3/0	2/8
1720	2/2	1/11	....	....	1768	2/6	2/6	2/8	2/6
1721	1/11	1/8	....	....	1769	2/4	2/4	2/6	2/6
1722	1/8	1/7	....	....	1770	2/2	2/2	2/6	2 8
1723	1/8	1/8	....	....	1771	2/4	2/4	2/10	2/8
1724	1/9	1/9	....	....	1772	2/8	2/6	3/0	2/10
1725	1/9	1/8	....	1/11	1773	2/6	2/6	3/0	2/10
1726	1/11	1/8	....	2/0	1774	2/6	2/6	3/2	2/10
1727	1/8	1/8	2/2	2/0	1775	2/4	2/4	3/0	2/10
1728	1/10	1/10	2/6	2/2	1776	2/4	2/6	2/10	2/10
1729	2/0	2/0	2/6	2/4	1777	2/6	2/4	2/10	2/10
1730	2/2	1/8	2/8	2/0	1778	2/6	2/6	3/0	2/10
1731	1/10	1/8	2/2	2/0	1779	2/6	2/6	3/0	2/8
1732	2/0	1/8	2/6	1/8	1780	2/4	2/4	2/6	2/6
1733	1/10	1/6	2/2	1/8	1781	2/4	2/4	2/8	2/4
1734	1/8	1/6	1/8	1/6	1782	2/4	2/6	2/6	2/8
1735	1/7	1/6	1/7	1/6	1783	2/6	2/8	2/8	2/8

NOTE.—The above are the prices *per stone of 8 lbs*. The *pieces of beef* are two rounds, chucks, clods, and leg mutton pieces. The *pieces of mutton* are legs and loins; the average quantity is about 32 stone per day. The extra quantity of mutton-fat is returned. The beef is delivered without bone, the weight of which was six stone and six pounds in making the 32 stone and 4 pounds of meat sent to the Hospital.

TABLE No. 10. — Continued.

SHOWING THE PRICE OF BEEF AND MUTTON AT ST. THOMAS'S HOSPITAL, SOUTHWARK, AT LADY-DAY AND MICHAELMAS, IN EACH YEAR FROM 1688 TO 1858.

Years.	BEEF. Lady Day Per Stone s. d.	BEEF. Michaelmas. Per Stone s. d.	MUTTON. Lady Day Per Stone s. d.	MUTTON. Michaelmas. Per Stone s. d.	Years.	BEEF. Lady Day Per Stone s. d.	BEEF. Michaelmas. Per Stone s. d.	MUTTON. Lady Day Per Stone s. d.	MUTTON. Michaelmas. Per Stone s. d.
1784	2/6	2/10	2/10	3/4	1823	2/6	3/4	3/6	3/8
1785	2/8	2/8	3/2	3/2	1824	3/4	3/4	3/8	3/8
1786	2/6	2/10	3/0	3/2	1825	4/0	4/4	4/8	4/8
1787	3/0	2/10	3/2	3/0	1826	4/0	4/0	4/8	4/4
1788	2/10	2/10	3/0	3/0	1827	4/0	4/0	4/4	4/4
1789	2/10	2/10	3/0	3/0	1828	3/8	3/8	4/0	4/0
1790	2/8	2/10	2/10	2/10	1829	3/6	3/4	3/10	4/0
1791	2/10	3/0	3/0	3/2	1830	2/8	3/0	3/2	3/6
1792	3/0	2/10	3/2	3/2	1831	3/4	3/4	4/2	4/2
1793	2/10	2/10	3/2	3/0	1832	3/4	3/0	4/2	3/10
1794	2/10	2/10	3/2	3/0	1833	3/4	3/4	3/10	4/2
1795	3/2	3/4	3/6	3/8	1834	3/0	3/0	3/10	3/6
1796	3/8	4/0	3/8	4/0	1835	2/10	3/2	3/0	3/4
1797	4/2	4/4	4/2	4/4	1836	3/6	3/4	3/8	3/10
1798	3/8	3/8	3/8	3/8	1837	3/4	3/4	3/10	4/2
1799	3/6	4/2	3/6	4/2	1838	3/0	3/4	3/6	3/10
1800	4/4	5/0	4/6	4/8	1839	3/4	3/8	3/10	3/10
1801	5/8	5/8	6/0	5/4	1840	3/4	3/8	3/8	4/0
1802	5/0	5/0	5/4	5/4	1841	4/0	3/8	4/4	4/0
1803	4/8	4/8	5/0	5/0	1842	3/4	3/0	3/8	3/4
1804	4/6	4/10	4/8	5/0	1843	2/8	3/0	3/0	3/4
1805	4/4	4/6	4/6	4/4	1844	2/8	2/8	3/0	3/4
1806	4/8	4/10	4/10	4/10	1845	2/8	3/4	3/4	4/0
1807	4/8	4/8	5/0	5/0	1846	3/8	3/4	4/4	4/0
1808	4/6	5/0	4/8	5/0	1847	3/8	4/0	4/4	4/8
1809	5/0	5/8	5/0	5/4	1848	4/0	3/4	4/8	4/0
1810	5/8	5/8	5/4	5/8	1849	3/0	3/0	3/8	3/8
1811	5/8	5/8	5/8	5/8	1850	2/8	2/8	3/4	3/4
1812	6/0	6/0	6/0	6/0	1851	2/6	2/8	3/4	3/8
1813	6/4	6/4	6/4	6/4	1852	2/8	3/0	3/6	3/8
1814	6/4	5/8	7/0	6/0	1853	3/2	3/6	3/10	4/4
1815	5/4	4/6	5/4	4/8	1854	3/2	3/4	4/2	4/2
1816	4/0	4/0	4/8	4/8	1855	3/2	3/8	4/2	4/8
1817	3/8	3/8	4/8	4/0	1856	3/0	3/6	4/0	4/8
1818	4/4	4/4	4/8	5/0	1857	3/2	3/2	4/8	4/8
1819	4/10	4/10	5/8	5/8	1858	2/10	2/10	4/4	4/6
1820	4/10	4/6	5/4	5/4	1859	3/4	3/2	4/8	4/6
1821	4/0	3/8	4/8	4/0	1860	3/2	....	4/6	....
1822	2/10	2/6	3/4	3/6					

NOTE.—The above are the prices *per stone of 8 lbs.* The *pieces of beef* are two rounds, chucks, clods, and leg mutton pieces. The *pieces of mutton* are legs and loins ; the average quantity is about 32 stone per day. The extra quantity of mutton-fat is returned. The beef is delivered without bone, the weight of which was six stone and six pounds in making the 32 stone and 4 pounds of meat sent to the Hospital.

TABLE No. 11.

Showing the Amount of the Funded and Unfunded Debt of the United Kingdom since 1691: the Amount of Interest Payable Thereon, and Charges for Management.

Years.	Funded.	Unfunded.	Interest and Charge.	Years.	Funded.	Unfunded.	Interest and Charge.
	£	£	£		£	£	£
1691	......	3,130,000	232,000	1744	50,049,532	6,692,886	2,293,302
1692	......	3,310,547	230,000	1745	52,049,532	7,668.285	2,428,329
1693	......	5,902,839	507,101	1746	56,073,070	8,544,774	2,650,231
1694	1,200,000	5,534,297	818,298	1747	61,473,070	7,642,344	2,882,538
1695	1,200,000	7,236,846	887,192	1748	68,420,147	7,391,985	3,165,765
1696	1,200,000	10,379,178	1,086,971	1749	71,492,619	5,996,321	3,204,858
1697	1,200,000	13,322,925	1,322,519	1750	71,657,717	5,202,093	2,789,351
1698	3,200,000	12,245,416	1,468,511	1751	71,480,824	5,716.202	2,769,484
1699	3,200,000	10,599,355	1,423,539	1752	70,964,793	5,466,890	2,735,312
1700	3,200,000	9,407,080	1,252,080	1753	70,964,793	4,070,022	2,694,038
1701	3,200,000	9,352,486	1,219.147	1754	70,869,162	1,259,120	2,648,452
1702	3,200,000	9,567,225	1,215,324	1755	71,769,162	736,410	2,650.041
1703	3,200,000	9,125,779	1,158,460	1756	73,759,470	815,555	2,753,566
1704	3,200,000	9,163,474	1,234,010	1757	76,759,470	1,065,927	2,736,254
1705	3,200,000	8,935,351	1,210,051	1758	81,756,147	1,371,862	2,918,707
1706	3,864,263	8,523,767	1,443,568	1759	89,346,147	1,927,312	3,181,895
1707	5,064,263	10,180,036	1,590,630	1760	97,862,793	4,151,225	3,576,275
1708	5,064,263	10,454,143	1,722.472	1761	109,908,947	4,386,040	4,148.999
1709	7,239,291	11,694,048	1,921,477	1762	122,088,947	4,705,990	4,747,849
1710	7,239,291	14,096,354	2,064,829	1763	129,160,193	3,555,856	5,032,733
1711	11,770,061	10,628,364	2,274,377	1764	128,257,089	5,030,851	5,002,865
1712	25,569,559	9,353,129	3,034,078	1765	128,849,647	2,966.526	4,028,250
1713	26,078,085	8,621,762	3,004,287	1766	129,561,835	2,075,096	4.887,346
1714	27,820,321	8,355,139	3,063,135	1767	130,181,716	1,929,106	4,875,558
1715	29,617,622	7,805,612	3,114,625	1768	130,322,486	2,264,918	4,870,163
1716	29,493,388	8,425,080	3,167,616	1769	128,567,870	1,745,410	4,786,941
1717	32,702,786	7,605,471	3,144,293	1770	127,132.485	2,065,148	4,712,679
1718	34,766,199	5,613,485	2,965,889	1771	127,198,393	1,787,619	4,733,694
1719	37,462,943	4,409,298	2,822,370	1772	125,790.701	2,245,832	4,706,326
1720	49,844,890	4,134,818	2,846,434	1773	125,763,009	3,108,488	4,749,567
1721	49,811,752	4,593,393	2,855,380	1774	124,763,009	2,399.404	4,698,313
1722	49,920,899	4,281,467	2,807,584	1775	123,763,009	3,079,802	4.703,519
1723	48,551,160	4,445,830	2,728,080	1776	125,899,532	5.337,751	4,870,534
1724	48,132,895	5,190,675	2,727,317	1777	131,052,578	5,724,059	5,112,344
1725	48,107,625	4,131,452	2,717,589	1778	137,052,578	6,000,056	5,487,323
1726	49,093,295	3,757,502	2,739.628	1779	144,052,578	9,521,772	6,100,060
1727	47,993,125	4,530,798	2,360,934	1780	156,246,424	11,214,550	6,931,739
1728	47,711,205	4,249,371	2,306,462	1781	177,283,347	11,975.314	7,451,052
1729	47,824,639	3,716,581	2,292,150	1782	197,773,347	16,956,239	8,413,441
1730	46,824,639	4,005,671	2,227,127	1783	212,773,347	19,070,284	9,065,585
1731	47,024,639	3,714,147	2,219,986	1784	228,627,049	14,436,096	9,541,256
1732	46,116,947	3,719,691	2,189,391	1785	239,693,900	5,892,570	9,678,942
1733	45,116,947	3,611,150	2,153,405	1786	239,200,719	6,266,136	9,664,541
1734	45,094,147	3,727,269	2,136,147	1787	237,697,666	6,581,559	9,595,379
1735	45,094,147	3,853,942	2,141,600	1788	236,191,315	7,446,101	9,572,217
1736	44,680,947	3,743,704	2,108.793	1789	234,632,465	8,120,446	9,567,359
1737	43,680,947	3,550,352	2,057,073	1790	233,044,965	9,416,615	9,585,712
1738	42,962,486	3,535,014	2,025,898	1791	231,537,865	10,138,134	9,513,507
1739	42,962,486	3,651,397	2,030,884	1792	229,614,445	10,048 976	9,432,179
1740	42,949,562	4,173,017	2.051,572	1793	234.034,716	13,839,718	9,711,238
1741	42,949,562	5,432.877	2,099,950	1794	247,877,235	15,445,420	10,396,645
1742	45,454,516	6,392,807	2,157,136	1795	301,861,304	19,601,375	12,699,310
1743	47,254,516	5,946,473	2,181,586	1796	355,323,772	8,575,123	14,765,095

TABLE No. 11.—Continued.

SHOWING THE AMOUNT OF THE FUNDED AND UNFUNDED DEBT OF THE UNITED KINGDOM SINCE 1691: THE AMOUNT OF INTEREST PAYABLE THEREON, AND CHARGES FOR MANAGEMENT.

Years.	DEBT. Funded.	DEBT. Unfunded.	Interest and Charge.	Years.	DEBT. Funded.	DEBT. Unfunded.	Interest and Charge.
	£	£	£		£	£	£
1797	381,525,835	7,434,755	15,575,330	1829	771,251,932	25,547,600	29,067,658
1798	414,936,332	12,589,570	16,887,399	1830	757,486,997	27,317,000	28,325,936
1799	423,367,546	18,956,831	17,560,127	1831	755,543,884	27,172,800	28,329,986
1800	447,147,163	23,747,117	18,582,950	1832	754,100,549	27,357,050	28,351,318
1801	497,043,488	20,468,383	19,819,839	1833	751,658,883	28,071,496	28,481,181
1802	522,231,786	15,421,222	20,268,551	1834	743,675,300	29,559,101	28,517,236
1803	528,260,642	19,472,154	20,812,962	1835	758,549,866	30,114,335	29,135,811
1804	545,803,318	25,328,000	21,658,890	1836	761,422,571	28,074,325	29,667,464
1805	573,529,932	26,339,915	22,568,359	1837	762,275,189	25,253,925	29,537,333
1806	593,954,868	27,141,815	23,196,582	1838	761,347,690	25,492,475	29,432,903
1807	601,733,073	32,073,339	23,373,092	1839	766,547,685	20,683,375	29,385,451
1808	604,287,475	39,258,308	23,595,013	1840	766,371,726	22,272,675	29,415,924
1809	614,789,092	39,672,219	24,292,276	1841	772,530,760	19,678,925	29,462,030
1810	624,301,937	37,891,919	24,553,162	1842	773,068,341	18,689,475	29,300,112
1811	635,583,448	42,616,988	25,484,765	1843	772,169,093	20,495,650	29,047,473
1812	661,409,958	44,844,629	26,853,846	1844	769,193,644	18,793,550	28,272,652
1813	740,023,535	48,070,246	29,893,737	1845	766,672,822	18,442,400	28,125,113
1814	752,859,907	60,280.269	31,105,644	1846	764,608,284	18,369,400	28,025,253
1815	816,311,941	44,727,108	32,645,618	1847	772,401,851	17,974,500	28,442,683
1816	796,200,191	49,768.292	32,055,350	1848	774,022,638	17,794,700	28,307,343
1817	776,742,403	62,639,742	31,591,927	1849	773,168,316	17,758,700	28,091,579
1818	791,867,314	48,715,350	31,485,753	1850	769,272,562	17,756,600	28,025,523
1819	794,980,482	41,550.500	31,168,540	1851	765,126,582	17,742,800	27,907,068
1820	801,565,310	33,335,650	31,354,749	1852	761,622,704	17,742,500	27,842,286
1821	795,312,767	32,671,731	31,105,319	1853	755,311,701	16,024,100	27,597,645
1822	796,530,144	38,677,150	29,722,533	1854	753,073,849	16,008,700	27,715,203
1823	791,701,614	35,778,550	30,142,582	1855	752,064,119	23,151,400	27,363,889
1824	781,123,222	37,900,450	29,174,122	1856	775,730,994	28,182,700	28,444,274
1825	778,128,268	31,703.200	28,987,773	1857	780,119,722	27,989,000	28,550,039
1826	783,801,740	25,024,850	29,415,102	1758	779,225,495	25,911,500	28,401,950
1827	777,476,892	27,622.050	29,328,782	1859	786,801,154	18,277,400	28,204,299
1828	772,322,539	27,709,750	29,167,877				

NOTE.—From 1854 the financial year ends 31*st March* ; thus 1859 represents the year ending 31st March, 1859.

TABLE No. 12.

Showing the Quantity of Raw Cotton, in Pounds Weight, Imported into the United Kingdom from Each of the Producing Countries since 1815.

Years.	United States.	Brazil.	Mediterranean.	B. E. Indies, Singapore, and Ceylon.	B. W. Indies and British Guiana.	Other Countries.	Grand Total.
	lbs.	lbs.	lbs.	lbs.	lbs.	lbs.	lbs.
1815	54,407,299	13,104,267	30,466	7,175,243	15,341,197	10,650,674	100,709,146
1816	51,291,997	20,131,581	239,966	6,972,790	12,731,822	3,912,809	95,280,965
1817	60,695,293	16,338,861	44,532	31,007,570	9,743,605	8,473,828	126,303,689
1818	68,217,656	24,987,979	1,109,982	67,456,411	11,249,851	5,723,698	178,745,577
1819	62,412,654	20,860,865	186,864	58,856,261	7,050,753	1,785,757	151,153,154
1820	89,999,174	29,198,155	472,684	23,125,825	6,836,816	2,040,001	151,672,655
1821	93,470,745	19,535,786	1,131,567	8,827,107	7,138,980	2,432,435	132,536,620
1822	101,031,766	24,705,206	518,804	4,554,225	10,295,114	1,732,513	142,837,628
1823	142,532,112	23,514,641	1,492,413	14,839,117	7,034,793	1,989,427	191,402,503
1824	92,187,662	24,849,552	8,699,924	16,420,005	6,269,306	953,673	149,380,122
1825	139,908,699	33,180,491	22,698,075	20,005,872	8,193,948	4,018,206	228,005,291
1826	130,858,203	9,871,092	10,308,617	20,985,135	4,751,070	833,284	177,607,401
1827	216,924,812	20,716,162	5,372,562	20,930,542	7,165,881	1,338,950	272,448,909
1828	151,752,289	29,143,279	7,039,574	32,187,901	5,893,800	1,743,799	227,760,642
1829	157,187,396	28,878,386	6,049,597	24,857,800	4,640,414	1,153,818	222,767,411
1830	210,885,358	33,092,072	3,428,798	12,481,761	3,429,247	644,216	263,961,452
1831	219,333,628	31,695,761	8,460,559	25,805,153	2,401,685	978,067	288,674,853
1832	219,756,753	20,109,560	9,163,692	35,178,625	2,040,428	583,467	286,832,525
1833	237,506,758	28,463,821	1,020,268	32,755,164	2,084,862	1,825,964	303,656,837
1834	269,203,075	19,291,396	1,681,625	32,920,865	2,293,794	1,484,670	326,875,425
1835	284,455,812	24,986,409	8,451,630	41,429,011	1,815,270	2,564,831	363,702,963
1836	289,615,692	27,501,272	8,226,029	75,949,845	1,714,337	3,951,882	406,959,057
1837	320,651,716	20,940,145	9,326,979	51,532,072	1,595,702	3,240,169	407,286,783
1838	431,437,888	24,464,505	6,409,466	40,217,734	1,529,356	3,791,628	507,850,577
1839	311,597,798	16,971,979	6,429,671	47,172,939	1,248,164	5,976,008	389,396,559
1840	487,856,504	14,779,171	8,324,937	77,011,839	866,517	3,649,402	592,488,010
1841	358,240,964	16,671,348	9,097,180	97,388,153	1,533,197	5,061,513	487,992,355
1842	414,030,779	15,222,828	4,489,017	92,972,609	593,603	4,441,250	531,750,086
1843	574,738,520	18,675,123	9,674,076	65,709,729	1,260,444	3,135,224	673,193,116
1844	517,218,622	21,084,744	12,406,327	88,639,776	1,707,194	5,054,641	646,111,304
1845	626,650,412	20,157,633	14,614,699	58,437,426	1,394,447	725,336	721,979,953
1846	401,949,393	14,746,321	14,278,447	34,540,143	1,201,857	1,140,113	467,856,274
1847	364,599,291	19,966,922	4,814,268	83,934,614	793,933	598,587	474,707,615
1848	600,247,488	19,971,378	7,231,861	84,101,961	640,437	827,036	713,020,161
1849	634,504,050	30,738,133	17,369,843	70,838,515	944,307	1,074,164	755,469,012
1850	493,153,112	30,299,982	18,931,414	118,872,742	228,913	2,090,698	663,576,861
1851	596,638,962	19,339,164	16,950,525	122,626,976	446,529	1,377,653	757,379,749
1852	765,630,544	26,506,144	48,058,640	84,922,432	703,696	3,960,992	929,782,448
1853	658,451,796	24,190,628	28,353,575	181,848,160	350,428	2,084,162	895,278,749
1854	722,151,346	19,703,600	23,503,003	119,836,009	409,110	1,730,081	887,333,149
1855	681,629,424	24,577,952	32,904,153	145,179,216	468,452	6,992,755	891,751,952
1856	780,040,016	21,830,704	34,616,848	180,496,624	462,784	6,439,328	1,023,886,304
1857	654,758,048	29,910,832	24,882,144	250,338,144	1,443,568	7,986,160	969,318,896
1858	833,237,776	18,617,872	38,248,112	132,722,576	367,808	11,148,032	1,034,342,176
1859	961,707,264	22,478,960	38,106,096	192,330,880	592,256	10,773,616	1,225,989,072

TABLE No. 13.

SHOWING THE CROPS OF COTTON YIELDED BY EACH STATE OF THE UNITED STATES, IN BALES, FROM 1824 TO 1859 INCLUSIVE.

Years.	ATLANTIC STATES.						GULF STATES.				TOTAL.
	Georgia.	South Carolina.	North Carolina	Virginia.	Philadelphia & Baltimore, overland.	New York, per Erie Canal.	Florida.	Alabama.	New Orleans and Louisiana.	Texas.	United States.
	Bales.	Bales.	Bales.	Bales.	Bales.	Bales.	Bales.	Bales.	Bales.	Bales.	Bales.
1824	152,735	134,518					4,500	44,924	126,481		509,158
1825	138,000	97,000		46,000			3,000	58,796	200,453		569,249
1826	190,592	111,978		72,000			2,817	74,201	251,959		720,027
1827	233,920	179,810		88,480			4,163	89,707	336,870		957,281
1828	153,749	109,733		112,811			3,940	71,563	304,186		720,593
1829	249,166	168,275		77,422			4,146	79,958	264,249		870,415
1830	253,117	183,871	36,862	104,621			5,787	102,684	354,024		976,845
1831	230,502	185,166	36,540	35,500			13,073	113,186	426,485		1,038,847
1832	276,437	173,872	28,461	33,895			22,651	125,921	322,635		987,477
1833	271,925	181,876	30,358	37,500			23,641	128,366	403,443		1,070,438
1834	253,665	227,359	33,220	30,829			36,738	149,978	454,719		1,205,894
1835	222,670	203,166	34,399	44,725			52,085	197,692	511,146		1,254,328
1836	270,121	231,237	32,057	33,170			79,762	236,715	481,636		1,360,725
1837	262,971	196,377	13,004	29,197	5,137		83,703	232,243	600,877		1,422,930
1838	304,210	294,334	21,439	28,618	2,280		106,171	309,807	731,256		1,801,497
1839	205,112	210,171	11,136	32,000			75,177	251,742	584,994		1,360,532
1840	242,693	313,194	9,394	22,200			136,257	445,725	953,672		2,177,835
1841	148,947	227,400	7,865	23,650			93,552	320,701	814,680		1,634,945
1842	232,271	260,164	9,737	20,800			114,416	318,315	727,658		1,683,574
1843	299,491	351,658	9,039	19,013			161,088	481,714	1,060,246		2,378,875
1844	255,597	304,870	8,618	11,139			145,562	467,990	832,171		2,030,409
1845	295,440	426,361	12,487	14,500			189,693	517,196	929,126		2,394,503
1846	194,911	251,405	19,637	25,200			141,184	421,966	1,037,144		2,100,537
1847	242,789	350,200	6,061	13,282		797	127,852	323,462	705,979	27,008	1,778,651
1848	254,875	261,752	1,518	13,991		175	153,776	436,336	1,190,733	8,317	2,347,634
1849	391,372	458,117	10,041	8,952		640	200,186	518,706	1,093,797	39,742	2,728,596
1850	343,635	384,265	11,861	17,550	9,100	3,440	181,344	350,952	781,886	38,827	2,096,706
1851	322,376	387,075	12,928	11,500	8,990	1,061	181,204	451,748	933,639	31,263	2,355,257
1852	325,714	476,614	16,242	19,940	6,600	2,086	188,499	549,449	1,373,404	45,820	3,015,029
1853	349,490	463,203	23,496	20,820	12,129	2,022	179,476	545,029	1,580,875	64,052	3,262,882
1854	316,005	416,754	11,524	25,783	8,990		155,444	538,684	1,346,925	85,790	2,930,027
1855	378,694	499,272	26,139	21,936	2,732	3,363	136,597	454,595	1,232,644	110,325	2,847,339
1856	389,445	495,976	26,098	31,000	6,261	47,175	144,404	695,738	1,661,433	80,737	3,527,845
1857	322,111	397,331	27,147	20,468	12,129	2,022	136,344	503,177	1,435,000	116,078	2,939,519
1858	282,973	406,251	23,999	23,773	6,261	3,363	122,351	522,364	1,576,409	145,286	3,113,962
1859	475,788	480,653	37,482	33,011	38,146	47,175	173,484	704,406	1,669,274	192,062	3,851,481

Note.—Down to 1840 the seasons end 30th September, since then it has been 31st August, so that the year given as 1859 in the table is the year ending 31st August, 1859.

TABLE No. 14.

Showing the Average Weight of Cotton Bales Imported Annually into the United Kingdom since 1816.

Year	lbs.	Year	lbs.
1816	256	1838	350
1817	266	1839	348
1818	263	1840	365
1819	264	1841	365
1820	249	1842	379
1821	262	1843	382
1822	267	1844	383
1823	281	1845	386
1824	266	1846	386
1825	270	1847	377
1826	295	1848	395
1827	303	1849	396
1828	293	1850	392
1829	297	1851	399
1830	300	1852	392
1831	310	1853	398
1832	319	1854	408
1833	327	1855	396
1834	337	1856	414
1835	331	1857	404
1836	342	1858	420
1837	347	1859	421

TABLE No. 14.—Continued.

Showing the Average Weight of each description of Cotton Bale Imported Annually into the United Kingdom since 1850.

Years.	United States.	Brazil.	West India.	Egypt.	East India.	All Kinds.
	lbs.	lbs.	lbs.	lbs.	lbs.	lbs.
1850	423	182	210	245	383	392
1851	425	182	210	245	384	399
1852	418	180	210	250	385	392
1853	425	182	210	248	380	398
1854	430	182	210	295	383	408
1855	422	182	210	306	383	396
1856	445	181	175	308	385	414
1857	443	181	175	313	387	404
1858	445	181	180	355	387	420
1859	447	181	180	369	385	421

TABLE No. 15.

Showing the Crops of Cotton in the United States, in Bales, and their Distribution since 1827.

Years.	Total Crops †	Exported to Great Britain.	France.	Other Countries.	Total.	Consumption of United States North of Virginia.	Estimated Consumption in Cotton Growing States, viz. south & west of Virginia.	Stock on Hand.
	Bales.	Bales.	Bales.	Bales.	Bales.	Bales.	Bales.	Bales.
1826-7	957,281	646,139	157,952	49,707	853,798	103,483	..	..
1827-8	720,593	424,743	148,519	26,738	600,000	120,593	..	..
1828-9	870,415	489,001	184,821	66,178	740,000	104,853	..	..
1829-30	976,845	595,713	200,791	42,212	838,716	126,512	..	34,895
1830-1	1,038,847	618,718	127,029	27,036	772,783	182,142	..	119,423
1831-2	987,477	628,148	207,209	56,371	891,728	173,800	..	41,599
1832-3	1,070,438	630,145	207,517	29,793	867,455	194,412	..	48,205
1833-4	1,205,394	756,291	216,424	55,236	1,027,951	196,413	..	29,617
1834-5	1,254,328	722,718	252,470	48,311	1,023,499	216,888	..	41,623
1835-6	1,360,725	771,148	266,188	79,267	1,116,603	236,733	..	43,341
1836-7	1,422,930	850,786	260,722	56,917	1,168,425	222,540	..	75,820
1837-8	1,801,497	1,165,155	321,480	88,994	1,575,629	246,063	..	40,305
1838-9	1,360,532	798,418	242,243	34,028	1,074,689	276,018	..	52,244
1839-40*	2,177,835	1,246,791	447,465	181,747	1,876,003	295,193	..	58,442
1840-1	1,634,945	858,742	348,776	105,759	1,313,277	297,288	..	72,479
1841-2	1,683,574	935,631	398,129	131,487	1,465,247	267,850	..	31,807
1842-3	2,378,875	1,469,711	346,139	194,280	2,010,130	325,129	..	94,486
1843-4	2,030,409	1,202,498	282,685	144,307	1,629,490	346,744	60,000	159,772
1844-5	2,394,503	1,439,306	359,357	285,093	2,083,756	389,006	65,000	98,420
1845-6	2,100,537	1,102,369	359,703	204,720	1,666,792	422,597	70,000	107,122
1846-7	1,778,651	830,909	241,486	168,827	1,241,222	427,967	80,000	214,837
1847-8	2,347,634	1,324,265	279,172	254,824	1,858,261	531,772	75,000	171,468
1848-9	2,728,596	1,537,901	368,259	321,684	2,227,844	518,039	110,000	154,753
1849-50	2,096,706	1,106,771	289,627	193,757	1,590,155	487,769	107,500	167,930
1850-1	2,355,257	1,418,265	301,358	269,087	1,988,710	404,108	60,000	128,304
1851-2	3,015,029	1,668,749	421,375	353,522	2,443,646	603,029	75,000	91,176
1852-3	3,262,882	1,736,860	426,728	364,812	2,528,400	671,009	90,000	135,643
1853-4	2,930,027	1,603,750	374,058	341,340	2,319,148	610,571	105,000	135,603
1854-5	2,847,339	1,549,716	409,931	284,562	2,244,209	593,584	85,000	143,336
1855-6	3,527,845	1,921,386	480,637	552,583	2,954,606	652,739	117,500	64,171
1856-7	2,939,519	1,428,870	413,357	410,430	2,252,657	702,138	117,000	49,258
1857-8	3,113,962	1,809,966	384,002	396,487	2,590,455	452,185	125,000	102,926
1858-9	3,851,481	2,019,252	450,696	551,455	3,021,403	760,218	143,000	149,237

* Down to 1840 the Seasons end 30th September, but after that, the 31st August.
† The totals of the Crops here given do not include the quantity consumed south and west of Virginia.

TABLE No. 16.

Showing the Expansion of the Cotton Trade of Liverpool, in the Imports of the Raw Material, since 1785.

Years.	Bales.	Years.	Bales.	Years.	Bales.	Years.	Bales.
1785	5	1804	153,126	1823	578,303	1842	1,249,811
1786	6	1805	177,508	1824	447,083	1843	1,557,597
1787	108	1806	173,074	1825	706,316	1844	1,490,984
1788	....	1807	196,467	1826	489,204	1845	1,652,731
1789	....	1808	66,215	1827	756,296	1846	1,134,194
1790	....	1809	267,283	1828	630,245	1847	1,087,058
1791	68,404	1810	320,594	1829	640,998	1848	1,568,000
1792	72,364	1811	174,132	1830	793,605	1849	1,732,700
1793	24,971	1812	171,551	1831	791,582	1850	1,573,100
1794	38,022	1813	141,188	1832	779,071	1851	1,748,946
1795	54,841	1814	182,626	1833	840,953	1852	2,205,700
1796	63,526	1815	270,635	1834	841,474	1853	2,028,400
1797	58,258	1816	276,715	1835	970,717	1854	2,065,700
1798	66,934	1817	314,181	1836	1,023,587	1855	2,142,700
1799	89,784	1818	425,344	1837	1,036,005	1856	2,308,700
1800	92,580	1819	365,365	1838	1,328,415	1857	2,250,500
1801	98,752	1820	458,736	1839	1,019,229	1858	2,334,500
1802	135,192	1821	413,182	1840	1,415,341	1859	2,709,400
1803	140,291	1822	453,732	1841	1,164,269		

TABLE No. 17.

Showing the Quantity of Raw Cotton Imported into the United Kingdom from the British East Indies, in each year since 1783.

Years.	lbs.	Years.	lbs.	Years.	lbs.	Years.	lbs.
1783	114,133	1803	3,182,960	1823	13,487,250	1843	65,658,696
1784	11,440	1804	1,166,355	1824	16,420,005	1844	88,638,824
1785	99,455	1805	694,050	1825	20,005,872	1845	58,255,306
1786	....	1806	2,725,450	1826	20,985,135	1846	34,033,721
1787	....	1807	3,993,150	1827	20,930,542	1847	83,542,864
1788	....	1808	4,729,200	1828	32,187,901	1848	83,773,078
1789	4,973	1809	12,517,400	1829	24,857,800	1849	70,162,364
1790	422,207	1810	27,783,700	1830	12,481,761	1850	118,065,379
1791	3,351	1811	5,126,100	1831	25,805,153	1851	120,010,443
1792	....	1812	915,950	1832	35,178,625	1852	84,857,584
1793	729,634	1813	497,350	1833	32,706,453	1853	179,447,850
1794	239,245	1814	4,725,000	1834	32,906,752	1854	116,744,096
1795	197,412	1815	7,175,243	1835	41,190,201	1855	143,486,672
1796	609,850	1816	6,972,790	1836	75,618,344	1856	178,378,592
1797	912,844	1817	31,007,570	1837	51,075,562	1857	248,301,312
1798	1,752,784	1818	67,456,411	1838	40,217,613	1858	129,398,752
1799	6,712,622	1819	58,856,261	1839	46,994,253	1859	190,520,400
1800	6,629,822	1820	23,125,825	1840	*76,148,296		
1801	4,098,256	1821	8,827,107	1841	*97,008,199		
1802	2,679,483	1822	4,554,225	1842	*88,365,250		

* A considerable increase took place in the imports of cotton from India in 1840-1-2, in consequence of the China War.

TABLE No. 18.

Showing the Weight of Cotton in, and Value of, Goods Exported from the United Kingdom to the East Indies;* and the Total Weight and Value of Raw and Manufactured Cotton Exported from India since 1840.

EXPORTS OF COTTONS FROM GREAT BRITAIN TO INDIA.

Years.	Goods. Yards.	Goods. lbs.	Yarn and Twist. lbs.	Total Weight of Yarn. lbs.	Declared real Value. £
1840	145,083,799	27,203,212	16,013,708	43,216,920	3,873,186
1841	145,881,219	27,352,729	13,144,648	40,497,377	3,427,612
1842	155,506,914	29,157,546	12,050,839	41,208,385	3,060,472
1843	215,862,174	40,474,158	16,802,958	57,277,116	3,937,414
1844	239,493,471	44,905,026	22,084,132	66,989,158	4,793,192
1845	229,260,682	42,986,378	16,823,846	59,810,224	4,210,423
1846	231,694,439	43,442,707	24,193,923	67,636,630	4,341,885
1847	149,414,176	28,015,158	15,688,997	43,704,155	3,178,535
1848	185,375,540	34,757,914	17,991,526	52,749,440	3,037,871
1849	269,833,885	50,593,853	21,096,702	71,690,555	3,977,805
1850	284,537,862	53,350,849	20,303,013	73,653,862	4,708,813
1851	323,930,636	60,736,994	24,400,116	85,137,110	5,046,221
1852	312,473,351	58,588,753	23,049,210	81,637,963	4,707,120
1853	321,413,627	60,265,055	23,392,329	83,657,384	5,078,668
1854	478,750,717	89,765,759	25,094,439	114,860,198	6,560,236
1855	424,631,817	79,618,466	27,447,590	107,066,056	5,842,974
1856	423,304,389	79,369,573	23,085,680	102,455,253	5,857,445
1857	419,266,233	78,612,419	17,846,904	96,459,323	6,083,266
1858	728,671,215	136,625,853	34,205,199	170,831,052	10,335,076
1859	886,604,546	166,238,352	39,655,995	205,894,347	‡13,800,000

† EXPORTS OF COTTON FROM INDIA TO ALL PARTS.

Piece Goods. Pieces.	Piece Goods. lbs.	Raw Cotton. lbs.	Total Weight of Cotton. lbs.	Computed Real Value of Imports into United Kingdom. £
3,176,517	8,258,944	159,182,311	167,441,255	No official record for these years.
2,904,441	7,551,546	194,255,879	201,807,425	
2,675,190	6,955,494	189,910,980	196,866,474	
2,692,092	6,999,439	202,501,768	209,501,207	
2,437,236	6,336,813	164,477,317	170,814,130	
2,501,013	6,502,633	126,277,550	132,780,183	
2,929,578	7,616,902	169,080,831	176,697,733	
2,451,513	6,373,933	160,317,295	166,691,228	
2,071,752	5,386,555	168,631,466	174,018,021	
2,227,260	5,790,876	165,665,220	171,456,096	
1,912,953	4,973,677	226,473,683	231,447,360	
2,246,079	5,839,805	253,552,831	259,392,636	
2,667,120	6,934,512	262,908,174	269,842,686	
2,147,106	5,582,475	197,761,765	203,344,240	
2,285,841	5,943,186	173,780,192	179,723,378	1,798,421
2,197,707	5,714,038	237,180,049	242,894,087	2,327,528
2,464,629	6,408,035	319,653,524	326,061,559	3,597,752
2,316,075	6,021,795	260,354,052	266,375,847	5,519,669
....	....	217,861,572	....	2,951,936
....	....	....	....	....

* Ceylon and Singapore are included previous to 1649.

† The figures showing the exports of cotton and cotton piece goods from India are for the years ending 31st March. Thus, the year 1857 ends 31st March, 1858.

‡ The declared real value of cottons exported to India for 1859 is estimated.

TABLE No. 19.

Showing the Progress and Value of the Trade with India since 1827; with Special Reference to the Textiles and their Manufactures.

Years.	EXPORTS FROM THE UNITED KINGDOM TO INDIA.								IMPORTS INTO UNITED KINGDOM FROM INDIA.			
	COTTON.			WOOLLEN AND WORSTED.					RAW COTTON.		All other Articles.	Total.
	Manufactures. Declared Value.	Yarns. Quantity.	Yarns. Declared Value.	Stuffs. Quantity.	Stuffs. Declared Value.	Other Kinds. Declared Value.	Other Articles of all Kinds. Declared Value.	Total Declared Value.	Quantity.	Official Value.*	Official Value.	Official Value.*
	£	lbs.	£	Pieces.	£	£	£	£	lbs.	£	£	£
1827	1,396,146	3,063,556	273,990	13,742	28,304	282,719	1,680,853	3,662,012	20,930,542	671,031	2,982,966	3,653,997
1828	1,365,748	4,316,899	369,924	8,869	23,607	215,884	1,495,500	3,470,663	32,187,901	1,048,947	3,716,837	4,765,784
1829	1,237,704	2,836,825	192,706	6,621	15,251	198,907	1,388,133	3,032,701	24,857,800	791,208	3,725,797	4,517,005
1830	1,513,088	4,632,875	319,705	16,806	41,398	270,488	1,196,269	3,340,948	12,481,761	397,559	3,925,791	4,323,350
1831	1,118,711	6,127,723	436,745	10,737	32,817	212,681	1,028,757	2,829,711	25,805,153	852,582	3,754,526	4,607,108
1832	1,298,728	4,076,645	287,671	15,090	34,772	155,326	1,192,626	2,969,123	35,178,625	1,100,360	3,846,621	4,946,981
1833	1,122,550	4,483,394	309,105	28,771	67,823	196,088	1,169,158	2,864,724	32,755,164	1,062,023	3,484,121	4,546,144
1834	956,881	4,267,653	315,583	7,576	27,431	216,905	1,059,429	2,576,229	32,920,865	1,054,935	4,028,429	5,083,364
1835	1,368,954	5,399,762	432,821	9,672	24,033	192,222	1,174,662	3,192,692	41,429,011	1,337,152	3,657,744	4,994,896
1836	2,020,343	6,592,310	561,878	23,809	57,200	267,471	1,378,937	4,285,829	75,949,845	2,355,335	4,670,934	7,026,269
1837	1,558,693	8,478,021	602,293	16,520	41,335	184,425	1,226,229	3,612,975	51,532,072	1,611,362	5,472,941	7,084,303
1838	1,805,449	10,710,136	640,205	10,330	21,079	183,821	1,225,642	3,876,196	40,217,734	1,245,720	4,899,127	6,144,847
1839	2,314,754	10,613,915	690,916	33,241	63,041	128,008	1,552,888	4,748,607	47,172,939	1,488,115	5,453,762	6,941,877
1840	3,025,656	16,013,708	847,530	63,422	122,784	168,254	1,858,968	6,023,192	77,011,839	2,412,542	5,671,311	8,083,853
1841	2,766,630	13,144,648	660,982	55,952	108,377	162,710	1,896,301	5,595,000	97,388,153	3,035,784	7,447,369	10,483,153
1842	2,515,397	12,050,839	545,075	34,924	79,926	130,577	1,898,913	5,169,888	92,972,609	2,752,361	6,835,064	9,587,425
1843	3,230,576	16,802,958	706,838	78,720	205,364	172,930	2,088,811	6,404,519	65,709,729	2,021,166	7,054,316	9,075,482
1844	3,768,962	22,084,132	1,024,230	96,120	194,620	244,022	2,463,832	7,695,666	88,639,776	2,716,933	8,065,761	10,782,694
1845	3,371,207	16,823,846	839,216	41,086	86,452	230,028	2,176,875	6,703,778	58,437,426	1,780,800	9,336,661	11,117,461
1846	3,254,141	24,193,923	1,087,744	27,676	67,177	170,769	1,854,625	6,434,456	34,540,143	1,087,563	8,541,475	9,629,038
1847	2,434,082	15,688,997	744,453	23,949	50,094	192,881	2,048,595	5,470,105	83,934,614	2,560,063	9,051,983	11,612,046
1848	2,344,763	17,991,526	693,108	28,972	64,947	153,091	1,821,237	5,077,146	84,101,961	2,598,071	8,594,444	11,192,515
1849	3,501,891	22,193,700	874,947	36,901	73,785	152,000	2,200,621	6,303,274	70,838,515	2,171,461	10,252,840	12,424,301
1850	4,180,386	20,965,471	1,039,808	27,154	41,768	282,857	2,477,846	8,022,665	118,872,742	3,615,182	10,543,721	14,158,903
1851	4,415,182	25,734,668	1,213,449	30,840	43,294	272,608	1,862,063	7,806,596	122,626,976	3,757,114	11,212,561	14,969,675
1852	4,388,374	24,802,091	1,070,068	26,944	41,449	199,521	1,753,495	7,352,907	84,922,432	2,566,208	11,081,647	13,647,855
1853	4,511,805	25,472,070	1,168,264	38,065	68,445	226,954	2,210,227	8,185,695	181,848,160	5,422,420	11,410,061	16,832,481
1854	5,921,449	26,531,939	1,280,766	30,279	55,558	327,646	2,490,550	10,025,969	119,886,009	*1,685,193	*11,288,420	*12,973,613
1855	5,174,155	28,944,460	1,283,931	20,965	31,924	277,356	4,160,328	10,927,694	145,179,216	2,268,425	12,490,296	14,758,721
1856	5,509,050	25,244,086	1,175,785	45,765	82,297	238,218	4,802,089	11,807,439	180,496,624	3,572,329	15,801,195	19,373,524
1857	5,786,471	20,027,859	1,147,379	50,271	84,168	437,772	5,623,863	13,079,653	250,338,144	5,458,426	15,635,875	21,094,301
1858	9,389,429	36,782,583	1,969,227	78,114	121,385	489,789	6,314,022	18,283,852	132,722,576	2,970,518	14,436,667	17,407,185

NOTE.—The above figures include also "Ceylon and Singapore."   * The value of imports since 1854 is the "Computed Real Value" in lieu of "Official," as previously given.

TABLE No. 20.

Showing the Progress and Value of the Trade with China and Hong Kong in Each Year since 1827.

EXPORTS FROM THE UNITED KINGDOM TO CHINA AND HONG KONG.

Years.	COTTONS. Manufactures. Declared Value.	COTTONS. Yarn. Quantity.	COTTONS. Yarn. Declared Value.	WOOLLEN AND WORSTED. Stuffs. Quantity.	WOOLLEN AND WORSTED. Stuffs. Declared Value.	WOOLLEN AND WORSTED. Other Manufactures. Declared Value.	All other Articles. Declared Value.	Total. Declared Value.
	£	lbs.	£	Pieces.	£	£	£	£
1827	67,280	300	25	119,783	274,444	187,028	81,860	610,637
1828	72,277	232,320	20,420	178,426	405,674	212,738	74,810	785,919
1829	57,906	304,814	14,146	135,126	285,747	205,375	64,343	627,517
1830	49,486	309,120	13,581	169,470	311,223	163,270	27,490	565,050
1831	77,835	497,100	31,116	153,060	257,280	142,805	38,665	547,701
1832	31,742	240,000	14,708	162,126	259,027	207,075	33,104	545,656
1833	51,097	300,400	15,248	167,983	283,960	250,710	29,562	630,577
1834	165,238	952,440	56,839	69,560	167,050	416,005	40,060	845,192
1835	291,853	2,833,362	170,390	109,567	203,572	318,562	85,331	1,074,708
1836	370,461	3,158,870	212,933	121,379	251,920	407,668	83,406	1,326,388
1837	273,387	1,873,965	103,908	59,619	134,584	111,952	54,544	678,375
1838	522,857	3,851,365	217,047	127,436	184,025	225,737	54,690	1,204,356
1839	386,775	1,389,760	76,862	99,517	175,863	159,347	53,122	851,969
1840	288,389	1,774,350	88,748	64,248	103,825	60,317	32,919	524,198
1841	422,957	3,402,100	156,580	54,899	116,209	96,356	70,468	862,570
1842	470,349	5,774,796	245,965	62,491	107,318	39,362	106,387	969,381
1843	655,276	5,683,775	216,663	124,714	258,025	159,790	166,426	1,456,180
1844	1,457,794	3,399,074	117,853	170,034	345,103	220,325	164,542	2,305,617
1845	1,635,183	2,609,850	99,958	132,819	245,886	293,332	120,468	2,394,827
1846	1,024,662	5,367,828	221,856	105,975	211,779	227,890	105,252	1,791,439
1847	848,814	4,104,040	164,264	113,635	241,766	148,671	100,454	1,503,969
1848	808,822	4,572,276	142,423	131,381	267,514	112,398	114,802	1,445,959
1849	883,189	3,352,994	118,094	192,267	254,392	116,487	164,947	1,537,109
1850	894,346	3,116,176	126,569	107,030	179,856	224,941	148,433	1,574,145
1851	1,409,782	4,319,330	189,047	103,376	188,110	186,498	187,831	2,161,268
1852	1,651,814	6,688,552	253,507	125,611	223,210	211,267	163,801	2,503,599
1853	1,209,948	5,234,617	198,485	63,955	118,741	84,258	138,165	1,749,597
1854	501,527	3,614,709	139,293	44,640	88,203	68,756	202,937	1,000,716
1855	788,474	2,864,500	95,511	23,411	37,280	96,790	259,889	1,277,944
1856	1,333,941	5,775,620	210,294	56,563	103,769	164,873	403,246	2,216,123
1857	1,573,828	3,462,611	158,081	60,189	116,618	170,234	481,221	2,449,982
1858	1,823,822	6,231,991	266,336	75,683	150,695	240,018	395,576	2,876,447

IMPORTS INTO THE UNITED KINGDOM FROM CHINA AND HONG KONG.

TEA. Quantity.	TEA. Official Value.	SILK. Quantity.	SILK. Official Value.	All other Articles. Official Value.	Total. Official Value.
lbs.	£	lbs.	£	£	£
39,746,147	3,974,614	128,431	47,256	75,488	4,097,358
32,678,546	3,267,855	212,895	78,061	135,471	3,481,387
30,544,382	3,054,438	120,978	44,384	128,459	3,227,281
31,897,546	3,189,755	19,200	7,045	35,483	3,232,283
31,648,922	3,164,892	8,419	3,232	38,882	3,207,006
31,708,956	3,170,896	28,111	10,320	26,141	3,207,357
32,057,747	3,205,775	22,186	8,151	52,534	3,266,460
32,029,052	3,202,905	582,857	213,773	90,251	3,506,929
42,052,047	4,205,205	737,802	271,539	88,022	4,564,766
48,520,508	4,852,051	1,281,889	474,088	96,757	6,422,896
36,502,345	3,650,234	1,807,690	703,483	179,974	4,533,691
38,998,572	3,899,857	721,517	279,104	131,004	4,309,965
37,191,762	3,719,176	360,882	129,731	129,011	3,977,918
22,576,405	2,257,640	247,762	90,870	40,159	2,388,669
27,639,817	2,763,982	277,097	101,614	99,083	2,964,679
37,409,544	3,740,954	180,148	66,131	149,115	3,956,200
42,779,265	4,277,927	275,308	110,194	243,423	4,631,544
51,754,485	5,175,449	353,016	140,788	249,353	5,565,590
50,714,657	5,071,466	1,175,866	436,508	312,968	5,820,942
54,534,248	5,453,425	1,836,872	678,056	511,183	6,642,664
55,355,590	5,535,559	2,021,765	748,247	418,727	6,702,533
47,346,817	4,734,682	2,241,011	861,955	222,042	5,818,679
53,102,129	5,310,213	1,861,537	695,949	164,510	6,170,672
49,368,001	4,936,800	1,812,370	700,101	212,124	5,849,025
69,487,979	6,948,798	2,099,134	841,981	180,712	7,971,491
65,295,202	6,529,520	2,470,029	945,203	238,048	7,712,771
68,639,727	6,863,973	2,996,411	1,211,435	180,207	8,255,615
83,301,550	*5,879,892	4,952,889	*3,592,836	*162,312	*9,125,040
81,560,207	5,118,752	5,048,997	3,432,739	195,099	8,746,590
84,795,802	5,123,080	4,195,849	4,106,208	192,360	9,421,648
60,295,610	4,310,205	7,187,090	6,910,630	227,804	11,448,639
73,359,599	5,036,293	2,521,080	1,886,645	170,151	7,043,089

* From 1854 the value given above is the "Computed Real Value," in substitution for the "Official Value" as previously given.

TABLE No. 21.

Showing the Quantity of Raw Cotton Imported into the United Kingdom from several of the British Colonies and Possessions since 1831.

BRITISH WEST INDIES AND BRITISH GUIANA.

Years.	Antigua.	Barbados.	Dominica.	Grenada.	Jamaica.	Montserrat.	Nevis.	St. Christopher.	St. Lucia.	St. Vincent.	Tobago.	Trinidad.	Bahamas.	Bermudas.
	lbs.	lbs.	lbs.	lbs.	lbs.	lbs.	lbs.	lbs.	lbs.	lbs.	lbs.	lbs.	lbs.	lbs.
1831	336	333,405	....	141,038	78,197	....	....	....	224	49,576	....	37,985	183,794	9,966
1832	....	129,874	....	139,742	22,825	....	....	....	655	60,830	....	43,441	131,134	....
1833	....	244,882	....	117,716	26,448	....	....	....	56	61,655	....	87,434	113,047	....
1834	....	264,457	....	133,263	26,394	....	3,511	957	672	103,203	....	117,751	435,210	193
1835	....	216,802	....	125,099	53,912	....	1,329	541	....	59,889	....	107,552	86,347	....
1836	....	121,752	....	117,935	37,015	311	10,310	....	....	71,864	....	108,239	157,118	20,146
1837	....	107,811	....	118,554	58,144	1,266	14,116	273	....	58,519	....	91,512	107,056	172,044
1838	....	130,576	....	109,945	18,354	1,110	4,619	5,189	....	56,813	....	206,977	151,078	58,695
1839	81	118,229	131	82,434	116,705	1,786	1,307	723	....	43,615	....	171,958	89,788	4,069
1840	....	65,561	....	108,549	101,855	....	1,680	179	....	60,416	....	46,792	337,994	28
1841	....	99,032	....	61,776	90,820	1,219	170	12	....	49,622	....	213,107	925,751	....
1842	....	60,590	....	90,438	81,040	....	....	....	....	110,280	....	103,793	121,138	43,558
1843	....	196,493	....	58,157	35,289	....	....	....	....	31,369	....	222,096	592,144	103
1844	....	222,066	....	49,118	83,914	....	....	....	....	38,110	....	212,608	1,046,010	30,661
1845	....	227,653	....	30,596	68,013	....	....	....	....	28,099	....	102,752	824,181	....
1846	36,388	380,248	....	9,335	49,392	....	....	....	....	53,382	....	26,066	257,507	....
1847	....	203,062	....	8,429	47,005	....	....	....	....	22,984	....	4,088	54,826	....
1848	....	99,486	....	2,524	65,232	....	....	....	....	26,497	....	27,602	184,050	....
1849	....	75,952	....	2,027	95,843	....	84	154	....	21,130	....	47,915	461,539	422
1850	....	16,031	....	3,265	28,056	....	587	634	....	22,796	....	9,243	3,393	....
1851	566	86,948	1,738	24,715	93,647	112	560	1,008	....	42,687	....	28,767	8,532	....
1852	4,592	230,384	2,912	4,368	47,600	....	392	6,368	....	38,976	....	46,480	96,992	....
1853	3,997	118,051	2,310	13,104	11,879	....	2,850	2,576	....	34,870	....	41,971	....	....
1854	1,644	60,590	1,512	59,234	7,027	....	409	....	....	40,153	3,543	105,681	5,376	....
1855	....	79,321	819	38,898	....	....	....	....	....	17,102	....	58,509	114,685	....
1856	31,024	51,632	....	67,760	15,232	....	....	896	560	35,616	336	49,728	....	....
1857	....	28,000	....	42,336	448	....	....	....	....	69,328	....	77,280	1,113,392	....
1858	....	3,472	....	57,456	5,712	....	....	....	....	57,120	112	16,240	....	....

TABLE No. 21.—Continued.

Showing the Quantity of Raw Cotton Imported into the United Kingdom, from several of the British Colonies and Possessions, since 1831.

Years.	BRITISH WEST INDIES, &c.				Mauritius. Total.	BRITISH POSSESSIONS IN THE EAST INDIES.			Total of the Three Presidencies.	Ceylon.	Singapore.	Grand Total.
	Tortola.	Demerara.	Berbice.	Total.		Bengal Presidency.	Madras Presidency.	Bombay Presidency.				
	lbs.	lbs.	lbs.	lbs.	lbs.	lbs.	lbs.	lbs.	lbs.	lbs.	lbs.	lbs.
1831	33,361	979,720	554,083	2,401,685	....	No official records for these years.	No official records for these years.	No official records for these years.	25,805,153	....	....	28,206,838
1832	20,191	937,791	553,945	2,040,428	....				35,178,625	....	....	37,219,053
1833	5,957	952,744	474,923	2,084,862	....				32,706,453	3,037	45,674	34,840,026
1834	19,587	929,459	259,830	2,293,794	....				32,906,752	....	14,113	35,214,659
1835	9,068	702,931	445,297	1,815,270	39,579				41,190,201	238,810	....	43,283,860
1836	11,749	818,648	262,049	1,714,309	....				75,618,344	307,012	24,489	77,664,154
1837	7,952	704,039	289,349	1,582,534	45,125				51,075,562	440,842	15,668	53,159,731
1838	11,387	487,762	176,937	1,529,356	....				40,217,613	....	121	41,747,090
1839	5,056	409,586	141,739	1,248,164	49,313				46,994,253	....	178,686	48,470,416
1840	4,141	107,433	26,213	865,797	56				76,148,296	863,543	....	77,877,692
1841	802	83,285	3,154	1,532,117	....				97,008,199	339,454	40,500	98,920,270
1842	....	24,190	....	592,271	....				88,365,250	4,607,359	....	93,564,880
1843	....	7,998	73,340	1,260,444	171,024				65,658,696	....	51,033	67,141,197
1844	224	....	55,265	1,707,194	739				88,638,824	952	....	90,347,709
1845	....	42,898	39,370	1,394,447	275				58,255,306	182,120	....	59,832,148
1846	....	275,901	113,638	1,201,857	739				34,033,721	506,422	....	35,742,739
1847	....	348,681	104,858	793,933	....				83,542,864	391,750	....	84,728,547
1848	....	235,046	....	640,437	....				83,773,078	326,766	2,117	84,742,398
1849	....	239,480	....	944,307	1,785				70,162,364	675,934	217	71,784,607
1850	....	145,891	....	228,913	....	85,789	5,571,450	112,408,140	118,065,379	807,363	....	119,101,655
1851	....	157,596	....	446,529	2,098	1,175,940	6,460,782	112,373,721	120,010,443	2,616,519	14	123,075,603
1852	....	229,824	....	703,696	....	557,088	3,808,224	80,492,272	84,857,584	64,848	....	85,626,128
1853	....	117,986	....	350,428	....	7,660,242	12,718,114	159,069,494	179,447,850	1,817,642	582,668	182,193,558
1854	....	122,467	....	409,110	19,040	5,420,576	110,179,104	116,744,096	....	3,044,135	47,778	120,264,159
1855	....	155,166	....	468,452	82,432	1,144,416	6,310,528	137,089,292	143,486,672	1,692,544	....	145,730,100
1856	....	210,560	....	462,784	....	86,912	8,696,128	168,263,536	178,378,592	1,966,384	151,648	180,959,408
1857	....	112,224	....	1,443,568	1,713,712	1,418,928	17,245,424	228,521,328	248,301,312	2,036,832	....	253,495,424
1858	....	227,696	....	367,808	1,678,656	2,554,560	5,438,944	123,769,408	129,398,752	3,323,824	....	134,769,040
190,400												

TABLE No. 22.

Showing the Quantity of Raw Cotton Exported from the United Kingdom, and the Countries to which Exported, since 1827.

Years.	Russia.	Germany,	Holland.	Belgium.	Austrian Territories.	France.	Sardinia.	Sweden.	Norway.	Prussia.	Other Countries.	Total.
	lbs.	lbs.	lbs.	lbs.	lbs.	lbs.	lbs.	lbs.	lbs.	lbs.	lbs.	lbs.
1827	1,292,877	4,676,886	7,471,834			100,279		138,559	19,769	336,064	4,097,902	18,134,170
1828	2,073,773	3,995,678	8,200,394			55,263		19,874	24,873	244,632	2,782,289	17,396,776
1829	2,862,541	5,898,750	12,508,726			738,554		99,492	34,354	1,087,956	7,058,742	30,289,115
1830	1,766,431	1,501,997	4,233,826			66,943		20,205	25,885	303,951	615,738	8,534,976
1831	1,274,815	3,380,635	11,443,021			181,068		124,335	83,566	629,306	5,191,809	22,308,555
1832	2,119,440	4,980,424	lbs. 8,800,717	lbs.		17,119	"Not defined in these years, included in 'Other Countries.'"	13,884	22,638	904,685	1,169,033	18,027,940
1833	1,253,639	3,585,872	4,253,665	6,480,159		62,095			32,932	111,236	1,584,284	17,363,882
1834	2,687,511	6,705,353	7,075,235	3,730,326		1,101,827		17,498	89,275	383,866	2,581,072	24,461,963
1835	4,972,559	8,324,767	8,798,406	5,856,127		339,760		183,588	39,227	548,026	3,717,294	32,779,734
1836	3,330,565	9,225,395	9,003,135	5,913,935		167,312		58,214	134,899	677,711	3,228,597	31,739,763
1837	5,079,681	9,300,792	13,293,548	7,764,861		59,595		108,868	63,463	972,391	3,078,832	39,722,031
1838	6,724,597	7,216,555	8,285,998	4,554,222		155,770		48,814	58,282	623,171	2,977,060	30,644,469
1839	7,532,951	8,260,805	9,381,974	6,349,669		628,696		244,969	102,913	504,014	5,732,247	38,738,238
1840	5,760,991	11,870,137	7,362,977	4,984,589		231,668		104,226	85,433	1,213,243	7,059,965	38,673,229
1841	8,098,735	11,318,612	9,086,342	5,982,614		196,273		38,947	52,039	665,974	2,234,049	37,673,585
1842	10,874,752	9,896,656	8,995,504	4,018,000		623,056		67,984	123,984	1,254,736	9,396,576	45,251,248
1843	11,627,392	10,258,752	7,805,392	3,519,712		137,872		866,544	105,168	1,070,048	4,229,120	39,620,000
1844	15,070,384	11,857,216	7,286,160	5,296,592		142,912		1,476,496	162,624	651,392	5,278,784	47,222,560
1845	13,962,816	8,164,016	11,242,000	5,163,088		40,992		681,632	192,080	1,847,664	1,622,096	42,916,384
		Hanse Towns.										
1846	14,539,616	15,713,936	17,745,504	4,077,024	7,080,864	157,248	1,562,064	1,170,400	614,992	1,515,248	1,750,112	65,930,704
1847	21,894,658	16,376,488	14,057,647	7,671,109	6,993,202	344,721	1,721,726	2,795,701	470,446	2,007,486	562,160	74,954,336
1848	36,475,824	9,990,176	Hanover. 257,936	13,828,416	6,400,240	904,736	264,208	887,824	1,879,360	738,192	645,120	1,747,760	74,019,792
1849	39,483,476	18,435,935	813,504	18,532,522	8,111,538	5,048,983	1,274,588	2,450,867	1,373,285	535,944	2,082,978	749,888	98,893,508
1850	40,563,074	23,860,101	702,585	16,720,072	8,667,711	3,337,171	1,127,521	2,710,116	1,840,096	1,285,695	1,178,585	477,090	102,469,717
1851	35,185,422	27,473,011	1,214,060	22,119,146	12,856,447	1,366,099	1,365,456	2,742,283	2,434,657	1,742,118	1,576,013	1,905,682	111,980,394
1852	45,605,805	22,472,042	1,826,219	15,834,261	12,657,713	1,957,071	2,225,477	2,238,158	3,591,869	1,660,270	674,272	1,141,164	111,884,321
1853	48,937,392	33,417,440	985,824	28,676,592	18,466,672	3,830,288	2,403,968	3,860,864	4,414,368	1,301,888	1,143,296	1,131,088	148,569,680
1854	208,544	36,055,264	598,192	26,934,544	14,040,768	4,811,856	2,759,232	3,821,328	5,866,560	1,835,904	23,444,624	2,949,296	123,326,112
1855	...	36,509,088	1,848,336	24,089,408	10,172,288	4,984,448	7,289,520	2,938,544	6,463,856	2,161,304	26,348,672	1,557,696	124,368,160
1856	37,109,072	34,387,248	11,679,024	23,481,360	11,591,776	8,272,208	7,049,840	3,468,512	2,483,152	2,366,784	802,256	4,069,632	146,660,864
1857	31,254,608	20,944,336	13,754,160	26,103,616	8,030,848	7,953,568	9,699,200	2,803,808	2,194,640	1,698,704	5,325,600	2,164,512	131,927,600
1858	48,093,696	27,977,376	14,165,984	19,111,344	12,216,064	6,237,840	5,261,200	537,936	4,329,808	2,464,224	7,751,184	1,462,944	149,609,600

TABLE No. 23.

SHOWING THE QUANTITIES AND VALUE OF EACH DESCRIPTION OF BRITISH COTTON MANUFACTURES EXPORTED FROM THE UNITED KINGDOM, FROM 1820 TO 1852.

Years.	White or Plain Cottons. Yards.	Declared Value.	Printed or Dyed Cottons. Yards.	Declared Value.	Hosiery & Small Wares. Declared Value.	Twist and Yarn. lbs.	Declared Value.	All Cotton Manufactures Declared Value.
1820	113,682,486	5,451,024	134,688,144	7,742,505	496,580	23,032,325	2,826,639	16,516,748
1821	122,921,692	5,713,722	146,412,002	7,454,243	619,999	21,526,369	2,305,823	16,093,787
1822	151,162,131	6,317,973	150,999,157	7,480,634	722,535	26,595,468	2,697,582	17,218,724
1823	152,184,705	5,884,935	149,631,387	7,095,709	720,014	27,378,986	2,625,946	16,326,604
1824	170,091,384	6,437,817	174,559,749	8,010,438	869,336	33,605,510	3,135,396	18,452,987
1825	158,039,786	6,027,892	178,426,912	8,205,117	919,788	32,641,604	3,206,729	18,359,526
1826	138,159,783	4,477,942	128,897,111	5,388,592	735,497	42,189,661	3,491,338	14,093,369
1827	183,940,186	5,762,576	181,544,618	7,184,459	1,144,552	44,878,774	3,545,578	17,637,165
1828	189,475,956	5,623,802	173,852,475	6,859,447	1,165,763	50,505,751	3,595,405	17,244,417
1829	222,550,344	5,853,625	180,012,152	6,662,623	1,041,884	61,441,251	3,976,874	17,535,006
1830	244,799,032	6,562,397	199,799,466	7,557,373	1,175,153	64,645,342	4,133,741	19,428,664
1831	239,191,261	6,065,478	182,194,032	6,098,035	1,118,672	63,821,440	3,975,019	17,257,204
1832	259,493,096	5,854,924	201,552,407	5,645,706	1,175,003	75,667,150	4,722,759	17,398,392
1833	259,519,864	5,847,840	236,832,232	6,603,220	1,331,317	70,626,161	4,704,024	18,486,401
1834	283,950,158	6,514,173	271,755,651	7,613,179	1,175,219	76,478,468	5,211,015	20,513,586
1835	277,704,525	6,910,506	279,811,176	8,270,925	1,240,284	83,214,198	5,706,589	22,128,304
1836	321,467,179	7,985,349	313,200,448	9,197,818	1,328,525	88,191,046	6,120,366	24,632,058
1837	286,164,256	6,085,789	245,209,407	6,642,200	912,192	103,455,138	6,955,942	20,596,123
1838	363,357,845	7,293,831	326,719,777	8,260,902	1,161,124	114,596,602	7,431,869	24,147,726
1839	380,168,656	7,535,799	351,281,467	8,842,646	1,313,737	105,686,442	6,858,193	24,550,375
1840	433,114,373	7,833,772	357,517,624	8,498,448	1,265,090	118,470,223	7,101,308	24,668,618
1841	421,884,732	7,213,075	329,240,892	7,772,735	1,246,700	123,226,519	7,266,968	23,499,478
1842	435,519,311	6,590,945	298,579,498	6,296,275	1,020,664	137,466,892	7,771,464	21,679,348
1843	562,575,205	8,024,287	356,065,000	7,144,177	1,085,536	140,321,176	7,193,971	23,447,971
1844	643,249,423	9,346,865	403,421,400	8,265,281	1,204,618	138,540,079	6,988,584	25,805,348
1845	678,415,780	9,661,014	413,270,289	8,368,794	1,126,288	135,144,865	6,963,235	26,119,331
1846	697,809,454	9,354,268	367,651,135	7,347,364	1,016,146	161,892,750	7,882,048	25,599,826
1847	541,143,488	8,057,815	401,396,672	8,149,288	1,168,142	120,270,741	5,957,980	23,333,225
1848	651,087,785	7,929,341	445,664,038	7,781,516	1,042,512	135,831,162	5,927,831	22,681,200
1849	795,112,525	9,817,721	542,423,591	9,337,243	1,276,082	149,502,281	6,704,089	26,775,135
1850	767,654,346	9,817,197	590,528,595	10,713,238	1,343,262	131,870,368	6,383,704	28,257,401
1851	963,489,894	11,725,538	579,671,895	10,323,664	1,405,608	143,966,106	6,634,026	30,088,836
1852	950,631,298	11,526,244	573,625,616	10,122,214	1,574,974	145,478,302	6,654,655	29,878,087

Note.—Since 1852 the accounts have been kept in another and more detailed form, and the continuation, therefore, will be found in Table No. 24,

TABLE No. 24.

Showing the Quantities and Value of British Cotton Manufactures (detailing each primary description), Exported from the United Kingdom since 1853.

Years.	CALICOES. White or Plain.	CALICOES. Dyed or Printed	CAMBRICS & MUSLINS. White or Plain.	CAMBRICS & MUSLINS. Dyed or Printed	Twist and Yarn.	Sewing Thread.	Fustians and Velvets.	Mixed Stuffs.	Stockings.
	Yards.	Yards.	Yards.	Yards.	lbs.	lbs.	Yards.	Yards.	Dozen Pairs.
1853	924,821,703	650,626,668	6,650,057	2,628,678	147,539,302	4,885,322	5,108,747	4,756,806	1,353,447
1854	1,089,861,773	583,539,736	9,263,536	3,003,915	147,128,498	4,622,404	4,884,249	2,345,913	950,766
1855	932,467,158	686,501,068	8,496,932	2,476,488	165,493,598	4,855,869	5,238,860	2,553,519	552,947
1856	1,211,281,686	803,132,156	6,063,034	3,261,667	181,495,805	5,371,643	7,544,870	3,992,056	1,009,839
1857	1,147,988,589	808,308,602	6,910,075	4,849,219	176,821,338	4,404,705	6,227,384	5,686,911	1,015,960
1858	1,517,308,665	785,666,473	7,277,370	3,952,534	200,016,902	4,517,730	7,335,580	2,598,463	498,133

TABLE No. 24.—Continued.

Years.	Hosiery and Small Wares. Entered at Value only.	Counterpanes. Entered at Value only.	Lace and Patent Net. Entered at Value only.	VALUE Yarn.	Thread.*	Calicoes, Cambrics, &c.	Other Ware.	Grand Total.
	£	£	£	£	£	£	£	£
1853	238,025	65,835	596,554	6,895,653	553,535	23,559,304	1,704,410	32,712,902
1854	189,091	43,367	514,413	6,691,330	524,241	23,212,568	1,317,718	31,745,857
1855	211,705	32,628	470,538	7,200,395	556,211	25,845,914	1,176,621	34,779,141
1856	325,403	41,424	424,778	8,028,575	582,410	28,133,998	1,487,758	38,232,741
1857	382,535	41,402	400,336	8,700,589	495,633	28,380,996	1,496,202	39,073,420
1858	269,848	34,359	389,438	9,579,479	525,970	31,672,566	1,223,307	43,011,322

Note.—This data for the earlier period may be found in the anterior Table No. 23.

* Sewing thread was previously included with "Hosiery and Small Ware."

TABLE No. 26.

Showing the Quantity of Cotton, Wool, Silk, Flax, and Hemp Imported into the United Kingdom since 1820.

Years.	Cotton.	Wool.	Silk.	Flax.	Hemp.
	lbs.	lbs.	lbs.	lbs.	lbs.
1820	151,672,655	9,775,605	2,641,866	42,827,568	47,730,256
1821	132,536,620	16,622,567	2,542,195	55,838,048	28,649,376
1822	142,837,628	19,058,080	2,680,568	68,331,872	69,042,848
1823	191,402,503	19,366,725	2,880,634	62,040,944	74,719,792
1824	149,380,122	22,564,485	3,477,648	83,163,472	64,056,832
1825	228,005,291	43,816,966	3,894,770	118,186,096	66,649,968
1826	177,607,401	15,989,112	2,665,225	77,125,664	54,804,960
1827	272,448,909	29,115,341	3,610,727	101,592,848	64,220,016
1828	227,760,642	30,236,059	4,765,241	98,133,168	56,461,440
1829	222,767,411	21,516,649	3,805,933	103,268,480	41,992,496
1830	263,961,452	32,305,314	4,318,181	105,738,752	56,758,352
1831	288,674,853	31,652,029	4,621,874	104,878,032	59,451,840
1832	286,832,525	28,128,973	4,224,897	110,041,792	66,479,168
1833	303,656,837	38,046,087	3,663,679	126,518,896	59,075,408
1834	326,875,425	46,455,232	4,848,612	90,912,864	75,466,720
1835	363,702,963	42,174,532	5,375,327	82,971,168	77,006,608
1836	406,959,057	64,239,977	6,458,030	171,260,992	65,635,584
1837	407,286,783	48,379,708	5,320,965	112,096,880	86,645,552
1838	507,850,577	52,594,355	4,669,484	182,142,912	81,802,112
1839	389,396,559	57,379,923	5,014,006	137,054,512	111,517,616
1840	592,488,010	49,436,284	4,748,836	140,362,880	76,615,616
1841	487,992,355	56,170,974	4,966,098	150,846,416	73,042,480
1842	531,750,086	45,881,639	5,785,507	128,325,008	65,621,360
1843	673,193,116	49,243,093	5,347,776	160,960,800	82,403,216
1844	646,111,304	65,713,761	6,300,173	177,351,328	102,282,096
1845	721,979,953	76,813,855	6,328,159	158,852,176	104,367,200
1846	467,856,274	65,255,462	5,735,338	128,474,304	98,884,128
1847	474,707,615	62,592,598	5,598,747	117,833,968	90,895,280
1848	713,020,161	70,864,847	6,588,755	163,930,032	94,726,352
1849	755,469,012	76,768,647	7,034,977	202,347,376	118,932,016
1850	663,576,861	74,326,778	7,159,176	204,166,816	117,447,120
1851	757,379,749	83,311,975	6,597,178	133,748,608	144,862,144
1852	929,782,448	93,761,458	8,015,211	157,775,968	119,633,360
1853	895,278,749	119,396,449	9,436,433	210,937,888	141,438,416
1854	887,333,149	106,121,995	10,739,053	145,962,320	137,531,968
1855	891,751,952	99,300,446	8,904,648	144,864,720	145,541,088
1856	1,023,886,304	116,211,392	10,251,926	188,948,592	171,105,312
1857	969,318,896	129,749,898	15,035,027	209,020,000	161,099,904
1858	1,034,342,176	126,738,723	8,513,525	143,797,360	183,496,320
1859	1,225,989,072	133,284,634	12,578,849	160,388,144	241,917,760

TABLE No. 27.
SHOWING THE QUANTITY OF RAW COTTON IMPORTED INTO THE UNITED KINGDOM FROM EACH SOURCE, IN BALES, SINCE 1801.

Years.	United States.	Brazil.	East Indies.	Egypt.	West India, &c.	Total.
	Bales.	Bales.	Bales.	Bales.	Bales.	Bales.
1801	86,360	Not defined.	14,610	....	Not defined.	260,485
1802	107,494	74,720	8,535	....	90,634	281,383
1803	106,831	76,297	10,296	....	45,474	238,898
1804	104,103	48,588	3,561	....	86,358	242,610
1805	124,279	51,251	1,983	....	75,116	252,629
1806	124,939	51,934	7,787	....	77,978	261,738
1807	171,267	18,981	11,409	....	81,010	282,667
1808	37,672	50,442	12,512	....	67,512	168,138
1809	160.180	140,927	35,764	....	103,511	440,382
1810	246,759	142,846	79,382	....	92,186	561,173
1811	128,192	118,514	14,646	....	64,879	326,231
1812	95,331	98,704	2,607	....	64,563	261,205
1813	37,720	137,168	1,429	....	73,219	249,536
1814	48,853	150,930	13,048	....	74,800	287,631
1815	203,051	91,055	22,357	....	52,840	369,303
1816	166,077	123,450	30,670	....	49,235	369,432
1817	199,669	114,518	120,202	....	44,872	479,261
1818	207,580	162,499	247,659	....	50,991	668,729
1819	205,161	125,415	184,259	....	31,300	546,135
1820	302,395	180,086	57,923	....	31,247	571,651
1821	300,070	121,085	30,095	....	40,428	491,678
1822	329,906	143,505	19,263	....	40,770	533,444
1823	452,538	144,611	38,393	5,623	27,632	668,797
1824	282,371	143,310	50,852	38,022	25,537	540,092
1825	423,446	193,942	60,484	111,023	31,988	820,883
1826	395,852	55,590	64,699	47,621	18,188	581,950
1827	646,776	120,111	73,738	22,450	30,988	894,063
1828	444,390	167,362	84,855	32,889	20,056	749,552
1829	463,076	159,536	80,489	24,739	18,867	746,707
1830	618,527	191,468	35,019	14,752	11,721	871,487
1831	608,887	168,288	76,764	38,124	11,304	903,367
1832	628,766	114,585	109,298	41,183	8,490	902,322
1833	654,786	163,193	94,698	3,893	13,646	930,216
1834	733,528	103,646	89,098	7,277	17,485	951,034
1835	763,199	143,572	117,965	43,721	22,796	1,091,253
1836	764,707	148,715	219,493	34,953	33,506	1,201,374
1837	844,812	117,005	145,174	41,193	27,791	1,175,975
1838	1,124,800	137,500	107,200	29,700	29,400	1,428,600
1839	814,500	99,300	132,900	33,500	36,000	1,116,200
1840	1,237,500	85,300	216,400	38,000	22,300	1,599,500
1841	902,500	94,300	273,600	40,700	32,900	1,344,000
1842	1,013,400	87,100	255,500	19,600	17,300	1,392,900
1843	1,396,800	98,700	182,100	48,800	17,700	1,744,100
1844	1,246,900	112,900	237,600	66,700	17,500	1,681,600
1845	1,499,600	110,200	155,100	82,000	8,800	1,855,700
1846	932,000	84,000	49,500	59,600	9,000	1,134,100
1847	874,100	110,200	222,800	20,700	4,900	1,232,700
1848	1,375,400	100,200	227,500	29,000	7,900	1,740,000
1849	1,477,700	163,800	182,200	72,600	9,100	1,905,400
1850	1,184,200	171,800	307,900	79,700	5,700	1,749,300
1851	1,393,700	108,700	328,800	67,400	4,900	1,903,500
1852	1,789,100	144,200	221,500	189,900	12,600	2,357,300
1853	1,532,000	132,400	485,300	105,400	9,100	2,264,200
1854	1,665,800	106,900	308,300	81,100	10,400	2,172,500
1855	1,623,600	134,700	396,100	114,800	8,900	2,278,100
1856	1,758,300	121,600	463,000	113,000	11,400	2,468,200
1857	1,482,000	168,900	680,500	75,900	11,300	2,418,600
1858	1,863,300	106,200	361,000	105,600	6,500	2,442,600
1859	2,086,300	124,900	510,700	101,400	6,800	2,830,100

TABLE No. 28.

Showing the Progress in the Demand for, and Supply of Raw Cotton in Europe and the United States, Quinquennially, in Bales, since 1827-8.

CONSUMPTION.

Years.	United States.*	Years.	Europe.	Total.	Rate of Increase.
	Bales.		Bales.	Bales.	
1827-8	121,000	1828	1,104,000	1,225,000	
1828-9	119,000	1829	1,219,000	1,338,000	
1829-30	127,000	1830	1,200,000	1,327,000	
1830-1	182,000	1831	1,305,000	1,487,000	
1831-2	174,000	1832	1,360,000	1,534,000	
1832-3	194,000	1833	1,350,000	1,544,000	
1833-4	196,000	1834	1,410,000	1,606,000	
1834-5	217,000	1835	1,475,000	1,692,000	4·812 o/o yearly
1835-6	237,000	1836	1,680,000	1,917,000	
1836-7	223,000	1837	1,760,000	1,983,000	
1837-8	246,000	1838	2,000,000	2,246,000	
1838-9	276,000	1839	1,708,000	1,984,000	
1839-40	295,000	1840	2,300,000	2,595,000	6·315 o/o yearly
1840-1	297,000	1841	2,285,000	2,582,000	
1841-2	267,000	1842	2,200,000	2,467,000	
1842-3	325,000	1843	2,450,000	2,775,000	
1843-4	347,000	1844	2,500,000	2,847,000	
1844-5	389,000	1845	2,356,000	2,745,000	2·300 o/o yearly
1845-6	423,000	1846	2,341,000	2,764,000	
1846-7	428,000	1847	1,745,000	2,173,000	
1847-8	532,000	1848	2,159,000	2,691,000	
1848-9	518,000	1849	2,477,000	2,995,000	
1849-50	488,000	1850	2,451,000	2,939,000	2·918 o/o yearly
1850-1	404,000	1851	2,618,000	3,022,000	
1851-2	603,000	1852	3,112,000	3,715,000	
1852-3	671,000	1853	3,013,000	3,684,000	
1853-4	610,000	1854	3,116,000	3,726,000	
1854-5	593,000	1855	3,316,000	3,909,000	4·850 o/o yearly
1855-6	694,000	1856	3,673,000	4,367,000	
1856-7	702,000	1857	3,079,000	3,781,000	
1857-8	452,000	1858	3,515,000	3,967,000	4·886 o/o yearly
1858-9	760,000	1859	3,821,000	4,581,000	

SUPPLY.

Years.	Crops of the United States.*	Years.	Other Imports into Europe.	Total.	Rate of Increase.
	Bales.		Bales.	Bales.	
1827-8	721,000	1828	444,000	1,165,000	
1828-9	870,000	1829	425,000	1,295,000	
1829-30	977,000	1830	423,000	1,400,000	
1830-1	1,039,000	1831	473,000	1,512,000	
1831-2	987,000	1832	466,000	1,453,000	
1832-3	1,070,000	1833	472,000	1,542,000	
1833-4	1,205,000	1834	371,000	1,576,000	
1834-5	1,254,000	1835	551,000	1,805,000	5·796 o/o yearly
1835-6	1,361,000	1836	755,000	2,116,000	
1836-7	1,423,000	1837	584,000	2,007,000	
1837-8	1,801,000	1838	533,000	2,334,000	
1838-9	1,361,000	1839	471,000	1,832,000	
1839-40	2,178,000	1840	473,000	2,651,000	4·456 o/o yearly
1840-1	1,635,000	1841	569,000	2,204,000	
1841-2	1,684,000	1842	545,000	2,229,000	
1842-3	2,379,000	1843	509,000	2,888,000	
1843-4	2,030,000	1844	511,000	2,541,000	
1844-5	2,395,000	1845	461,000	2,856,000	2·878 o/o yearly
1845-6	2,101,000	1846	319,000	2,420,000	
1846-7	1,779,000	1847	481,000	2,260,000	
1847-8	2,348,000	1848	401,000	2,749,000	
1848-9	2,729,000	1849	538,000	3,267,000	
1849-50	2,097,000	1850	747,000	2,844,000	3·834 o/o yearly
1850-1	2,355,000	1851	680,000	3,035,000	
1851-2	3,015,000	1852	739,000	3,754,000	
1852-3	3,263,000	1853	882,000	4,145,000	
1853-4	2,930,000	1854	630,000	3,560,000	
1854-5	2,847,000	1855	783,000	3,630,000	4·757 o/o yearly
1855-6	3,529,000	1856	843,000	4,372,000	
1856-7	2,940,000	1857	1,096,000	4,036,000	
1857-8	3,114,000	1858	717,600	3,831,600	3·073 o/o yearly
1858-9	3,851,000	1859	700,000	4,551,000	

Note.—The figures in this Table differ somewhat from those given in Table No. 15, in respect of the Statistics of the United States; the information in the two Tables is received from different sources,—the result of distinct estimates.
* The consumption in the cotton growing states of the United States is not included; nor is the quantity so consumed included in the United States' Crops.

TABLE No. 29.

Showing the Monthly Average Price of Fair Upland Bowed Cotton in the Liverpool Market in Each Year since 1826.

	1826.	1827.	1828.	1829.	1830.	1831.	1832.	1833.	1834.	1835.	1836.	1837.	1838.	1839.	1840.	1841.	1842.
January	$7\frac{5}{8}$	7	$5\frac{5}{8}$	$6\frac{1}{4}$	$6\frac{1}{8}$	$6\frac{1}{4}$	$5\frac{7}{8}$	$7\frac{1}{4}$	$8\frac{1}{4}$	$9\frac{3}{4}$	$9\frac{3}{4}$	$10\frac{3}{8}$	8	$8\frac{3}{8}$	$6\frac{3}{4}$	$6\frac{3}{4}$	$5\frac{3}{4}$
February	$7\frac{1}{4}$	$6\frac{7}{8}$	$5\frac{1}{2}$	$5\frac{7}{8}$	$6\frac{20}{1}$	$6\frac{1}{8}$	$6\frac{1}{8}$	$7\frac{1}{4}$	$8\frac{1}{2}$	10	$10\frac{1}{4}$	$8\frac{7}{8}$	$7\frac{1}{2}$	$8\frac{1}{2}$	$6\frac{1}{4}$	7	$5\frac{5}{8}$
March	$7\frac{1}{4}$	$6\frac{5}{8}$	$5\frac{1}{2}$	$5\frac{3}{4}$	$6\frac{5}{8}$	6	$6\frac{5}{8}$	$7\frac{1}{4}$	$8\frac{5}{8}$	$10\frac{1}{4}$	$10\frac{3}{4}$	7	7	$8\frac{7}{8}$	$6\frac{1}{4}$	$7\frac{1}{8}$	$5\frac{5}{8}$
April	$6\frac{7}{8}$	$6\frac{3}{8}$	$6\frac{1}{4}$	$5\frac{5}{8}$	7	6	$6\frac{3}{8}$	$7\frac{1}{4}$	$8\frac{1}{2}$	$10\frac{3}{4}$	$11\frac{3}{8}$	$7\frac{1}{8}$	$6\frac{3}{4}$	9	$6\frac{3}{8}$	7	$5\frac{5}{8}$
May	$6\frac{7}{8}$	$6\frac{1}{4}$	$6\frac{1}{4}$	$5\frac{1}{2}$	$6\frac{7}{8}$	$5\frac{7}{8}$	$6\frac{1}{2}$	$7\frac{1}{4}$	$8\frac{1}{2}$	$11\frac{1}{4}$	11	$6\frac{3}{8}$	7	$8\frac{5}{8}$	$6\frac{1}{8}$	$6\frac{3}{4}$	$5\frac{5}{8}$
June	$6\frac{7}{8}$	$6\frac{3}{8}$	$6\frac{1}{2}$	$5\frac{5}{8}$	$6\frac{5}{8}$	$5\frac{3}{4}$	$6\frac{1}{2}$	$7\frac{7}{8}$	$8\frac{3}{4}$	$11\frac{1}{4}$	$10\frac{3}{4}$	$6\frac{1}{4}$	7	$8\frac{3}{8}$	6	$6\frac{1}{2}$	$5\frac{5}{8}$
July	$6\frac{5}{8}$	$6\frac{1}{8}$	$6\frac{1}{2}$	$5\frac{1}{4}$	$7\frac{1}{8}$	$5\frac{1}{2}$	$6\frac{3}{8}$	9	$8\frac{3}{4}$	$11\frac{1}{4}$	$10\frac{1}{2}$	$6\frac{1}{4}$	$6\frac{7}{8}$	$7\frac{1}{4}$	6	$6\frac{3}{8}$	$5\frac{1}{2}$
August	$6\frac{1}{4}$	$6\frac{1}{8}$	$6\frac{3}{8}$	$5\frac{1}{2}$	$7\frac{1}{8}$	$5\frac{1}{2}$	$6\frac{3}{8}$	$10\frac{1}{4}$	$8\frac{3}{4}$	$10\frac{3}{4}$	$10\frac{1}{2}$	$6\frac{3}{8}$	$6\frac{3}{4}$	$7\frac{1}{8}$	6	$6\frac{1}{4}$	$5\frac{1}{2}$
September	$6\frac{1}{2}$	$6\frac{1}{8}$	$6\frac{1}{4}$	$5\frac{1}{2}$	7	$5\frac{3}{8}$	$7\frac{1}{4}$	$10\frac{1}{4}$	9	$10\frac{3}{4}$	$10\frac{1}{2}$	$7\frac{1}{8}$	$6\frac{3}{4}$	7	6	$6\frac{1}{8}$	$5\frac{3}{8}$
October	$6\frac{3}{4}$	6	$6\frac{5}{8}$	$5\frac{5}{8}$	7	$5\frac{3}{8}$	$7\frac{1}{2}$	$9\frac{1}{2}$	9	$9\frac{3}{4}$	$10\frac{3}{4}$	$6\frac{7}{8}$	$6\frac{3}{8}$	7	6	$6\frac{1}{8}$	$5\frac{3}{8}$
November	$6\frac{7}{8}$	$5\frac{3}{4}$	$6\frac{5}{8}$	$5\frac{5}{8}$	$6\frac{3}{4}$	$5\frac{7}{8}$	7	$7\frac{3}{4}$	$9\frac{1}{4}$	$9\frac{3}{4}$	$10\frac{3}{4}$	$7\frac{3}{4}$	$7\frac{1}{4}$	7	6	6	$5\frac{3}{4}$
December	7	$5\frac{7}{8}$	$6\frac{1}{4}$	$6\frac{1}{8}$	$7\frac{7}{8}$	$5\frac{3}{4}$	$7\frac{1}{8}$	$8\frac{1}{4}$	$9\frac{7}{8}$	$9\frac{1}{4}$	$10\frac{3}{8}$	$8\frac{1}{2}$	$7\frac{7}{8}$	$6\frac{3}{4}$	$6\frac{1}{4}$	$5\frac{7}{8}$	$5\frac{3}{8}$

TABLE No. 29.— Continued.

Showing the Monthly Average Price of Fair Upland Bowed Cotton in the Liverpool Market in Each Year since 1826.

	1843.	1844.	1845.	1846.	1847.	1848.	1849.	1850.	1851.	1852.	1853.	1854.	1855.	1856.	1857.	1858.	1859.
January	$5\frac{3}{8}$	$5\frac{5}{8}$	$4\frac{1}{4}$	$4\frac{3}{8}$	$7\frac{1}{4}$	$4\frac{7}{8}$	$4\frac{1}{4}$	$6\frac{3}{8}$	$7\frac{5}{8}$	5	$5\frac{7}{8}$	$6\frac{1}{4}$	5	$5\frac{5}{8}$	$7\frac{3}{8}$	$6\frac{3}{4}$	$6\frac{7}{8}$
February	$4\frac{7}{8}$	$6\frac{1}{8}$	$4\frac{1}{2}$	$4\frac{3}{8}$	$6\frac{7}{8}$	$5\frac{1}{4}$	$4\frac{3}{8}$	$6\frac{7}{8}$	$7\frac{1}{4}$	$5\frac{1}{8}$	6	$6\frac{1}{4}$	$5\frac{3}{8}$	$6\frac{1}{8}$	$7\frac{3}{4}$	$7\frac{3}{10}$	7
March	$4\frac{3}{8}$	6	$4\frac{1}{2}$	$4\frac{3}{8}$	$6\frac{1}{8}$	$4\frac{3}{4}$	$4\frac{3}{8}$	$6\frac{3}{8}$	$7\frac{1}{4}$	$5\frac{1}{4}$	6	$6\frac{1}{8}$	$5\frac{3}{4}$	$6\frac{1}{4}$	$7\frac{5}{8}$	$7\frac{1}{8}$	$7\frac{1}{8}$
April	$4\frac{3}{8}$	$5\frac{1}{2}$	$4\frac{20}{1}$	$4\frac{3}{8}$	$6\frac{3}{4}$	$4\frac{3}{4}$	$4\frac{1}{2}$	$6\frac{7}{8}$	$6\frac{5}{8}$	$5\frac{1}{4}$	$6\frac{1}{4}$	6	$5\frac{1}{2}$	$6\frac{1}{2}$	7	$7\frac{1}{4}$	$7\frac{1}{4}$
May	$4\frac{5}{8}$	$5\frac{1}{4}$	$4\frac{1}{4}$	5	$6\frac{1}{2}$	$4\frac{1}{2}$	$4\frac{3}{8}$	$7\frac{1}{4}$	6	$5\frac{1}{2}$	$6\frac{3}{8}$	$6\frac{1}{4}$	$5\frac{3}{8}$	$6\frac{5}{8}$	7	$7\frac{1}{4}$	$6\frac{7}{8}$
June	$4\frac{7}{8}$	5	$4\frac{1}{4}$	$5\frac{1}{8}$	$7\frac{1}{8}$	$4\frac{1}{4}$	$4\frac{7}{8}$	$7\frac{1}{2}$	6	$5\frac{1}{2}$	$6\frac{1}{2}$	$6\frac{1}{4}$	$6\frac{1}{4}$	$6\frac{5}{8}$	$8\frac{1}{4}$	$7\frac{1}{8}$	$7\frac{1}{8}$
July	$4\frac{1}{2}$	5	$4\frac{1}{2}$	5	$7\frac{1}{2}$	$4\frac{3}{8}$	$5\frac{1}{8}$	$8\frac{1}{4}$	$5\frac{3}{4}$	$5\frac{3}{4}$	$6\frac{3}{8}$	$6\frac{3}{4}$	$6\frac{3}{4}$	$6\frac{1}{2}$	$8\frac{1}{4}$	$7\frac{3}{8}$	$7\frac{3}{8}$
August	$4\frac{1}{2}$	5	$4\frac{3}{8}$	5	$7\frac{1}{8}$	$4\frac{1}{4}$	$5\frac{1}{4}$	$7\frac{3}{4}$	$5\frac{1}{2}$	6	$6\frac{5}{8}$	6	$6\frac{5}{8}$	$6\frac{5}{8}$	$8\frac{1}{2}$	$7\frac{1}{4}$	$7\frac{1}{2}$
September	5	$4\frac{3}{8}$	$4\frac{3}{8}$	$5\frac{38}{1}$	$5\frac{3}{4}$	$4\frac{1}{4}$	$5\frac{3}{4}$	$8\frac{1}{4}$	$5\frac{1}{2}$	6	$6\frac{3}{8}$	6	$6\frac{1}{2}$	$6\frac{3}{8}$	$8\frac{3}{8}$	$7\frac{1}{4}$	$7\frac{1}{4}$
October	$5\frac{1}{4}$	$4\frac{1}{4}$	$4\frac{3}{8}$	$5\frac{3}{4}$	$5\frac{3}{4}$	4	$6\frac{1}{8}$	8	$5\frac{1}{4}$	$6\frac{1}{4}$	$6\frac{1}{4}$	6	6	7	$9\frac{1}{4}$	7	$7\frac{3}{8}$
November	$5\frac{1}{4}$	$4\frac{1}{2}$	$4\frac{1}{2}$	$6\frac{1}{8}$	$5\frac{1}{4}$	$4\frac{1}{4}$	$6\frac{5}{8}$	$7\frac{3}{4}$	5	$5\frac{7}{8}$	$6\frac{3}{8}$	6	5	$7\frac{1}{4}$	$9\frac{1}{4}$	$7\frac{1}{4}$	$7\frac{3}{8}$
December	$5\frac{3}{8}$	$4\frac{1}{4}$	$4\frac{1}{4}$	$7\frac{1}{4}$	$4\frac{7}{8}$	$4\frac{1}{4}$	$6\frac{3}{8}$	$7\frac{1}{4}$	5	$5\frac{3}{4}$	$6\frac{3}{8}$	$5\frac{1}{2}$	$5\frac{1}{4}$	$7\frac{3}{8}$	$6\frac{1}{4}$	7	$7\frac{1}{8}$

TABLE No. 30.

Showing the Quantity or Value of Foreign Cotton Manufactures Imported Into, Exported From, and Consumed in the United Kingdom; with the Amount of Revenue Collected Thereon since 1831.

Years.	IMPORTED. Cotton Piece Goods of India.	IMPORTED. Cotton Manufactures entered at Value.	IMPORTED. Cotton Yarn.	EXPORTED. Cotton Piece Goods of India.	EXPORTED. Cotton Manufactures entered at Value.	EXPORTED. Cotton Yarn.	CONSUMED. Cotton Piece Goods of India.	CONSUMED. Cotton Manufactures entered at Value.	CONSUMED. Cotton Yarn.	Revenue on All Kinds.
	Pieces.	£	lbs.	Pieces.	£	lbs.	£	£	lbs.	£
1831	1,064,416	31,211	196,796	784,317	18,089	86,643		26,619	94,204	4,094
1832	506,184	18,477	184,859	811,716	9,078	116,839		25,390	111,203	3,715
1833	300,823	34,537	177,333	583,843	16,386	33,267		28,577	118,707	4,030
1834	298,966	57,982	103,830	674,459	18,919	40,562		47,989	80,689	6,006
1835	306,086	71,796	117,826	478,027	29,392	87,348		50,133	76,607	6,351
1836	384,943	114,201	199,109	377,826	52,011	126,360		67,577	52,339	8,279
1837	550,104	86,751	146,883	335,178	52,401	93,242		39,792	63,486	5,351
1838	270,545	92,662	277,113	384,966	53,263	133,756		43,793	106,570	6,380
1839	444,143	134,457	447,315	321,368	87,029	357,158		51,310	89,955	7,145
1840	379,179	164,595	424,635	299,740	99,977	419,920		66,978	83,460	8,159
1841	173,267	151,416	532,204	264,462	84,183	458,598		68,480	72,774	8,363
1842	126,764	74,891	452,528	212,700	34,257	431,663		41,974	39,149	5,305
1843	130,862	76,960	664,322	209,531	45,270	590,505		32,483	62,082	3,956
1844	128,085	106,068	513,628	189,584	67,757	446,040		39,132	55,565	4,715
1845	272,970	141,506	664,269	216,599	85,576	553,228		56,813	19 March, free.	6,434
1846	336,215	202,115	1,153,542	249,754	94,181	1,041,347				1,613
1847	379,491	258,244	1,011,358	246,884	68,060	967,577				1,289
1848	193,849	304,560	511,445	152,404	105,990	575,243			No Records.	1,026
1849	178,418	287,212	413,478	152,956	128,877	375,367		No Records.		1,769
1850	186,010	341,388	905,966	147,895	117,271	777,957	No Records.			2,040
1851	302,572	390,572	999,789	194,217	120,495	819,504				2,075
1852	315,144	355,161	711,101	170,957	106,734	617,814				1,134
1853	451,822	484,306	1,126,741	151,945	107,295	674,305				2,612
1854	388,094	540,193	1,407,864	220,014	73,887	540,814				3,880
1855	243,959	382,457	1,029,237	173,968	50,022	435,827				3,091
1856	257,720	472,833	1,116,226	106,379	77,944	530,548				3,321
1857	357,866	534,296	956,652	98,465	90,237	363,559				6,431
1858	170,685	520,932	799,827	89,899	75,518	321,167				4,619

TABLE No. 31.

Showing the Value of Raw Cotton Exported from the Three Presidencies of Bombay, Madras, and Bengal, to all Foreign or External Ports, since 1834-5.

Years.	Bombay.	Madras.	Bengal.	Grand Total.
	£	£	£	£
1834-5	1,159,780	64,663	312,531	1,536,974
1835-6	1,856,084	255,109	631,620	2,742,813
1836-7	1,765,310	357,154	383,799	2,506,263
1837-8	1,392,276	60,953	181,205	1,634,434
1838-9	1,430,945	146,533	218,155	1,795,633
1839-40	1,463,583	271,593	183,376	1,918,552
1840-1	1,898,408	270,328	196,650	2,365,386
1841-2	2,167,866	363,744	119,997	2,651,607
1842-3	1,892,544	325,704	173,129	2,391,377
1843-4	2,093,565	197,335	202,553	2,493,453
1844-5	1,327,463	354,613	201,874	1,883,950
1845-6	1,102,866	139,846	93,507	1,336,219
1846-7	1,611,760	173,119	115,809	1,900,688
1847-8	1,234,752	131,970	155,373	1,522,095
1848-9	1,581,967	157,571	35,771	1,775,309
1849-50	2,018,260	160,482	22,436	2,201,178
1850-1	2,943,021	250,505	281,263	3,474,789
1851-2	2,903,340	221,112	495,537	3,619,989
1852-3	2,837,216	385,176	407,102	3,629,494
1853-4	2,469,760	162,739	169,651	2,802,150
1854-5	2,166,402	169,490	92,872	2,428,764
1855-6	3,067,475	89,361	158,115	3,314,951
1856-7	3,912,253	316,362	209,334	4,437,949
1857-8	4,010,997	279,407	11,365	4,301,769
1858-9	3,892,479	197,379	4,242	4,094,100

TABLE No. 32.

Showing the Quantity of Raw Cotton Exported from Egypt (Port of Alexandria), and the Countries to which Exported, from 1855 to 1857 inclusive.

Countries Whither Exported.	1855.	1856.	1857.
	lbs.	lbs.	lbs.
Great Britain	26,520,270	31,609,704	27,875,120
France	10,608,304	9,280,796	10,765,300
Austria	13,760,376	11,942,574	9,246,398
Tuscany	48,118	11,368	....
Sardinia, Turkey, Syria, and Barbary	109,760	35,280	13,230
Greece and Ionian Islands	....	29,008	214,816
Grand Total	51,046,828	52,908,730	48,114,864

TABLE No. 33.

Showing the Official and Computed Real Value of Raw Cotton, and Foreign and Colonial Merchandise Imported into the United Kingdom; the Official and Computed Real Value of Foreign and Colonial Merchandise Re-Exported; and the Official and Declared Real Value of British Cotton and other Manufactures Exported from the United Kingdom since 1801.

	OFFICIAL VALUE.				ACTUAL VALUE.				
	IMPORTS	EXPORTS.			IMPORTS.		EXPORTS.		
			British Produce and Manufactures.					British Produce and Manufactures.	
Years.	All Foreign and Colonial Merchandise	All Foreign and Colonial Merchandise.	Cotton Manufactures.	All Kinds.	All Foreign and Colonial Merchandise	Raw Cotton.	All Foreign and Colonial Merchandise.	Cotton Manufactures.	All Kinds.
					Computed Real Value.	Computed Real Value.	Computed Real Value.	Declared Real Value	Declared Real Value.
	£	£	£	£	£	£	£	£	£
1801	31,786,262	10,336,966	7,050,809	24,927,684					39,730,659 *
1802	29,826,210	12,677,431	7,624,505	25,632,549					45,102,330 *
1803	26,622,656	8,032,643	7,081,641	20,467,531					36,127,787 *
1804	27,819,552	8,938,741	8,736,772	22,687,309					37,135,746 *
1805	28,561,270	7,643,120	9,525,465	23,376,941					38,077,144
1806	26,899,658	7,717,555	10,490,049	25,861,879					40,874,983
1807	26,734,425	7,624,312	10,309,765	23,391,214					37,245,877
1808	26,795,540	5,776,775	12,975,996	24,611,215					37,275,102
1809	31,750,557	12,750,358	19,445,966	33,542,274					47,371,393
1810	39,301,612	9,357,435	18,951,994	34,061,901					48,438,680
1811	26,510,186	6,117,720	12,013,149	22,681,400					32,890,712
1812	26,163,431	9,533,065	16,517,690	29,508,508					41,716,964
1813		Records	destroyed by	fire.					No Records.
1814	33,755,264	19,365,981	17,655,378	34,207,253				20,070.824	45,494,219
1815	32,987,396	15,748,554	22,289,645	42,875,996				20,712,227	51,603,028
1816	27,431,604	13,480,780	17,564,461	35,717,070				15,684,161	41,657,873
1817	30,834,299	10,292,684	21,259,224	40,111,427				16,061,230	41,761,132
1818	36,885,182	10,859,817	22,589,130	42,700,521				18,795,623	46,603,249
1819	30,776,810	9,904,813	18,282,292	33,534,176				14,709,258	35,208,321
1820	32,438,650	10,555,912	22,532,079	38,395,625				16,533,754	36,424,652
1821	30,792,760	10,629,689	23,541 615	40,831,744				16,122,537	36,659,630
1822	30,500,094	9,227,589	26,911,043	44,236,533				17,279,256	36,968,964
1823	35,798,707	8,603,904	26,544,770	43,804,372				16,324,715	35,458,048
1824	37,552,935	10,204,785	30,155,901	48,735,551				18,450,537	38,396,300
1825	44,137,482	9,169,494	29,495,281	47,166,020				18,359,999	38,877,388
1826	37,686,113	10,076,286	25,194,270	40,965,735				14,093,752	31,536,723
1827	44,887,774	9,830,728	33,182,898	52,219,280				17,640,601	37,181,335
1828	45,028,805	9,946,545	33,467,417	52,797,455				17,235,063	36,812,756
1829	43,981,317	10,622,402	37,269,432	56,213,041				17,526,703	35,842,623
1830	46,245,241	8,550,437	41,307,429	61,140,864				19,418,885	38,271,597
1831	49,713,889	10,745,071	39,577,866	60,683,933				17,249,908	37,164,372
1832	44,586,741	11,044,869	43,932,993	65,026,702				17,392,907	36,450,594
1833	45,952,551	9,833,753	46,412,420	69,989,339				18,481,239	39,667,347
1834	49,362,811	11,562,036	51,080,273	73,831,550	Not recorded earlier than 1854.	Not recorded earlier than 1854.	Not recorded earlier than 1854.	20,504,930	41,649,191
1835	48,911,542	12,797,724	52,315,780	78,376,731				22,119,896	47,372,270
1836	57,230,967	12,391,711	58,578,424	85,229,837				24,622,036	53,368,571
1837	54,737,301	13,233,622	51,130,290	72,548,047				20,585,616	42,214,938
1838	61,268,320	12,711,318	64,812.529	92,459,231				24,133,867	50,060,970
1839	62,004,000	12,795,990	67,892,675	97,402,726				24,534,391	53,233,580
1840	67,432,964	13,774,306	73,129,192	102,705,372				24,654,293	51,308,740
1841	64,377,962	14,723,151	69,779,270	102,180,517				23,489,446	51,545,116
1842	65,204,729	13,584,158	68,687,872	100,260,101				21,672,214	47,284,983
1843	70,093,353	13,956,113	82,189,599	117,877,278				23,445,612	52,206,447
1844	75,441,555	14,397,246	91,039,575	131,564,503				25,803,449	58,534,705
1845	85,281,958	16,280,870	93,665,834	134,599,116				26,119,331	60,111,082
1846	75,953,875	16,296,162	93,385,819	132,288,345				25,599,826	57,786,876
1847	90,921,866	20,036,160	82,237,190	126,130,986				23,333,224	58,842,377
1848	93,547,134	18,368,113	93,185,103	132,617,681				22,681,200	52,849,445
1849	105,874,607	25,561,890	112,416,294	164,539,504				26,775,135	63,596,025
1850	100,460,433	21,893,167	113,775,380	175,416,709				28,257,401	71,367,885
1851	110,679,125	23,732,703	126,366,489	190,658,314				30,088,836	74,448,722
1852	109,331,158	23,328,308	125,040,858	196,176,601				29,878,087	78,076,854
1853	123,099,313	27,733,537	131,710,646	214,327,452				32,712,902	98,933,781
1854	124,426,159	29,803,044	136,160,974	214,071,848	152,389,053	20,175,395	18,636,366	31,745,857	97,184,726
1855	117,284,881	31,494,391	153,711,478	226,920,262	143,542,850	20,848,515	21,003,215	34,779,141	95,688,085
1856	131,937,763	33,423,724	163,922,118	258,505,653	172,544,154	26,448,224	23,393,405	38,232,741	115,826,948
1857	136,215,849	30,797,698	159,088,484	255,396,713	187,844,441	29,288,827	24,108,194	39,073,420	122,066,107
1858	138,159,144	33,887,888	182,221,181	271,654,822	164,583,832	30,106,968	23,174,023	43,001,322	116,608,756
1859	....	....	....	....	179,334,981	34,559,636	25,203,163	48,208,444	130,444,725

* The Declared Value of British Produce and Manufactures Exported in the years 1801 to 1804, applies to Great Britain only, the real value of Exports from Ireland not having been recorded earlier than 1805.

TABLE No. 34.

Showing the Quantity of Raw Cotton Exported from the British East Indies, and the Countries to which Exported, from 1850-1 to 1857-8 inclusive.

Countries Whither Exported.	1850-1.	1851-2.	1852-3.	1853-4.	1854-5.	1855-6.	1856-7.	1857-8.
	lbs.	lbs.	lbs.	lbs.	lbs.	lbs.	lbs.	lbs.
Great Britain	141,446,798	81,104,223	181,360,994	138,183,429	119,513,537	170,771,510	253,410,036	197,221,247
France	3,250,691	95,952	....	598,288	256,540	737,972	1,873,711	14,143,874
Holland	30,021	....	....	....	....	....	2,534,160	4,090,984
Belgium	....	....	12,008	....	176,008	438,144	3,141,432	1,026,648
Austria	....	....	....	....	....	....	1,301,944	2,922,164
Germany	30,021	....	....	97,360	....	896	1,172,312	3,262,822
Turkey	....	....	....	....	....	....	155,904	....
Arabian and Persian Gulf	333,224	979,755	1,193,489	1,423,968	1,076,973	402,388	193,136	537,211
China	77,050,629	160,717,651	75,671,742	55,777,008	45,893,923	56,691,112	48,784,561	20,524,119
Islands and Shores of the Indian Seas	3,458,132	10,049,428	3,149,125	392,388	4,457,320	5,685,409	1,412,691	5,996,436
Sardinia	....	....	119,920	350,448	....	1,058,904	2,724,176	4,970,560
Ceylon	679,525	361,834	1,266,875	693,406	1,084,179	1,246,946	2,404,200	1,928,503
All Other Places	194,642	243,988	134,020	245,470	1,321,712	146,668	545,261	3,729,484
Grand Total	226,473,683	253,552,831	262,908,173	197,761,765	173,780,192	237,179,949	319,653,524	260,354,052

TABLE No. 35.

Showing the Quantity of Raw Cotton Exported from the United States of America, and the Countries to which Exported, from 1851 to 1858 inclusive.

Countries Whither Exported.	1851.	1852.	1853.	1854.	1855.	1856.	1857.	1858.
	lbs.	lbs.	lbs.	lbs.	lbs.	lbs.	lbs.	lbs.
Great Britain	670,645,122	752,573,780	768,596,498	696,247,047	673,498,259	899,327,988	683,997,972	780,952,389
France	139,164,571	186,214,270	189,226,913	144,428,360	210,113,809	221,767,611	174,234,678	178,789,761
Holland	5,508,670	10,259,042	7,088,994	6,048,165	4,941,414	13,096,530	10,434,227	8,497,751
Belgium	16,335,018	27,157,890	15,494,442	13,980,460	12,219,553	23,171,784	12,247,423	9,345,329
Hanse Towns	16,716,571	22,138,228	22,671,782	37,719,922	30,809,991	62,066,653	44,902,760	29,435,863
Russia	10,098,448	10,475,168	21,286,563	2,914,954	448,897	4,643,384	31,933,534	32,110,204
Sweden and Norway	5,160,974	5,939,025	6,099,517	9,212,710	8,428,437	17,289,637	10,038,095	4,057,593
Denmark	....	37,042	435,169	32,983	209,186	1,168,081	1,176,366	....
Austria	17,309,154	23,948,434	17,968,642	14,961,144	9,761,465	18,653,154	7,614,592	6,980,136
Sardinia and Italy	10,320,406	17,934,268	17,487,984	12,725,830	16,087,064	20,854,867	17,239,859	19,497,950
Spain	34,272,625	29,301,928	36,851,042	35,024,074	33,071,795	58,479,179	45,557,067	39,630,463
Portugal	....	98,235	87,691	121,059	144,006	388,393	56,439	....
British North American Colonies	23,525	16,582	12,295	72,790	883,204	4,158,530	857,490	130,617
Mexico	845,960	6,700,091	7,463,851	12,146,080	7,527,079	6,010,395	7,958,638	9,084,609
Cuba	113,572	294,852	196,392	250,633	9,620	4,950	2,000	1,871
Other Countries	722,473	141,803	652,595	1,946,895	270,822	350,565	31,335	109,476
Grand Total	927,237,089	1,093,230,638	1,111,570,370	987,833,106	1,008,424,601	1,351,431,701	1,048,282,475	1,118,624,012

APPENDIX TO DIAGRAMS.

TABLE No. 36.—SHOWING THE FIGURES EMPLOYED IN THE COMPILATION OF THE DIAGRAM—SHOWING THE DEMAND FOR, AND SUPPLY AND STOCK OF COTTON IN THE UNITED KINGDOM SINCE 1825.

Years.	SUPPLY. Imported.	Exported.	DEMAND. Consumed.	Total.	Stock.
	lbs.	lbs.	lbs.	lbs.	lbs.
1825	228,005,291	18,004,953	202,546,869	220,551,822	115,500,000
1826	177,607,401	24,474,920	162,889,012	187,363,932	110,900,000
1827	272,448,909	18,134,170	249,804,396	267,938,566	164,800,000
1828	227,760,642	17,396,776	208,987,744	226,384,520	147,000,000
1829	222,767,411	30,289,115	204,097,037	234,386,152	115,500,000
1830	263,961,452	8,534,976	269,616,640	278,151,616	118,800,000
1831	288,674,853	22,308,555	273,249,653	295,558,208	114,400,000
1832	286,832,525	18,027,940	259,412,463	277,440,403	103,700,000
1833	303,656,837	17,363,882	293,682,976	311,046,858	94,400,000
1834	326,875,425	24,461,963	302,935,657	327,397,620	82,300,000
1835	363,702,963	32,779,734	326,407,692	359,187,426	89,600,000
1836	406,959,057	31,739,763	363,684,232	395,423,995	116,300,000
1837	407,286,783	39,722,031	368,445,035	408,167,066	115,600,000
1838	507,850,577	30,644,469	455,036,755	485,681,224	160,900,000
1839	389,396,559	38,738,238	352,000,277	390,738,515	125,800,000
1840	592,488,010	38,673,229	528,142,743	566,815,972	207,000,000
1841	487,992,355	37,673,585	437,093,631	474,767,216	216,700,000
1842	531,750,086	45,251,302	473,976,400	519,227,702	242,300,000
1843	673,193,116	39,619,979	581,303,105	620,923,084	342,000,000
1844	646,111,304	47,222,541	554,196,602	601,419,143	390,200,000
1845	721,979,953	42,916,332	606,600,000	649,516,332	453,500,000
1846	467,856,274	65,930,732	614,300,000	680,230,732	245,400,000
1847	474,707,615	74,954,336	441,400,000	516,354,336	184,100,000
1848	713,020,161	74,019,790	576,600,000	650,619,790	220,100,000
1849	755,469,012	98,893,508	629,900,000	728,793,508	240,300,000
1850	663,576,861	102,469,717	588,200,000	690,669,717	231,600,000
1851	757,379,749	111,980,394	658,900,000	770,880,394	225,900,000
1852	929,782,448	111,884,321	739,600,000	851,484,321	300,900,000
1853	895,278,749	148,569,680	760,900,000	909,469,680	306,900,000
1854	887,333,149	123,326,112	776,100,000	899,426,112	271,200,000
1855	891,751,952	124,368,160	839,100,000	963,468,160	208,900,000
1856	1,023,886,304	146,660,864	891,400,000	1,038,060,864	196,200,000
1857	969,318,896	131,927,600	826,000,000	957,927,600	211,700,000
1858	1,034,342,176	149,608,480	905,600,000	1,055,208,480	189,958,000
1859	1,225,989,072	175,143,136	976,600,000	1,151,743,136	230,257,000

The quantities given as imported and exported are those returned by the Board of Trade.

Consumption, down to 1844 is that returned by the Board of Trade; thereafter it is the quantity *taken by the trade*, being the computation of Messrs. G. Holt and Co. of Liverpool.

Stock, is the quantity held in merchants', dealers' and spinners' hands in the United Kingdom as far as can be ascertained, and is also the computation of the last-named firm.